ROMANTICISM
AND THE RISE OF ENGLISH

ROMANTICISM
AND THE RISE OF ENGLISH

Andrew Elfenbein

Stanford University Press

Stanford, California

Stanford University Press
Stanford, California

Printed in the United States of America on acid-free, archival-
quality paper.

Library of Congress Cataloging-in-Publication Data

Elfenbein, Andrew.
  Romanticism and the rise of English / Andrew Elfenbein.
    p. cm.
  Includes bibliographical references and index.
  ISBN 978-0-8047-6025-6 (cloth : alk. paper)
  1. English language--18th century--Usage. 2. English language--
19th century--Usage. 3. English literature--18th century--History
and criticism. 4. English literature--19th century--History and
criticism. 5. English philology--History. 6. Romanticism--Great
Britain. I. Title.
  PE1083.E44 2009
  420.9034--dc22

                                2008019788

Typeset by Bruce Lundquist in 10.9/13 Adobe Garamond

Contents

Acknowledgments

On the top floor of my university's library, catalogued in an obsolete system, tucked away in a far corner, lurk books on the history of English. The literal and figurative distances of this material from more familiar concerns in literary criticism are part of this book's content and have been a challenge in its production. I have nevertheless been lucky to find sympathetic readers and audiences. Special thanks to Leslie Brisman, James Chandler, Anna Clark, Brian Goldberg, Michael Hancher, Gordon Hirsch, Peter Manning, James McKusick, Maureen McLane, Andrew Scheil, Susan Wolfson, and the members of my university's Nineteenth-Century Subfield. My readers for Stanford University Press, William Keach and Stuart Curran, saved me from many oversights: the book is better for their help. I also am grateful to past and present members of the Textgroup at the Center for Cognitive Sciences: Paul van den Broek, David Rapp, Randy Fletcher, Brooke Lea, Mija Van Der Wege, and others. Danika Stegeman was a valuable research assistant, and Anne Carter has been of great help in the final preparation of the manuscript. Emily-Jane Cohen and Emily Smith of Stanford University Press have given this book speedy and helpful assistance.

Vital financial support came from the American Philosophical Society and the Howard Foundation; my own institution provided a single-semester leave, sabbatical support, and a Summer Faculty Fellowship and McKnight Summer Research Support. I am grateful to the staffs of the British Library Sound Archives, Yale University's Sterling Memorial and Beinecke Libraries, Chicago's Newberry Library, and the University of Minnesota's Wilson Library for their help.

Earlier versions of portions of chapters 2 and 6 appeared in *Modern Philology* (© 2004 University of Chicago); earlier versions of portions of chapters 3 and 5 appeared in the *Cambridge Companion to British Romantic Poetry* (© 2008 Cambridge University Press). I am grateful for permission to reprint. A special thanks to Dino Felluga and Michael Eberle-Sinatra for inviting me to give a plenary at the 2005 meeting of the North American Society for the Study of Romanticism that became an early version of chapter 4 and parts of chapter 6.

I owe a peculiar kind of debt to a group of scholars whom I have never met, yet whose efforts undergird this book. R. C. Alston founded the Scolar Press, and during a brief period in the late 1960s and early 1970s, reprinted hundreds of books about English linguistics in the series *English Linguistics, 1500–1800: A Collection of Facsimile Reprints.* These formed the backbone of my research: the book would have been impossible without them. Other historical linguists, like Michael McMahon, David Denison, Ingrid Tieken-Boon van Ostade, Joan Beal, Carol Percy, and Lynda Mugglestone, whose work is largely unknown to literary historians, have been indispensable intellectual companions.

When my study has been so filled with books that I have all but disappeared beneath them, my son Dima and my partner John Watkins have been there to dig me out: I thank them both for their patience. The lofty indifference of my cats, Brandy, Muffin, and Charlotte, has been a gift that I can hardly measure. I dedicate the book to my teacher of philology, Marie Borroff, master of verbal arts.

ROMANTICISM
AND THE RISE OF ENGLISH

Introduction

The Dust of Philology

In 1967, William Riley Parker, a distinguished Miltonist and editor of *PMLA*, allegorized the birth of academic English:

> English was born about 100 years ago. Its mother, the eldest daughter of Rhetoric, was Oratory . . . Its father was Philology or what we now call linguistics. Their marriage . . . was shortlived, and English is therefore the child of a broken home. This unhappy fact accounts, perhaps, for its early feeling of independence and its later bitterness toward both parents. I date the break with the mother . . . not from the disgraceful affair she had with Elocution, but rather from the founding of the Speech Association of America in 1914 . . . I date the break with the father, not from his happy marriage to Anthropology, but from the founding of the Linguistic Society of America in 1924, and the developing hostility of literary scholars to non-prescriptive grammar, new terminology, and the rigors of language study. ("Where Do English Departments Come From?" 340)

Although Parker's soap opera simplifies English's rise as a discipline, it pinpoints the bitterness that literary criticism feels toward older forms of the discipline. This bitterness goes beyond the usual boundary markings of any discipline: historians can still respect work over a century old, and psychologists routinely refer to William James's findings. Most literature professors, however, would think it ridiculous to be held responsible for philology, much less oratory. Such older modes are not hallowed ancestors but figures of contempt.

Of the two parents described by Parker, Father Philology has been far more threatening than Mother Oratory. In histories of English studies, oratory generally receives less space than philology, whose demise appears as a key episode, the Liberation of Scholarship from Pedantry.[1] Gerald Graff, for example, condemns nineteenth-century textbooks that do "not get beyond the analysis of isolated words and constructions" and snickers at an edition of *Julius Caesar* for providing "82 pages of philological notes to 102 pages of Shakespeare's play" (*Professing Literature* 38, 39).[2] According-ing to Graff, philologists choked the life out of literature in their attempt to make it respectable.[3] In the standard narrative of English's history, a brave band of New Critics substituted probing close readings for dull investigations into obscure verb forms or archaic pronunciations. While the work of the New Critics has in its turn undergone substantial revi-sion, the rejection of philology has remained unquestioned as an obvious good. Philology had a longer life in departments devoted to literatures other than English, but Sander Gilman in 1987 noted that "the number of chair holders in foreign literature today who are primarily 'philologists' has sunk to virtually zero; the number of historical linguists is reduced each year" ("Quiet Revolutions" 44).

Specter-like, philology has almost risen from the grave several times, only to be killed off yet once more. After Roman Jakobson in 1960 ar-gued that linguists needed to know poetics, several linguistically oriented approaches to literary criticism flowered and faded in ensuing decades. Nothing secured their rapid death more than exposés of their claims to objectivity: these approaches had to be chastened for smuggling sci-ence into the humanities.[4] Not surprisingly, the linguistic turn that won out in English departments, poststructuralism, rejected the certainties that allowed other linguistic approaches to seem naive.[5] Moreover, in keeping with the tide of post-Saussurean linguistics, all these approaches were firmly ahistorical, loudly preferring synchronic over diachronic analysis.

It might seem that diachronic philology would have found its moment with the arrival of historicism in the 1980s. Nevertheless, despite calls in the 1980s for critics to situate their understanding of literary language historically, historicism for the most part went ahead with little atten-tion either to the traditional insights of philology or to the possibilities of reinventing philology from a historicist standpoint.[6] Instead, historicist scholarship provided detailed contextualization of everything about a lit-erary work except the English in which it was written, as if language alone remained immune from history.

Through a peculiar pseudo-resuscitation, philology has sometimes become a catch-all term used by critics wanting to lament the passing of an older scholarly moment. For example, in "The Return to Philology," Paul de Man praised the teaching of Harvard's Reuben Brower. Although de Man's title promises a defense of philology, Brower's teaching, as described by de Man, has nothing to do with the historical investigation of English. It instead models good close reading: Brower's students "were not to make any statements that they could not support by a specific use of language that actually occurred in the text" (23). Similarly, various scholars have re-assessed the legacy of Eric Auerbach as if "philologist" were the right word to describe him, even though philology plays only a minor role in his masterpiece, *Mimesis*. Auerbach does not focus on linguistic history, but on the transformation of representational traditions; he offers dazzling stylistic analyses, but always in relation to particular works. The pseudo-resuscitation of philology also surfaces in its casual conflation with the fields of book history, bibliography, editing, or the study of any ancient language. While these fields often use philological knowledge, they remain conceptually and practically different from the study of English's history.

English professors now study everything except English. Philological investigation, when it survives at all, persists in the study of Anglo-Saxon. The idea of studying the history of English during an era as recent as the Romantic period seems so unthinkable that some readers of this book's title may initially assume that the "rise of English" refers not to linguistic history but to the emergence of literary criticism as an academic discipline. Traditional philology itself focused on Old and Middle English. The melodramas of Viking invasions and the Great Vowel Shift supposedly gave way to the serene finality of Present Day English, which could be treated as existing in a vacuum from around 1750 to the present.[7] Although dating the arrival of modern English to the eighteenth century is not an obvious truth but a loaded scholarly move, it has rarely been contested.[8] It excuses scholars of literature written after 1750 from needing to know anything about linguistic history: supposedly the minor differences between English then and now do not matter.

If English professors have had little time for English, they have had much for language. Most important has been stylistics, the investigation of the systematic patterning of literary language. Yet an investment in stylistics has occurred at the expense of philology, which threatens its fundamental assumptions. Philology contests the tendency of stylistics to explain all linguistic features, no matter how minute, as the product of a conscious decision about meaning; that consciousness is often, though not always, located in the author's mind. Philology, instead, locates them as aspects of *langue* rather than of *parole*, of a collective and impersonal linguistic history rather than of individual genius.

Likewise, stylistics, unlike philology, binds small linguistic details to larger thematic concerns, as if these details, supposedly meaningless in themselves, gained significance only as allegories of content. In his sketch of the elements of verbal communication, Roman Jakobson distinguished the context (circumstances described in the message) from the code (the language system that lets the message be put into words) ("Linguistics and Poetics" 66). Most literary scholarship on language absorbs code into context, rather than recognizing its potential autonomy. The code becomes merely a second-order reflection of the more important message. Criticism that links small linguistic details to larger thematic concerns is prized for its perceived sensitivity; criticism that describes usage without making the metaphoric leap to a larger significance is condemned as dull. The literary critical vocabulary of the "interesting" thus acquires a strongly coercive power to shore up conventional modes of thinking.

Philology's autonomy threatens literary criticism. The vocabulary, syntax, morphology, and pronunciation of English have histories of their own, quite apart from the social uses to which they have been put, and certainly independent of the history of literature. Philology is a kind of history, but, from the point of view of literary criticism, a bad one because it does not fit well with other histories. It hardly seems vital to the success of the British Empire, for example, that "do" in the eighteenth century became an obligatory dummy auxiliary in negatives, questions, and emphatic affirmations, although not in simple assertions (Traugott, *History of English Syntax* 176). Yet this development is part of the history of Britain, just not a history that anyone cares about.[9] The gap between this formal linguistic development and more familiar historical masterplots looks absolute. It is possible to link a large-scale development like eighteenth-century linguistic standardization to other eighteenth-century efforts to schematize difficult and confusing phenomena; for example, Foucault in *The Order of Things* compares the rise of comparative philology in England and Germany to the rise of the concepts of labor in economics and organism in evolutionary biology.[10] Yet even if we acknowledge the truth of such connections, they do not help to historicize the particular rules that the standardizers developed, to explain why certain forms were chosen over others, or to describe why some irregularities persisted while others did not. The closer one comes to the granular tidbits of English's history, the less easily they fit into the history of Britain. Philology presents in an acute form what Mary Poovey calls "the epistemology of the modern West: the tension between the desire to construct (or discover) some order that supports meaningful generalizations and the kind of sloppiness or disorder that inheres in discrete particulars" (*History of the Modern Fact* 268).

Literary criticism has shown its independence from philology by ignoring such minutiae and turning to the agency of authors or, for those wishing to avoid expressivism, of discursive movements and institutional determinants. Literature appears in all cases as purposive (however agency is theorized), rather than as an instance of the rules of language obtaining at a particular time and place. According to Andrew Bennett, "what critics talk about when they talk about literature is the problem of authorship" (*Author* 127). Philologists, however, do something else. To analyze a literary work philologically is to disintegrate it into isolated crumbs of usage that lead to no satisfying conclusions, to make it dusty; as Walter Benjamin (quoting Karl Kraus) notes, "The more closely you look at a word the more distantly it looks back" (267). Philology's pile-up of evidence can lead to the feeling that the history of English is really a nonhistory, a block of observations so autonomous that it cannot be meaningfully integrated into literary study. What makes the facts about usage especially unsettling is their deracinated agency: just who or what belongs to the history of English? Philology raises in stark terms the question of where a literary work comes from, since it threatens to divorce the study of language from intention. Too close an attention to philological detail disperses the building blocks of literary criticism, so that philology becomes at once too theoretically threatening and too boring.

In addressing itself to language as a whole, philology uncomfortably points out the arbitrariness of the designation "literature." As John Mowitt notes about linguistic literary criticism, "the attempt to specify literary specificity linguistically recast the disciplinary object of literary criticism in a manner that plunged literature back into the vastness of language practices" (*Text* 86). If the point is to study the history of English, why privilege literary works over any other English? If the point is to study literature, then you need somehow to distinguish literary language from any other kind. Philology's death has left literary critics with three choices. First, they can commit to its unacknowledged successor, cultural studies, in which all signifying practices are open to analysis, just as philology is potentially open to any manifestation of language. Cultural studies, via semiotics, simply expands what counts as such a manifestation. Second, critics can study authors designated by academic tradition as literary, whose English is assumed to be special. The third option has been to arrive at uncomfortable hybrids, in which approaches from cultural studies are applied to works recognized as canonical or at least literary, even though the historical contingency of their literariness is never acknowledged.

I find philology a more useful category for literary history to reappropriate than contemporary linguistics for several reasons: philology takes place through historical analysis, especially in the examination of change in a complex system; it elevates writing over speech; and it prefers the workings of a particular language to the universalizing ambitions of linguistics. Most of all, the outlines of a contemporary philology that would be useful to literary criticism remain uncertain enough to encourage investigation, whereas linguistics has largely rejected literature. It should be possible to develop a philological stylistics that uses philology to pry open assumptions usually taken for granted by stylistics and by most practical criticism. For example, the figure of the intending author itself has a philological history, one that became especially prominent during the Romantic period.[11] The nature of the division between *langue* and *parole* changed after English's eighteenth-century standardization because English's systematic and rule-bound nature became visible as an overt object of study. Not coincidentally, the nature of English literary *parole* changed as well, since a work could be perceived as original only after English had been re-created as a system. Only four years separated Edward Young's *Conjectures on Original Composition* (1759), which defended the aesthetic importance of original genius to art, from Samuel Johnson's *Dictionary* (1755). One could become an original genius who is prior to or even superior to English only once English itself was coherent enough to provide a worthy adversary: if you were going to prove your genius by breaking the rules, you needed rules to break. The result was the emergence that Foucault describes of the distinctive questions that could be asked of a literary text: "We now ask of each poetic or fictional text: From where does it come, who wrote it, when, under what circumstances, or beginning with what design?" ("What Is an Author?" 109).

The philological effects of English's standardization on literature are the central concern of this book, and I focus on Romanticism because Romantic writers were the first to confront fully standardized English. In foregrounding the rise of English, my approach differs from that of previous Romanticists interested in language. Rather than concentrating on philology, Romanticists have traced the history of ideas about language and language use, and examined their manifestation in literary practice. The pioneering work of Hans Aarsleff has been a fundamental reference point for understanding the rich history of Enlightenment theories of language. Scholars such as James McKusick, William Keach, and Richard Marggraf Turley have provided invaluable guides to Romantic authors and their knowledge of philosophical claims about how language originated, how best to describe it, and how it should function in a modern society.[12] In addition, scholars have treated language as a system reinforcing hierarchies of power, in which anyone who did not use the prestige language suffered. Olivia Smith, John Barrell, Tony Crowley, Janet Sorensen, and Lynda Mugglestone are some of the most prominent scholars who have developed this picture of language use during the Romantic period.[13] They have shown how insidious the social reception of eighteenth-century prescriptivism could be through its power to denigrate the working class, members of the Celtic areas of Britain, and women in general.

These approaches to Romanticism and language have produced distinguished scholarship upon which I rely throughout this book. Yet *Romanticism and the Rise of English* foregrounds what these studies bypass, the fact that English's history does not overlap entirely either with literary style, philosophies of language, or social values attached to usage. English's standardization in the eighteenth century divided what a literary work represented into two large parts, each with internal subdivisions: the expression of original genius and an instantiation of better or worse English usage. This division never became too visible because the two parts operated at different levels of textuality. The original author seemed safe at the broader level of subject matter, but the closer one looked at specifics of word choice, the more the authority of English chipped away at the imagination's autonomy.

For example, content words (nouns, verbs, adjectives, and adverbs) might be imagined to originate with an author, but the rules of English seem to supply function words (articles, conjunctions, auxiliary verbs, pronouns, prepositions). When Charlotte Smith begins *The Emigrants* (1793) with the lines, "Slow in the Wintry Morn, the struggling light / Throws a faint gleam upon the troubled waves" (1–2), one may feel that "slow," "Wintry," "Morn," and "struggling," belong to Smith, while "in," "the," "a," and "upon" belong to English: they are hard-wired into language use. Yet this distinction immediately raises questions that are at once important and absurdly unanswerable, as if even to raise them is to go down the wrong path. It's at least arguable, for example, that the choice of "the Wintry Morn" rather than "a Wintry Morn" may reflect some level of individual decision, but making such an argument depends on a complex and often unexamined set of assumptions about what "individual decision" means. Similarly, certain collocations in Smith's lines, such as "faint gleam," are such commonplaces in late eighteenth-century poetry that it is not clear to what extent they should be understood as hers, or even what it means to posit Smith as an origin for English in the poem.

Beyond such questions about the origins of word choice, the movement from linguistics to semiotics has meant that literary criticism has lost touch with aspects of language use that philology once covered, such as pronunciation and syntax. In Smith's lines, do we imagine the second syllable of "struggling" to be realized with a final /n/ or /ŋ/?: both were present during the period, and the most prominent guide to pronunciation in the period, John Walker, noted that the "best speakers" preferred /n/ (*CPD* 49). Likewise, at the level of syntax, the sentence's subject-verb-object construction might be imagined as belonging transhistorically to English, while its frequent adjective-noun connections ("Wintry Morn," "struggling light," "faint gleam," "troubled waves") look like inheritances from conventions of eighteenth-century poetic diction. Saussure's *langue/parole* division gives way to a spectrum of sociolects and idiolects determined by the conventions of language use associated with particular activities, like writing poetry.

Philology's challenges to the idea of agency are especially pressing for questions of revision. For example, in the first draft of Keats's *Lamia*, Lamia tells Hermes that she saw him fly to Crete in pursuit of a nymph "swiftly as a mission'd Phœbean dart." Keats later changed "mission'd" to "bright" (78).[14] To interpret the change, the standard critical move would be stylistic: in moving from "mission'd" to "bright," Keats eliminates the sense of internal, mental purposiveness in the past participle that points to an agent behind the dart; "mission'd dart" floats between a pretty periphrasis for a ray of sunshine and a more threatening image of an aggressive, even murderous arrow. "Bright" eliminates the complicated internality of "mission'd" and replaces it with an externalizing adjective that overlaps semantically with "Phœbean." As such, a traditional student of style might find in the revision a telling comment about Lamia herself, whose story about external appearances overwrites one about internal motivations: Lamia's uncertain mission also lurks beneath her more obvious brightness.

Yet our description of Keats as the origin of these revisions may change if we acknowledge that he also made these other revisions:

Original: Ravish'd, she lifted up her Circean head
Final: Ravish'd she lifted her Circean head (115)

Original: Delicate, put to proof the [lythe] Caducean charm
Final: Delicate, put to proof the lythe Caducean charm. (133)

Original: The rugged paps of little Perea's rills
Final: The rugged founts of the Peræan rills (176)

Original: In harbour Cencreas, from Egina isle
Final: In port Cenchreas, from Egina isle (225)[15]

In each case the pronunciation of the Greek or Greek-derived words in each line changes to increase by one the number of phonemes, with the penultimate syllable getting stress in the revision. (The second example is complex: Keats initially took out "lythe" in accordance with the other revisions; it was later restored, in a way that made an already hypermetric line even stranger.) According to Jack Stillinger, Richard Woodhouse recommended these changes to Keats; they are also more in line with the previous usage of such adjectives in poetry. Keats's first versions were not aesthetically inadequate or even debatable. They were changed because they were wrong, from the point of view of the eighteenth-century standardization of English, which, as Lynda Mugglestone has demonstrated, had raised the stakes for correct pronunciation of even non-English words.[16] While it would be crude to claim that the historical state of attitudes toward pronunciation should eliminate minute stylistic criticism, we are nevertheless left with the problem of assessing the relative importance of multiple determinations behind Keats's revisions.

Keats wrote out these changes in manuscript, but to leave the question
of agency there is to miss the point. Any act of writing involves not just
physical writing, but the cognitive act of generating the language and the
social act of claiming responsibility for it. In this case, Keats physically
produced the changes and came up with the words, but the importance of
the change attests to an authority beyond Keats, that of standardized pronunciation. Stillinger uses this example, along with many others, to dis-
pute the myth of "solitary genius": Woodhouse's intervention proves that
Keats's poems were not just by Keats.[17] While his analysis substitutes multiple agencies for a single agency, it still privileges the creative imagination
as poetry's origin. Yet the demands of English as code, as institutionalized
by eighteenth-century prescriptivism, have as good a claim as the demands
of Keats's circle to agency in a historical account of Keats's poem.

A standard literary critical rescue would be to invoke the New Critical
intentionalist fallacy and claim that the origin of Keats's changes is irrelevant to their effects; trying to figure out exactly who or what is responsible, word by word, for a literary work begs too many questions about just
what being responsible for a work means. Even worse, doing so directs attention away from the work itself toward fruitless questions about origin,
since what the critic should care about is not why the changes happened,
but what they do to Keats's poem. Yet such an answer runs into trouble
by inviting an inconsistent approach to historical context. *Lamia* as the
work of a revising author belongs to a particular time and place, but the
effects of the changes are supposedly ahistorical, to be judged by the stylistic sensitivity of a critic centuries later. If the words of the work are to
be severed from their origin, however defined, then just exactly how does
one describe their historical status?

Another way out of the problem would be to declare that how we view
a work's language depends on what kind of author we want, or, following
Foucault, what kind of interpretive act we perform when we designate
certain historical agencies under the sign of an author: for Foucault, the
author's name "permits one to group together a certain number" of texts,
define them, differentiate them from and contrast them to others" ("What
Is an Author?" 107). Distressingly, such moves have tended to collapse
into quasi-theological assertions of the life or death of the author, rather
than leading to investigations of the role that the author's name plays in
interpretation. Yet it has been easier to acknowledge the potentially multiple agencies played by the author's name than to concretize them usefully

in actual analysis. Key essays about the status of the author are widely assigned in theory classes and widely ignored in practical criticism.

Relevant questions involve not the attributed agencies of the author *per se*, but the multiple agencies made available by interactions among historically situated authors, texts, and readers. Foucault's varying author functions depend on varying textual and reader functions as well. Characteristically, using the author as a figure in literary criticism enables the critic to bypass the linguistic determination of English either because it threatens authorial autonomy or because it introduces historical determination at the wrong level, that of the code rather than of the context. For example, recent criticism admits various historical determinants in relation to Keats's creativity, such as his class, politics, and gender. Yet in such analyses, Keats is understood as having a self-reflexive and even critical relation to these determinants that reinstates authorial agency as soon as it is threatened.[18]

Even if one adopts a steely-eyed Foucaultianism, demystifies the last traces of expressivism, and surrenders to the classificatory power of the author, as defined at particular historical moments, one has by no means resolved philology's challenges. They cannot be answered by an appeal to philosophy of intention or the sociology of agency because these are not sensitive enough to the particular situation of authorship. As Paul de Man noted, "the impersonal precision of grammar" has the power to put into question "a whole series of concepts that underlie the value judgments of our critical discourse: the metaphors of primacy, of genetic history, and, most notably, of the autonomous power to will of the self" (*Allegories* 16). The discipline of literary criticism has not provided useful classificatory schemes that would make sense of the multiple constraints involved in the deployment of English in texts. On the contrary, it has largely made such questions disappear.

I understand linguistic determination in reference to literature as the satisfaction of constraints in language production. These constraints are multiple and operate at global and local levels. At a global level, the field of printable English, as historically situated, constrains choices on syntax, semantics, and phonology by limiting the pool of possible words and their combination; further constraints appear at such levels as mode (as in poetry, prose, or drama), genre (Gothic, satiric, sentimental), audience (coterie, general), occasion (formal, casual), and gender (acceptable feminine versus masculine language). Within a particular text, constraints shift constantly during language production: to begin a sentence with a noun phrase immediately narrows the field of possible terms for the rest of the sentence. Constraints are probabilistic rather than absolute, though what counts as "probable" will shift. For example, some uses of function words are so common as to be routinized; some syntactic patterns harden into convention (as in the eighteenth-century adjective-noun combination discussed earlier). Constraints also operate in parallel rather than serially: they are all simultaneously present.[19]

For example, when Felicia Hemans begins "The Wife of Asdrubal" (1819) with the lines "The sun sets brightly—but a ruddier glow / O'er Afric's heaven the flames of Carthage throw" (1–2), constraints function at multiple levels, including but not limited to standard English syntax, phonology, poetic diction, rhyme, and prosody (iambic pentameter). At a global level, Hemans begins a narrative poem with a scenic description, following a convention of contemporary narrative poetry. At a more local level, beginning with "the" makes the next syllable more likely to be a content word and more likely to be a stressed syllable. Beginning with "the sun" narrows the possible verbs that can be governed by the noun phrase within the historically defined field of poetic English: Hemans uses the high-frequency collocation "the sun sets." Since in standard English syntax, "sets" is intransitive, the next word is unlikely to be a noun or noun phrase. Hemans could end the sentence here, but such a stop would be unlikely (though not impossible) within the field of early nineteenth-century poetic convention. Instead, an adverb/adverb phrase or preposition/prepositional phrase is most likely to follow; the next word should also be one that can receive stress and that has a strong semantic overlap with "sun." Given these constraints, "brightly" is not inevitable, but is more probable than a host of other words.

The standardization of English in the eighteenth century increased the salience of many of these determinants by codifying more sharply than ever before which usages were correct and which were not. Any deviation from linguistic correctness could be taken as a sign of authorial incompetence, unless it was justified by constraint at some other level, as in the case of dialect literature. Literary writing had always been subject to linguistic determination, but the stakes in that determination suddenly became much higher for those writing in English.

Eighteenth-century prescriptivism arose both as a social movement and as a set of autonomous linguistic rules. Romantic works negotiated both aspects of prescriptivism, the ideological implications of its distinction between correct and vulgar usage and its specific rules and regulations regarding vocabulary, spelling, syntax, and pronunciation. These coalesced through the development of literary sociolects belonging to particular modes of writing. Traditionally, the linguistic analysis of literature has sought to define literary language. The Romantic period creates not literary language in the abstract, but a set of prototypical relations to English associated with modes of writing: poetry, novels, and familiar prose. In the Romantic period, poetry becomes poetic; novels, novelistic; and prose, prosaic. To make such a generalization is not to claim absoluteness. Plenty of works written in the early nineteenth century challenged these prototypical uses of English. Yet Romanticism had winners in the broader history of literature: the period is remarkable for how long-lasting certain solutions to the problems of literary language became. My book offers less a history of literature than an account of new forms of literariness possible only after the standardization of English in the eighteenth century.

Analyzing these changes involves bringing to bear unfamiliar bodies of knowledge on the study of Romanticism. Philology fits badly into the genre of the essay, since it originally started as a separate and far more ambitious discipline than literary criticism; as Hans Aarsleff notes, philology in Germany became "no less than the study of the history and knowledge of all human thought and activity" (*Study of Language* 180). Great works of philology like Otto Jespersen's monumental *Modern English Grammar on Historical Principles* are organized as lists, pages and pages of examples that do not add up to satisfyingly definitive pronouncements. Philology loves tables, charts, and graphs, not essays or chapters.

The traditional mode linking philological knowledge to a literary work was not the essay but the gloss, often contained within an editorial apparatus; many of the great nineteenth-century philologists, like W. W. Skeat, were also editors. The gloss gave not sustained interpretations but flashes of potential insight, which depended on the reader's creation of links between work and language. In it, the isolated textual moment and its relation to the history of the language crowded out the integrity of author, work, or culture.[20] Rather than privileging the unities described by de Man, the gloss provided competing or even contradictory information about a given textual moment, without necessarily drawing conclusions about overall meaning; such minuteness earned it contempt from critics like Graff. Philology, as manifested in the gloss, resists the coercion whereby analysis of a particular must be justified by an "interesting" appeal to the general, either at the level of the individual work or of the culture.

Romanticists may recognize a familiar passage behind my description of the gloss, Keats's letter on negative capability. Keats famously criticizes Coleridge because he "would let go by a fine isolated verisimilitude caught from the penetralium of Mystery, from being incapable of remaining content with half-knowledge" (*JK* 78). Philology as applied to literature encourages the "isolated verisimilitude" that is consistent with "half-knowledge." Literary criticism, in contrast, prefers full knowledge, or at least its rhetorical accoutrements. In this book, analyses shuttle among the pile-up of facts characteristic of philology, the isolated insight encouraged by the philological gloss, and the more traditional thesis of literary criticism. I offer not readings of works as totalities, but rather insights into isolated moments. Authors and their agency do not disappear, but I understand them in relation to totalities defined not at the level of works or careers, but of the history of English.

My first chapter examines philology and the problems associated with describing the history of English. I focus especially on the element of traditional philology most relevant for the Romantic period, prescriptivism, or, to use the eighteenth-century term, "purification." Prescriptivism is a much-maligned term in contemporary linguistics, and this bias has colored histories of eighteenth-century language use. Yet for the many men and women who took part in the eighteenth-century purification of English, whom I refer to collectively as the "English experts," the reinvention of English revolutionized communication in light of print capitalism. Print created a crisis of common ground, in which the potential gap between author and audience widened frighteningly. Pure English rushed to fill that gap by creating rules for authors to follow and readers to recognize. Consequently, printed English became more accessible than it had ever been, and led to a golden age of amateur authorship. Yet pure English also had a darker side, at least for some. Not only did it create barriers between those who did and did not use the prestige language variety, it could also drain the life from English in ways that made "primitive" uses of the language look more vital.

The next chapter examines micro-effects of prescriptivism. By focusing on two of the most notorious rules created by the English experts, the prohibition on double negatives and the will/shall distinction, I uncover the new sets of relations between author, text, and audience that these rules made available. Wordsworth's "Tintern Abbey" provides the test case for the relevance of linguistic negation for an understanding of Romantic poetry. Examining the will/shall distinction in Romantic literature more generally makes visible the repertoire of linguistic agencies potentially exercised by all modes of literary writing during the period.

The next chapter moves from the micro-level of usage to the macro-level of authorial career. Theatrical treatment of dialect represented one of literature's first responses to the purification of English at the level of pronunciation. Playwrights generated fantasy examples of bad English associated with particular ethnic groups. Dialect realized otherness in ways that manifested a literary love/hate relationship with pure English: dialect users were vulgar, but they usually had more vitality and energy than refined speakers. Proto-liberal eighteenth-century dramatists invented a linguistic masterplot of purification, in which dialect speakers who are meant to be sympathetic characters reform linguistically during the course of the plot.

Eighteenth-century experimental poets, in contrast, took over dialect as their marker of literariness, usually by associating it with older and supposedly more authentic forms of English, as in the cases of Chatterton and Burns. Their work offered a possible model for poetic English that Romantic writers for the most part rejected. Their responses gave shape to authorial careers in terms that paralleled those of the eighteenth-century masterplot of purification. By the end of the period, two modes of defining poetic language, personal style and transpersonal poeticity, had emerged to distinguish poetry both from dialect and from novelistic, dramatic, or nonfictional uses of English.

The next two chapters link micro- and macro-levels of analyses by examining the two major developments through which schools disseminated pure English in the late eighteenth century: elocution, as pioneered in London, and expository prose, as developed in the Scottish universities. Each solved the problems of print communication in radically different ways, and the literature of the Romantic period negotiated both. The novel revised the hermeneutic ambitions of elocution by reassigning elocutionary markers to the description of reported speech, while the third-person omniscient narrator became the representative embodiment of expository prose. Poetry, in contrast, rebelled against elocution at varying levels, from the inconsistent representation of rhyme sounds to the proliferation of weirdly unpronounceable names. It also developed a

counter-technology of voice through the production of what I call percussive Romanticism, a form of poetry in which the force of meter overcame
distinctions prized by elocution.

The history of the sentence, understood not as a syntactic unit but as a
conceptual frame for organizing print, occupies chapter 5. The atomized
self-sufficiency of the well-formed sentence advocated by the English experts posed a crisis for the novel, evident as early as Johnson and Sterne,
and resolved through varying methods in Jane Austen and Walter Scott.
Poetry engaged the problematic of the well-formed sentence not at the
level of the syntactic sentence but at the level of the stanza and verse paragraph, the primary site of its potential excerptability. Prose in the work
of Macaulay and Carlyle reproduced the division within poetry between
the generic, all-purpose familiar style and the distinctive stylistic stamp
of genius.

By the end of the Romantic period, Romantic writers had developed
lasting solutions to the challenges posed by English's purification. The
final chapter addresses the later history of these responses within English
studies. Philologically inspired pedagogy provided a widely used model
of learning that encouraged attention to English apart from the unifying
context of the author. Oral recitation in schools kept alive the tradition of
percussive Romanticism, until it in turn was supplanted by a new culture
of vocal production. This culture contrasted with the rise of the academic
voice, which repudiated the expressiveness prized in the earlier history of
oral performance. The later history of familiar prose depended on the unlikely reception of the most admired nineteenth-century sentence writer,
Thomas Babington Macaulay. Macaulay's reception institutionalized
a problematic ideal of composition, which concentrated on the formation of the sentence and promoted what was taken to be a universally
valid model of style. My conclusion addresses the directions to which the
recovery of philology in an era of global English, obsolescent national
monolingualism, and the rise of computer code might point.

This book confronts questions often passed over in practical literary
study, however much attention may be paid to them at the level of theory: what happens if we talk about "English" instead of "language"? What
does taking the code of English seriously mean for how we understand
the basic tools of literary analysis? What kinds of shortcuts become widespread when English as the object of history disappears? What would it
mean to privilege philology over linguistics? What is lost in analyzing

literature primarily at the level of representation? Philology in this book becomes the privileged venue for exploring these questions, in ways that move far from governing paradigms of current literary criticism. Yet my goal is less to recover philology *per se* than to (re)activate questions that it encourages a critic to ask.

§ 1 Purifying English

Histories of English all agree, as Murray Cohen notes, that "there is more of almost everything linguistic in the second half of the eighteenth century than in the first: more grammars and more kinds of grammar, more theories of language, more sorts of questions asked about language, more dictionaries, spelling books, proposals for reordering pedagogy, and more languages taught" (*Sensible Words* 78). Philologists, grammarians, lexicographers, and orthoepists (codifiers of correct pronunciation) developed rules about usage that changed how English was defined, taught, analyzed, judged, and printed. While guides to English had existed for centuries, they had previously helped foreigners wanting to learn English; if people (usually foreigners) spoke "good English," the phrase meant that they were comprehensible. The eighteenth century saw the rise of books of usage for natives, which aimed to teach readers not how to speak English, but how to do it correctly. Good English was now not just comprehensible: it followed rules for right usage.

Traditional philological histories have treated this prescriptivism as a very bad thing. Hatred of prescriptivism runs deep in linguistics. The first chapter of a standard linguistics textbook, for example, insists that "all grammars are equal" and commands that "any statement of the rules and conventions for speech and writing must reflect the way language is actually used, not someone's idealized vision of how it should be used" (O'Grady et al., *Contemporary Linguistics* 6, 7).[1] Since linguistics long ago renounced prescriptivism in order to enter into the academy as a respectable scientific discipline, such textbooks make sure to teach the uninitiated that prescriptivism is deluded and harmful.

Historians of English follow the general trend of linguistics by carrying back to the eighteenth century the mistrust of prescriptivism: "One cannot escape the feeling that many of them [the prescriptivists] took delight in detecting supposed flaws in the grammar of 'our most esteemed writers'" (Baugh and Cable, *History of the English Language* 273); "Such writers fail to see that language has to remain variable in order to be able to respond to all kinds of changes as a result of developments in technology, culture and global communication generally. To think that language could be fixed in the same way as, say, the metre or shoe sizes or video systems is an illusion" (Nevalainen and van Ostade, "Standardisation" 285).[2] Such comments turn later linguistic historians into unwitting prescriptivists, sternly separating good from bad linguists just as earlier writers separated good from bad usage. Yet the English experts have the last laugh, since the English of later historians obeys all their rules and helps to guarantee their continued power.

The changes in English in the eighteenth century are more profound than traditional philology has admitted. These changes meant less that English became rule-bound than that the nature of what it meant to be an English-using person changed. The English experts transformed English so as to recast personal identity, intra- and inter-group bonds, and collective agency. Their work drastically expanded the potential functions and results that could be expected of actions that took place in English. Most of all, they created a new urgency and excitement surrounding practices enabled by English.[3]

At the center of this change was print. While Britons spoke many language varieties during this period, English ruled print: no utopian upheavals were needed to create print monolingualism. For many, print meant the diffusion of liberty and civilization themselves; as Samuel Johnson told Adam Fergusson, "The mass of every people must be barbarous where there is no printing" (Boswell, *Life of Johnson* 477). Print changed not only the amount of English available to readers but also the link between author and audience. As Michael McKeon notes, in discussing Defoe,

> Publication is represented as an act of depersonalization that abstracts both author and reader from the concrete presence of face-to-face exchange; and yet the very impersonality of the exchange imposes upon the author an unprecedented burden of personal and ethical obligation. Publication is here

felt to be an act of supreme mastery . . . and yet by virtue of this mastery it is also felt to entail an alienation, a loss of control over what has been said, a disowning of what henceforth remains in the possession of others. (*Secret History* 54)

The abstraction and depersonalization described by McKeon had a side effect: English became the assumed source of commonality between author and reader. As other sources of common ground vanished, understanding printed English was left as the chief and possibly the only bond that an author had with an audience. Instead of writing for particular readers, authors faced an amorphous general public, of whom little could be known beyond the fact that it read English.[4] As a result, print made the stakes in a common linguistic ground higher than ever before, and the standardizers of English worked hard to make it a reality.

The English experts' works glory in the dazzle of print. J. Paul Hunter has noted that by the beginning of the eighteenth century, novelists made up for the lack of a previous connection with their readers through devices aiming to mimic orality, such as introductions, direct addresses, and appeals to common interest (*Before Novels* 156–61). The English experts did the opposite. Rather than masking their print status, their books showcased the art of the page. At the level of layout, they feature elaborately varied formats, with beautifully aligned lists, columns, charts, and tables. At the level of typeface, they varied fonts and the size of type to distinguish between major topics, minor topics, exceptions, and examples. New symbols appeared for intonation, emphasis, syllabification, and special notes.[5] Although these books rarely mention print explicitly, their visuality proved that print had revolutionized communication. English would now be defined not through speech or handwriting, but through print. Even works about spoken English would be works in print, so that the meaning of pronunciation itself needed to be redefined.

Although later historians have called the work of the English experts "prescriptivism," they thought of it as purification. George Campbell defined "pure English" in his *Philosophy of Rhetoric* (1776):

Pure English then, implies three things; *first*, that the words be English; *secondly*, that their construction, under which, in our tongue, arrangement also is comprehended, be in the English idiom; *thirdly*, that the words and phrases be employed to express the precise meaning which custom hath affixed to them. (1:408)[6]

Campbell singles out three components of pure English: lexis, syntax, and semantics. Controversy swirled around each. Just which words counted as English had long been a problem in English because of its heteroglot history: was "chef" French or English? Which Scottish words were English, and which were not? In terms of syntax, the "English idiom" underwent rethinking in the period since it was not clear where it was located: in a region, in a city, in a rank, or in an institution. Finally, claiming that "custom . . . affixed" a meaning to a word or phrase assumed an obviousness about "custom" that was easy to invoke in the abstract but harder to use when defining specific terms.

If the details of Campbell's definition were questionable, the myth of pure English was not. The adjective "pure" exalted English into a sacred vessel, an intact virgin needing defense from gross impurities. Those who used English well became knights of romance, defending her spotless purity; those who used bad English were vile ravishers, eager to turn the virgin into a whore. At the same time, the terms in which Campbell defined purity compromise its absoluteness by suggesting that the virgin is always already a whore, since her purity depended on the vagaries of custom, not on transcendent categories. In the eighteenth century, however, rather than wrecking the mythic purity of English, this seed of impurity only increased the ardor of those defending it, since custom ended up being whatever the individual believed it to be.

Before the eighteenth century, printed English, either as a group fantasy or as a body of actual linguistic and social practices, had not served as a common ground for England, Wales, Scotland, or Ireland. I use "common ground" in the sense of the psycholinguist Herbert H. Clark: "Common ground is a form of self-awareness. Two people, Susan and Bill, are aware of certain information they each have. To be common ground, their awareness must be reflexive—it must include that very awareness itself. Ordinarily, people can justify a piece of their common ground by pointing to a shared basis for it—a joint perceptual experience or a joint action" (*Using Language* 120). English experts dreamed that access to print would be the "shared basis" for making pure English common ground for all Britons. Before English's standardization, linguistic common ground for educated men meant Latin and Greek, along with the entire apparatus of learning that accompanied knowledge of those languages; for members of particular language communities, the spoken vernacular, in the form of local languages ranging from Scots to Manx, was part of common ground. What was missing was a language that could, at least at the level of social myth, be common ground for all Britons.

The discourse that should have had the greatest unifying power, Protestantism, came up against the fact that not everyone in Britain was Protestant, and not all Protestants were the same. By the end of the eighteenth century, printed English had done what religion had not. Protestantism had for centuries celebrated the vernacular, and by the end of the eighteenth century, the vernacular, as remade by print, took over for Protestantism: pure English has never lost the glow of sanctity that it earned as an unrecognized supplement to, or even replacement for, God. It had become an attainable ideal of commonality supposedly open to all Britons, unlike Protestantism. If they shared nothing else, Dissenters, Catholics, Anglicans, Jews, and atheists could all aspire to pure English. As such, it became what Benedict Anderson calls a national "print-language," allowing those "who might find it difficult or even impossible to understand one another in conversation" to become "capable of comprehending one another via print and paper" (*Imagined Communities* 47).[7] Print alone did not create national consciousness: printed Latin and Greek, for example, had long fostered not national consciousness but a pan-European scholarly community. Yet eighteenth-century English experts worked hard to link pure English to Britishness.

This was not as easy a task as it might have seemed, largely because of the peculiar uncertainty around just what Britain was. Rather than being a secure site of identity, Britain was an unstable political image, made up of regions with independent and messy pasts. Its monarch led a German principality, and it was subject to some spectacular internal divisions, as in the American War of Independence and the 1798 Irish rebellion. The place of Britain in the larger world was unclear: it was both a nation unto itself, a nation tied to its European allies (as the Napoleonic wars proved), and a nation whose rising colonial power rendered old geographical limits obsolete.

As Linda Colley has noted, this uncertainty meant that "active commitment to Great Britain was not, could not be a given. It had to be learnt; and men and women needed to see some advantage in learning it" (*Britons* 295). Pure English as a national print language fostered an influential version of Great Britain: a unity of England, Scotland, Wales, Ireland, and numerous colonial possessions, in which England, especially London, was first among unequals. Using pure English would supposedly allow the peoples of England, Scotland, Wales, Ireland, and the colonies to participate in the mystic dominion of London, even if they lived and worked far from it, and even if other aspects of their identities had nothing to do with it.

In 1762, Thomas Sheridan dreamed of a Britain transformed by pronunciation:

> An uniformity of pronunciation throughout Scotland, Wales, and Ireland, as well as through the several counties of England, would be a point much to be wished; as it might in a great measure contribute to destroy those odious distinctions between subjects of the same king, and members of the same community, which are ever attended with ill consequences, and which are chiefly kept alive by difference of pronunciation, and dialects. (*Course of Lectures* 206)

For Sheridan, "pronunciation, and dialects," more than any other factors, alienated people from each other, and he hoped that a standard would let the English, Scottish, Welsh, and Irish learn that they were really "members of the same community." One might have imagined that religion or economic disparity, for example, would be far greater roadblocks to unity than linguistic differences, but Sheridan singled out pronunciation. There was an obvious reason for his focus: of all modes of creating national unity, print English seemed the most achievable. The infrastructure needed for such purification, including a functioning public sphere, a book trade that reached throughout Great Britain, a widespread, if uneven, system of education, and a commitment to the liberty of the press, made Sheridan's vision seem not like utopianism but a practical goal.[8]

As Charles Jones notes, "by the 1780s and 1790s, it is difficult to find writers dealing with pronunciation characteristics who do not address them in a judgmental, prescribing or attitudinal fashion" (*English Pronunciation* 117). Blunt appeals to national unity accompanied this prescriptivism, and by the time of John Walker's *Critical Pronouncing Dictionary* (1791), the most influential work on English pronunciation ever written, the projection of bad English onto the Scottish, Irish, and working-class Londoners had become entrenched. Walker included in his prefatory material detailed "rules to be observed by the Natives of Ireland in order to obtain a just Pronunciation of English," "rules to be observed by the Natives of Scotland in order to obtain a just Pronunciation of English," and a list of the faults of "my Countrymen, the Cockneys." For Walker, London English ruled supreme: "Though the pronunciation of London is certainly erroneous in many words, yet . . . it is undoubtedly the best" (*CPD* ix, xi, xii, xiii).

For the English experts, national linguistic unity predicted imperial greatness: "Do not the Arts and Sciences in every Kingdom participate to a great Degree the Fate of its Language? . . . How dear then ought the Honour of the English Language to be to every Briton! And how regarded but with an Esteem equal to, and becoming the Glory of our Arms?" The author, James Buchanan, makes explicit the military analogy behind the purification of English: Britons should be as proud of pure English as of the finest artillery or battleships of the day. Inspired by his theme, Buchanan quotes from Nahum Tate's "Upon this Noble Design of an English Education":

> Hark! Honour calls my Sons to new Alarms,
> To grow in Arts victorious, as in Arms,
> Our Language to advance, and prove our Words
> No less design'd for Conquest than our Swords!   (*British Grammar* xxxiv)[9]

For Buchanan and Tate, English "Words" rhyme with British "Swords." Britain's imperial might needed English, and, although the rhyme was imperfect, this claim was not empty rhetoric. British military power required prolific soldier-writers who penned reports, sent intelligence, and maintained a broad correspondence.[10] At the most basic level of military operations, good soldiers needed good English.

While English's purification had been in progress long before the Romantic period, the Napoleonic wars gave it new urgency. More than ever before, pure English became not only a symbol for national pride but a critical aspect of a wartime communications. To use bad English was not simply to offend against rules: it was a kind of political treason, an offense against the nation. In *Belinda* (1801) by Maria Edgeworth (daughter of an Irish landowner), for example, Harriot Freke, dangerous supporter of French ideas, speaks markedly sloppy English: "And how d'ye go on here, poor child? . . . I hope you're of my way o' thinking . . . Now we talk o'looks" (204). The virtuous Belinda, in contrast, speaks in perfectly composed, almost exaggeratedly formal sentences: "Is it possible, sir . . . that you should suspect me of such wretched hypocrisy, as to affect to admire what I am incapable of feeling?" (215). In Jane Austen's

Pride and Prejudice (1813), a woman capable of saying "Kitty and me were to spend the day there" (244) is dangerous enough to be able, a few pages later, to threaten the unit cohesion of British military operations.

In general, tributes to the glories of English abounded in the period. William Mitford compared it favorably to other major modern languages: "It has given us nothing of the offensive guttural of the German, nothing of the offensive nasal of the French, nothing of that strong peculiarity of tones which distinguish its northern sister from all other dialects. Such as our language is, it is the speech of a people spread in all quarters of the globe, a principle remaining bond of two divided empires, and, for the benefit of both, richly fraught with excellent writings on all subjects" (*Inquiry* 430). The first edition of the *Encyclopædia Britannica* ended its article on English by claiming that it had "become the most copious, significant, fluent, courteous, and masculine language in Europe, if not in the world" ("English" 2:499).[11] Writing to Lady Beaumont, Dorothy Wordsworth noted about a quotation from Pascal that "there is always something wanting to the fullness of my satisfaction in the expression of elevated sentiments in the French language; and I cannot but think . . . that if Pascal had been an Englishman . . . there would have been more of dignity in the language of the sentences you have quoted" (*Letters* 2:108).

Robert Nares's *Elements of Orthoepy* (1784) predicted the rise of global English: "Employed in the noblest works of human genius, diffused by colonization over a prodigious extent of territory, where it flourishes in purity and vigour, the English language (could it be secured from internal depravation) seems to defy the effects of any thing less than a political convulsion as violent as those which silenced for ever the superior melody of the Greek and Roman tongues" (xxii). Elements of Nares's description were wishful thinking: already, the English spoken in North America had deviated from that of Britain, so the "purity and vigour" of colonial English was questionable. Nevertheless, Nares's larger point was plain: Britain's might had earned English the right to be the heir to Greek and Latin.

Nothing attests to the excitement of creating a common national language than the energy that eighteenth-century writers devoted to it. Walker's *Critical Pronouncing Dictionary* noted that "the greatest abilities in the nation have been exerted in cultivating and reforming [English]; nor have a thousand minor critics been wanting to add their mite of amendment to their native tongue" (iii). In his hands, pure English appears as a cooperative project in which greater and lesser talents join to perfect the language. A nascent group of intellectual laborers, ranging from pro-vincial schoolmasters to urban academics, fed a limitless appetite among eighteenth-century readers for guides to good English. An educated class that had never had much effect on public life and that had even been the object of contempt suddenly created a communications revolution.

Important as the nationalist ideal was to pure English, the goals of pure English reached farther. Like the arrival of the world wide web, the purifi-cation of English held out hopes that the doors of communication would be open to all willing to learn an easily accessible set of rules. Those who used bad English were not simply vulgar: they were dangerous. In the my-thology of pure English, bad English was like a computer virus or worm, what Nares called "internal depravation," a dangerous threat that could quickly multiply until it destroyed the very ground of communication. Just as the web has increased the possibility of authorship in ways that are still hardly imaginable, so the spread of pure English, in tandem with the rise of print media, especially periodicals, enabled a golden age of amateur authorship in the late eighteenth century.

The increase of authorship was initially felt at a level largely invisi-ble to literary scholars: a rise in letter writing so dramatic as to require John Palmer's overhaul of the British postal system in 1784–85.[12] This increase led Vicesimus Knox to worry that tradesmen would begin to write literature: "The manuscripts which they should delight in compos-ing should be day-books, ledgers, bills, and letters to correspondents . . . . But when figures give place to rhymes, and posting to prosing, beware of a commission of bankrupt" (*Essays* 1:246). Knox acknowledges the key point: tradesmen were now writing. Yet the real authors were from a slightly higher level of respectability, though not necessarily of income. As Robert D. Mayo notes, "The eagerness of provincial clergymen, blue-stockings, and college and university students to publish essay-serials and volumes of verses and literary essays, was matched in the miscellanies by a stream of poems, stories, sketches, mathematical demonstrations, charac-ters, and moral disquisitions, designed to exhibit their authors' learning, taste, ingenuity, and knowledge of the proprieties" (*English Novel* 323). The most important of these "proprieties" was pure English, the golden key to culture, which guaranteed access to the new sphere of print in a way that Greek and Latin never had.

It seemed incomprehensible to many in the eighteenth century that anyone would not want to learn pure English. To know its rules was to employ what looked like the sleekest, most sophisticated tool for communication ever devised. To use bad English, when good English seemed so easily accessible (whether or not it actually was), looked like sheer stubbornness, a refusal to acknowledge the obvious benefits of the English experts' work. In 1809, for example, a colonel of the Bedford militia established an evening school and ordered all the sergeants and corporals to attend "in order that they might learn to read and write": when several did not attend, they were "tried by a court-martial for this offence, and being found guilty, were punished for it" (Taunton, *Reports of Cases* 67).

Pure English, importantly, was accessible to many who were not natives of England. While it would be an overstatement to claim that the non-English invented pure English, many of those not born in England had a high stake in developing and mastering it because it held out the possibility, as Sheridan had claimed, of creating an equal footing for all Britons, regardless of birthplace. Sheridan may have been particularly sensitive to the internal divisions of Great Britain because he himself was from Ireland. Lindley Murray, whose *English Grammar* (1795), along with his other textbooks, had estimated sales of three million in the first half of the nineteenth century, was born in Pennsylvania. Hugh Blair, whose *Lectures on Rhetoric and Belles Lettres* (1783) sold approximately 18,500 copies during the Romantic period, was Scottish, like George Campbell and James Buchanan; his lectures, which became one of the best known guides to English style, originated in his courses at the University of Edinburgh.[13] As Robert Crawford has noted, "while the metropolis and English Court may have taken it for granted that their own standards should be adopted as universal, it was none the less Scots, and generally 'provincials', who encouraged other Scots and provincials to adopt these standards so as to improve and, ultimately, to benefit themselves and their community"(*Devolving* 38).

Even standardizers native to England spent parts of their careers outside it, where they heard Englishes that differed from those of England itself. Before becoming an elocutionist, John Walker was an actor on the Dublin stage; Robert Lowth, whose *Short Introduction to English Grammar* (1762) was the most prevalent grammar before Lindley Murray's, had ecclesiastical appointments in Ireland; William Cobbett, author of a grammar designed for the laboring classes, lived in the United States from 1792 until 1800. Admittedly, books by these writers either do not mention the English of Scotland, Ireland, or the United States or denigrate it as obviously incorrect; they usually assume that their English is that of England itself. Nevertheless, while their introductions often claim to reflect general usage, their specific decisions arose from their own sense of what they liked. Given their biographies, these linguistic preferences cannot be treated as a record of a pre-existing English of England: they are a mosaic arising from collective experiences of Englishes from throughout Great Britain and its colonies.

Pure English was also an important tool for those traditionally excluded from writing on the basis not only of nationality, but also of gender, race, and class. In Jane Austen's *Northanger Abbey* (1818), Henry Tilney tells Catherine Morland that women's letters were characterized by "a general deficiency of subject, a total inattention to stops, and a very frequent ignorance of grammar" (20).[14] As if conscious of his scorn, women writers of the period work particularly hard to make sure that their English follows the rules of the English experts. They were especially aware of the implied contractual nature of pure English: if one used it, then one had a right to be taken seriously. As I have noted earlier, women writers like Edgeworth and Austen ridicule female figures whose English is wanting, partly to underscore the correctness of their own work. In the 1830s, Maria Jane Jewsbury, looking back at an older generation of female writers, noted that "amongst the elders . . . the distinguishing features are nerve, simplicity, vigour, continuity, unambitious earnestness, and good English" ("On Joanna Baillie" 337): she saves the key quality for last. The same investment in pure English can be found in an Anglo-African writer like Olaudah Equiano or a working-class author like Ann Yearsley. Pure English was their admission to the common ground of literate Britain.

This appeal of pure English may help to explain why it quickly spread through English-speaking society even though no official body, like the French Academy, propagated it. Indeed, English experts were as successful as they were partly because there was no obvious central unit, but a multilayered proliferation of works about pure English and a wide range of practices in everyday life (reading, writing, speaking, learning) that could be reshaped by new ideals. Foucault describes "power" in terms of such a proliferation of agencies and practices to insist on its weblike, decentralized nature (*History of Sexuality* 94–96). Yet in his case studies, power usually turns out to be more centralized in practice than he wants it to be in theory. The spread of pure English, in contrast, does a better job of manifesting what Foucault calls power than most of Foucault's actual examples because the effects of pure English were never securely localized in a single discourse or institution.

Although Jonathan Swift imagined the benefits of an academy for English, it never materialized.[15] Instead, monuments of usage like Johnson's dictionary and the works of Lowth, Sheridan, Walker, Murray, and others were the work of enterprising individuals with differing backgrounds, levels of education, professions, and links to the book trade. Nothing prevented the marketing of competing works, stopped writers from disagreeing with each other, or denied the power of individual usage. Walker's *Critical Pronouncing Dictionary*, for example, had many different pronunciations from the previous major work on the subject, Sheridan's *General Dictionary of the English Language* (1780). If authorities disagreed, then the force of any particular prescription was weakened, so that prescriptivism could only reach so far.

The English experts themselves loudly defended their resistance to standardization. In the "Preface" to his *Dictionary*, Samuel Johnson wrote, "I, who can never wish to see dependence multiplied, hope the spirit of *English* liberty will hinder or destroy" the establishment of "an academy . . . for the cultivation of our stile" (108). This is a remarkable claim: in the preface to the most influential work of English prescriptivism ever written, Johnson protests against an academy that might standardize English too completely.[16] Similarly, grammarians avoided fanatical rhetoric about purity. John Fell noted that "the laws of our speech, like the laws of our country, should breathe a spirit of liberty: they should check licentiousness without restraining freedom" (*Essay* xi). When the anonymous author of *A Vocabulary of Such Words in the English Language as are of Dubious or Unsettled Accentuation* described his project, he did so humbly: "Let it not be thought . . . that I mean to advance arrogant opinions of pronunciation; in a case of such difficulty, where men of the first talents disagree, far be it from me to presume to decide; but the seeming necessity of giving a preference has often led me to declare my sentiments" (iii). Even though his work was indeed designed to choose the best pronunciation, he worried about seeming "arrogant." Purification might be a good thing, but it had to appear not as a tyrannical set of arbitrary rules but an organized reflection of the best usage.[17]

The result was a provocative doubleness within pure English. Bad English, like that given by Maria Edgeworth to Harriot Freke, rebelled against the nation by refusing the signs of real Englishness. At the same time, slavishly adhering to rules was also un-English, a pedantic rejection of traditional English liberty and custom. Part of what the English experts codified was resistance to codification. Purification should be seen less as a set of rules than as a nuanced outlook on practical language use that acknowledged both the need for clear guides to good usage and the limitations of such guides.

The archetypal gesture behind such hesitation came in a famous moment in English letters: Samuel Johnson's rejection of Chesterfield's patronage. While this gesture has usually been seen as an assertion of professionalism against patronage, it also changed the relation of English to Britain. Chesterfield's patronage would have tied pure English to Britishness as embodied by a particular social group, the aristocracy. Johnson rejected the power of the aristocracy, symbolic or actual, to control English in favor of the professional author's sense of common usage.[18] Although the rejection created a consequent vagueness about just where to locate such usage, this vagueness was itself part of English's appeal: since common usage was not located in any one body, it could potentially belong to everyone and be found anywhere.

Pure English was present not only in dictionaries and grammars, but also in actors' voices, the work of corrector and compositor in the publishing house, the field correspondence and journals of soldiers throughout the empire, and the writing that everyday readers made in books when they corrected errors in spelling, grammar, and punctuation.[19] Sir James Mackintosh, traveling back to England from his post in India, was frustrated by the ship's slow progress; to pass the time, he noted in his diary, "I have been giving myself an employment which 'to its sweetness brought no satiety.' It was marking a copy of Lindley Murray for F—— and E——, as my text-book for instructing them in grammar" (*Memoirs* 2:230). Mackintosh was no professional grammarian, but an experienced, respected Whig political theorist, heir to the most sophisticated thinking of the Scottish Enlightenment. Yet, coming home to London, he spent hours preparing a copy of Murray's *English Grammar* for his children. What strikes me is how deeply fulfilling he found his task: he adapts Adam's praise of Raphael's teaching in *Paradise Lost* to describe what might seem a tedious job. Grammar wove itself for Mackintosh into the affective structure of everyday family relations. It offered not a dull set of arbitrary rules, but a language of love.

Yet pure English had a dark side. Most obviously, its supposedly common ground was hardly common: it became an excuse for widespread forms of exclusion. As noted in the previous chapter, scholars have discussed well the nastier sides of purification. Their accounts describe the oppressive power of pure English to reinforce a national and imperial sociopolitical system with the ability to stigmatize and marginalize all who did not conform. While I agree with much in these accounts, a causal fallacy tends to haunt them, as when Tony Crowley notes, "Heteroglot divisions, at the level of class and regionality, caused particular anxiety and needed to be banished forever in an attempt to solidify bourgeois hegemony" (*Language in History* 92).The statement assumes that, because English had an important role in bourgeois hegemony, the experts who purified English did so in order to "solidify" this power. As Jane Hodson argues, "the linguistic theories of the late eighteenth century cannot be mapped directly onto political beliefs" (*Language and Revolution* 7). Creating such correspondences attributes a transparent motive to the activity of eighteenth-century English experts that their works do not support.

In addition, discussions of the socially stratifying effects of prescriptivism ascribe more agency to language use than it strictly deserves. Much as Sheridan imagined that language alone could have socially transformative effects, so later scholars have treated language as the tool of a peculiar form of condensation. It comes to stand for the myriad discriminatory strategies and sites of identification available in British society, as if every form of hegemonic power relation could be channeled through English. Such condensation attests to the intimacy of English as a practice of everyday life: it can easily be felt as the chief site at which discrimination occurs. Nevertheless, this intimacy should not lead scholars to mistake effects for causes. Language use cannot be isolated from a host of other factors as a source of social stigmatization. While it is true that the English experts held the English used by most Britons (slaves, laborers, Cockneys, Jews, women, the Irish, the Scottish, the Welsh, and the native inhabitants of the colonies) to be inferior to that of respectable London society, it is hardly clear that the status of these marginalized groups would have been better even if attitudes to English had been different. In terms of its efficacy as an independent cause, pure English probably did more to empower those on the borders of respectability than it did to disempower those already marginalized by other factors.

If in their programmatic statements, English experts praised the unity that pure English would give to Britain, the actual content of their books creates a different impression. English did not let itself be reduced to a set of rules without a fight, and traces of the struggle are everywhere evident in long lists of exceptions and in detailed fine print. Although histories of English often treat the prescriptivists as having reduced English to a neat set of rules, a few minutes actually looking at the English experts' work is enough to destroy that impression: Johnson's *Dictionary* exposes the polysemy of English words; Murray's *English Grammar*, the liability of rules to be broken; and Walker's *Pronouncing Dictionary*, the variety of possible pronunciations available. In eighteenth-century works on language, English battles its own purification, and English experts win at best a very partial victory. Quite apart from the resistance to codification that I attributed to the English experts themselves, their works preserve an entropic drive within English guaranteeing that an exhaustive description would never happen.

Even worse, the rules provided by one expert did not necessarily agree with those of another. As John Clare noted in frustration, "Every writer on grammar seems to be at loggerheads . . . with each other" ("[Grammar]"). The result could make their works look not like a generally available resource for all, but the site of in-house battles between rivals. The accessibility of pure English warred with the potential pedantry of describing a language as complex as English. The rigor of pure English could go too far and end up seeming effete and lifeless.

Nestling beside the happy celebrations of pure English lurked a suspicion, even dread, of its potential. One source came from a long tradition of satirizing the dullness of Greek and Latin as taught in grammar schools, as in William Combe's Dr. Syntax, famously illustrated by Thomas Rowlandson.[20] After English experts had turned English into a language as rule-governed as Greek and Latin, this stereotype of dullness could shift from classical to vernacular pedagogy, as in this passage from George Crabbe:

> These are the Sons of Farmers, and they come
> With partial fondness for the Joys of Home;
> Their Minds are coursing in their Fathers' Fields,
> And e'en the Dream a lively pleasure yields;
> They, much enduring, sit th' allotted hours,
> And o'er a Grammar waste their sprightly powers.
>   (*The Borough*, "Letter 24: Schools" 326–31)

Crabbe shows that English grammar bores farmers' sons as much as Greek and Latin grammar bored gentlemen's sons. The farmer boys are not intrinsically stupid: Crabbe stresses that they have "sprightly powers," in which "sprightly" carries some of its older meaning concerning the powers of the mind. But, in Crabbe's view, grammar is deadening; vampire-like, it drains the boys' powers. All their vitality goes instead to dreaming of "their fathers' fields" where they long to work, rather than wasting their time with pure English.

Another source for the suspicion of pure English was Protestant mistrust of the letter. St. Paul famously described God as the one who "hath made us able ministers of the new testament; not of the letter, but of the spirit: for the letter killeth, but the spirit giveth life" (2 Corinthians 3:6). Paul's anti-Semitic description associates the New Testament with the spirit; the Old, with the letter. Although Paul is not writing about linguistic rules, his theology could be moved to a linguistic realm so as to make pure English look like surrender to the letter's lethal power. John Wesley's *Explanatory Notes Upon the New Testament* (1755), for example, draws upon this suspicion of grammar when discussing the verse "So we also, when we were children, were in bondage under the elements of the world" (Galatians 4:3). Wesley glosses "under the elements of the world" by noting, "Under the typical Observances of the Law, which were like the first Elements of Grammar, the ABC of Children; and were of so gross a Nature, as hardly to carry our Thoughts beyond this World" (506). Nothing in Paul's epistle specifically points to grammar. Wesley instead introduces it as the obvious comparison for a form of crude, child-like knowledge, a bondage to the law that the greater spirituality of Jesus will surpass.

Two other sites for potential suspicions of pure English are Enlightenment politics and history. As I have noted, even the English experts worried that too much purification could seem tyrannical. Imposed rules could look like a tyranny of language, which the standardizers strove to avoid by citing custom. A motley group of politically liberal "anti-English" experts went even further. They published numerous works demonstrating the continuing vitality of older forms of English. In many cases, their scholarship was impressive, often surpassing in antiquarian knowledge anything that the English experts presented, as in the case of Francis Grose's *A Classical Dictionary of the Vulgar Tongue* (1785), Joseph Ritson's *Robin Hood* (1795), and many investigations of local speech.[21] Samuel

Pegge's discussion of London Cockney, for example, argued that "what is called *vulgarity* is barely a residuum of what was antiently the established national dialect, at different periods, from time immemorial" (*Anecdotes* 3).

This association between vernacular forms of English and liberty is not an obvious truth, although literary critics have often treated it as if it were. A linguistic code, in itself, is value-neutral. Yet scholarship on this topic often champions, more or less explicitly, the good rebels against pure English versus the evil English experts, as when Tom Paulin writes, "John Clare wrote before the long ice age of standard British English clamped down on the living language and began to break its local and vernacular energies" ("John Clare in Babylon" 401). Such a championship depends on confusion between the actual prescriptions of the English experts and the social mythology attached to pure English. It also mystifies power relations by granting power to "standard British English" and to the "living language" that they, on their own, never possessed. Arguably, formulations like Paulin's keep alive the mythology of pure English more than prescriptivism ever could by attributing magical abilities to a code.

Finally, Enlightenment histories of language linked poetry and imagination to primitivism, and prose and reason to modernity. Admirable as pure English might be, it killed the supposed wildness and passion of pre-civilized language. Joseph Priestley's "Observations on Style" (1761) narrated a familiar story:

> Both language and arts, in their infancy, are composed of rough unpolished materials, that barely answer the purposes for which they were intended: in process of time . . . they acquire an elegance of construction, and beauty of finishing . . . but, at last, strength and service are sacrificed to useless and superfluous ornaments; following the universal changes of taste, which are, from the rough and unpolished, to the cultivated and manly; and from the cultivated and manly to the effeminate and vitiated. (58–59)

If English had been purified, then it had reached its "cultivated and manly" stage. All that was left was a depressing collapse into the "effeminate and vitiated." As Murray Cohen notes about the eighteenth century, there "is a sense among authors that language has been impoverished, or more extremely, that it is an enemy of poetry" (*Sensible Words* 81).

The most haunting link between purification of English and exhaustion concludes Johnson's "Preface" to his *Dictionary*: "I may surely be contented without the praise of perfection, which, if I could obtain, in this gloom of solitude, what would it avail me? I have protracted my work till most of those whom I wished to please have sunk into the grave, and success and miscarriage are empty sounds: I therefore dismiss it with frigid tranquillity, having little to fear or hope from censure or from praise" (112–3). The shock of this ending overflows the bounds of its literal meaning: metaphorically, purifying English has killed Johnson. This distressing conclusion makes it seem not only that those whom he wished to please are dead, but that he has died as well: he speaks from beyond the grave, in "this gloom of solitude," with "frigid tranquility." Although he does not explicitly connect pure English with death, the downbeat grimness of the "Preface"'s ending suggests that creating good English is lethal.

The combination of enthusiasm and dread surrounding pure English meant that its legacy for later writers was vexed: to use Blake's terms, it was simultaneously the prolific and the devourer. In either case, however, it was there to stay. By the beginning of the Romantic period, the English experts had composed most of pure English's core works, and these had become authoritative. Eighteenth-century grammar books and their examples had long afterlives: John Walker's *Critical Pronouncing Dictionary* and Lindley Murray's *English Grammar* were standards well into the twentieth century, though often in revised form. Indeed, they were almost too successful: production of new works by English experts dropped during the Romantic period because reprints of older ones saturated the market. Writers of the Romantic period were the first in the history of English literature to confront a literary field thoroughly transformed by English's purification and all its social and ideological repercussions.[22] Traces of the new order created by pure English appear in the most basic aspects of what it meant to write. Readers of the Romantic period wanted Murray's *English Grammar* or Walker's *Critical Pronouncing Dictionary* far more than they wanted Wordsworth or Shelley.[23] The works that literary scholars have come to think of as major publications of the early nineteenth century were, for the most part, small drops in a flood of works disseminating pure English. The prestigious house of Longman was bankrolled for decades after it acquired the copyright to Murray's bestseller, and brought out revised versions to extend their copyright for as long as possible (Reibel, "Introduction" ix).[24] In a pamphlet about it, one writer noted in 1809 that it had "eclipsed all former" grammars and that "it has been chiefly owing to his publication, that instruction in English grammar is now so much the wish of all ranks of people" ("A Member of the University of Oxford," *Lindley Murray Examined* 4). The radical publisher Joseph Johnson published numerous works of English grammar and elocution designed for classroom use. Even John Taylor, publisher of Keats and Clare, planned to write a *Grammar Made Easy*, though he did not finish it (Chilcott, *A Publisher and His Circle* 17). In 1805, Isaac D'Israeli wrote to John Murray (later Byron's publisher) about his friend, the bookseller Sir Richard Phillips: "He owns his *belles-lettres* books have given no great profits . . . but he makes a fortune by juvenile and useful compilations . . . he thinks all *belles lettres* are nonsense" (Smiles, *A Publisher and His Friends* 1:49). Phillips owned up to the hard truth: useful books sold; poetry did not. During Wordsworth's lifetime, the poem by him that most readers would have seen was "The Pet-Lamb" because Lindley Murray included it in his *Introduction to the English Reader*, which went through thirty-six editions by 1836 (Bauer, "Wordsworth and the Early Anthologies" 40).

The English experts permeated not only the booksellers' shelves but also the literate knowledge of the Romantic writers. Coleridge, Byron, and Scott all used John Walker's pioneering rhyming dictionary of the English language, which listed both perfect rhymes and merely "allowable" ones.[25] It became an indispensable tool for poets. Scott, for example, wrote to John Ballantyne, "I wish James could bring me Walkers Dict[ionar]y of rhymes from my lib[rar]y. It is on a shelf on my right hand as I sit at desk" (*Letters* 1:460).[26] Scott's letter is a good example of how pure English was not a disembodied set of abstractions, but an everyday practice. It involved not just cold rules but something as detailed as the personal organization of space: Scott's letter suggests that he had reached for Walker's dictionary many times.

Hazlitt and Cobbett both published English grammars in which they engaged in lengthy contestations of earlier English experts like Lowth and Murray.[27] Even Byron, notorious for his indifference to English usage, boasted of having "compiled the major part of two Armenian & English Grammars" (*Byron's Letters and Journals* 9:31). I have already noted the importance of pure English to the work of women writers like Austen and Edgeworth, who strove to combat the perceptions that women's English was inevitably faulty. Although John Clare railed against the tyranny of grammar, he did so in terms that came directly from the English experts. When Clare praised "a man who learns enough of grammer to write sufficiently plain so as to be understood by others as well as to understand his own consceptions himself" ("[Grammar]" 481), he sounds much like Lindley Murray arguing that the "fundamental rule" for composition is "to communicate, in the clearest and most natural order, the ideas which we mean to transfuse into the minds of others" (*EG* 222). Their assumptions were the same; their means of realizing them, different.

Whatever a writer's personal relationship to English, all writers could expect their manuscripts to be altered to fit a publisher's sense of correct English; according to Philip Luckombe in 1771,

> Most authors expect the Printer to spell, point, and digest their Copy, that it may be intelligible and significant to the Reader; which is what a Compositor and the Corrector jointly have regard to . . . It shews how necessary it is for Master Printers to be deliberate in chusing Apprentices for the Case, and not to fix upon any but such as have either had a liberal education or at least are perfect in writing and reading their own language. (*History and Art of Printing* 377)

Although authors in the period complained about the mistakes made by printers' devils, Luckombe reminds us of the coin's other side: many compositors and correctors labored long and hard to turn messy manuscripts into pure English. Caleb Stower in *The Printer's Grammar* (1808) made a similar point: "Where a corrector understands the language and characters of a work, he often finds occasion to alter and to mend things that he can maintain to be either wrong, or else ill digested" (213). Pure English was not simply a pristine ideal located in the minds of a few grammarians: it quickly became part of the multi-tiered stages of transforming manuscript pages to marketable print.

If corrections were not made, critics were quick to attack perceived faults, and they usually pounced on the author, not the compositor or corrector.[28] Whig critics accused Tory writers of bad grammar, and vice versa: the desirability of pure English and the evils of its opposite were shared assumptions across the political spectrum.[29] So powerful was the ideal of usage that critics would attack even mistakes that were not especially obvious. For example, Francis Jeffrey, in reviewing Byron's *The Corsair*, quoted the lines, "He sate him down in silence, and his look / Resumed the calmness which before forsook." Jeffrey then scolded, "Forsook what?—The verb is unquestionably active, and not neuter. The whole passage indeed is clumsy in diction, and, we would almost say, vulgar in expression" ("Review of *The Corsair*" 63). He objects because Byron's "forsook" needs a direct object; the verb is transitive ("active"), not intransitive ("neuter"). One might have responded to Jeffrey that Byron's meaning is nevertheless plain enough: he has simply elided "him" after "forsook." Yet Jeffrey dislikes Byron's poetry enough that he is determined to add bad grammar to his list of Byron's supposed faults. The perception of bad poetry demands bad grammar as evidence. Moreover, Romantic authors themselves absorbed such prescriptions in their response to each other. Wordsworth, for example, upon reading the preface to the second edition of William Godwin's *Enquiry Concerning Political Justice*, noted, "Such a piece of barbarous writing I have not often seen. It contains scarce one sentence decently written" (*Letters* 1:170–71).

Such attacks, along with the fact that books like Blair's *Lectures on Rhetoric and Belles Lettres* far outsold the works of Romantic writers, meant that purification and its effects undercut Romantic writers' exclusive control over or responsibility for English. For all the vitality that the rise of pure English gave to the spread of authorship, it also marked a distinct loss of power for authors. A long-cherished myth in literary history had been that great authors had a magical power to shape English. Spenser in *The Faerie Queene* praised Geoffrey Chaucer as the "well of English undefyled" (4.2.32), as if Chaucer had been the origin of all pure English, and would be its everlasting repository. Closer to the Romantic period, Thomas Warton had written a widely noted *History of English Poetry* (1774–81), a history of the collective efforts of poets to create "the growing elegancies of the English language" (4:1). In his preface to his edition of Shakespeare, Samuel Johnson had repeated a commonplace when he wrote that to Shakespeare "we must ascribe the praise, unless Spenser may divide it with him, of having first discovered to how much smoothness and harmony the English language could be softened" (321). Great writers had refined the supposed crudeness of English.

English experts let it be known that, whatever had happened in the past, for the future, they, and not great writers, would determine the course of English. Admittedly, their books often cited literary works for examples; their most frequently cited sources were Swift, the New Testament, Hume, Addison, Pope, *The Spectator*, the Old Testament, Shakespeare, Dryden, and Milton (*DENG* 35).[30] Of the poets on the list, all were dead—in some cases, long dead—as if whatever the English language needed to get from poetry, it had gotten long ago. John Walker's rhyming dictionary underscored this point: "It is highly probable that our prosody has passed its meridian, and that no reformation can possibly be made without injuring it. The delicate ears of a Pope or an Addison, would scarcely have acquiesced in the usage of imperfect rhymes, and sanctified them so often by their practice, if such rhymes had been really a blemish" ("Preface to the Index" 301). For Walker, Pope and Addison were English poetry's "meridian," and their "delicate ears" had defined which imperfect rhymes were allowable. Any later rhyming would be guilty of "injuring" English prosody unless it followed the models established by Addison/Pope/Walker.

The case was similar for prose. Joseph Priestley, in his "Observations on Style" (1761), noted that English had reached its peak:

> The conjectures and apprehensions we find in the writings of *Addison*, *Pope*, *Swift*, and others, their cotemporaries, that the language of their time would, at length become obsolete in this nation, are absolutely groundless. And it may be taken for granted, that the schemes of some still more modern writers, to add something considerable to the perfection of the English language, in order to contribute to the permanency of it, cannot, according to the course of nature, produce any effect. If the English language hath not already attained to its maturity, we may safely pronounce that it never will. (60)

Although Priestley means this to be good news for authors, he sends mixed signals. Modern writers can be comforted that English will not change dramatically, so later readers will understand what they write. Yet Priestley also suggests that modern writers have suddenly become irrelevant: English no longer needs them. If all writing in English suddenly ceased, it would have little effect on the language's "permanency."

Not all English experts were as sure as Walker and Priestley that the English of the best authors was good enough. Charles Coote noted that, although it was "particularly incumbent" upon authors "to observe a strict adherence to grammatical propriety," they rarely lived up to their responsibility: "This is a point to which the greater part even of our most esteemed writers have not sufficiently attended" (*Elements of Grammar* v–vi). William Hazlitt noted with irritation that Lindley Murray's best-selling grammar made it appear that "hardly any of our best writers ever wrote a word of English" ("Late Mr. Horne Tooke" 11:57n).

By the Romantic period, English had a canon, a standard language, more than enough exemplars of good and bad usage, and a decided bias toward prose, especially Addison's.[31] There hardly seemed any pressing need for new literature at all. In seeming to exclude contemporary writing from shaping English, the English experts were creating more than a linguistic challenge. Given the importance of pure English to the politics of nationhood, they were also implicitly removing literature by living writers from a significant role in the future of Great Britain. They had stolen the language and the nation, to say nothing of the market.

It was an open question whether writers would choose to align themselves with or against the sectors of their society enforcing pure English. Particularly vexing was the fact that, whatever side they chose, the outcome might not matter: since all the authors quoted by the grammarians were dead, English needed no new authors anyway. If literature was not going to provide models of correct English usage, what good was it?

The answer was that literature could model usage in a different way. Freed from having to model a usage that would be common to all, literature was free to explore how English might become specialized, adapted to particular aims and purposes. Literary critics have long questioned the notion that there is a distinctively literary mode of English, good for all times and places, because any definition of such English erases the roles of readers and of institutions in creating what is considered literary.[32] Yet such questioning has often avoided the fact that, while a transhistorical definition of literary language may not be possible or useful, there are large-scale, general trends characterizing the history of literary English, as Josephine Miles and others noted long ago.[33] As a concept, literary English should be thought of less as an absolute category than as a prototype that varies historically. The visibility and quality of its variance altered dramatically after the standardization of English and its emergence as a print standard.

Previously, specialized English had meant specialized vocabulary, the words that Samuel Johnson notoriously refused to include in his dictionary. After English's purification, specialization could be more far reaching. In literature, it took two forms. The first was the manifestation of literary genius as an aftereffect of a distinctive style, which supposedly became a linguistic mirror of personality. Although attention to style had a history as long as the history of literary criticism itself, the association between style and individual genius blossomed only after the purification of English, once it could stand out against a background of supposedly unmarked rules defined by a standardized language. Style gave language a peculiar position: it was both prominent and a mere echo of the author's personality.

Style as manifestation of personality is a more coherent concept the farther one gets away from actual textual details. If a personal style is marked by distinctive traits, then are moments in a work not marked by those traits not really by the author? The notion of style also seems to promise that usage can be siphoned off from content, except that a list of an author's characteristic words, syntactic formations, or phonological combinations rarely adds up to much of a sense of generative personality. Rather than being a phenomenon solely of language, style as an expression of personality might best be thought of as a gist representation, combining generalized memories, strips of actual language, and emotional moods that create the impression of a distinctively textured reading experience in connection with a particular author. Although the reader contributes much to creating this impression of style, the mythology of genius encourages readers to imagine that it comes entirely from authors themselves. The belief that authorial personality has a mysterious ability to stamp itself in unique ways on language is an enduring result of the Romantic response to English's purification.

Wordsworth's career is exemplary. In his "Preface to *Lyrical Ballads*" (1800), Wordsworth, having explained the subject matter of his poems, then turns to "apprize" the reader "of a few circumstances relating to their *style*." His ideas about style turn out to be a purification of English as well, one that involves abandoning "poetic diction" for the "language of men" (*Lyrical Ballads and Other Poems* 747). Wordsworth aims to purify the language of poetry not only of poetic diction but also, evidently, of poets as well (though he later retracts this claim): to write in "the language of men" is to claim that the poems are not authored by an individual, but by language itself. Yet Wordsworth's subsequent reception guaranteed that what he thought was an attempt to write in an extrapersonal mode came to be seen as a peculiar style belonging to him alone. Such an individualizing of Wordsworthian language is, for example, the chief project of Coleridge's discussion of Wordsworth in the *Biographia Literaria*. Wordsworth purifies the language of poetry from poetic diction; Coleridge purifies Wordsworth from anything in his poetry that cannot be admired as a mark of individual genius.

Yet style is not enough. Intersecting with and to some extent interfering with the link between English and personal style was the rigidification of conventions defining the English of certain forms of writing (poetry, the novel, and familiar prose); these conventions functioned for the vernacular in the way that classical topoi had done in earlier literary periods. These conventions arose not only from the rules of the English experts but also from two influential models for using pure English: the London-based elocutionary movement and the rise of expository prose, based in the Scottish universities. Both defined competing modes for making pure English an effective vehicle of communication. Important distinctions between poetry, novels, and the familiar essay arose through different relations to these models, which set up far more visible walls among modes than had previously existed.

The result was a tension about English at the heart of modern literary authorship. Authors aspiring to literariness had to situate themselves between the linguistic demands of an individual style and those of a literary mode. We have become used to seeing phrases like "the poet Shelley" or "the novelist Scott," but the Romantic period opened up a potential gap between the kind of English belonging to the job title and that belonging to the proper name. What it meant to be "Shelley" in English might differ from what it meant to be a "poet" in English. To be a literary author, it was not enough to write good English, as it had been for a time in the eighteenth century. Now, one had to write poetic (or novelistic or essayistic) English that was at the same time recognizably yours: one had to conform and not conform.

In light of this tension, there is a long history of reading the Romantic encounter with English as a catastrophe, dating back to the attacks on Wordsworthian simplicity, Keats's Cockneyism, and the sloppiness of Scott's prose. In 1828, De Quincey lamented that "the most eminent English writers do not write their mother tongue without continual violations of propriety. With the single exception of Mr. Wordsworth, who has paid an honourable attention to the purity and accuracy of his English, we believe that there is not one celebrated author of this day who has written two pages consecutively, without some flagrant impropriety in the grammar (such as the eternal confusion of the preterite with the past participle, confusion of verbs transitive with intransitive, &c. &c.), or some violation more or less of the vernacular idiom" ("Rhetoric" 2:270). De Quincey's accusations cast a long shadow. Romanticism as a field has been especially sensitive to language because key figures in New Criticism, from T. S. Eliot to Donald Davie, condemned Romantic poetry for its bad style.[34] The philosophical complexity of the Romantics' understanding of language has been scholars' defensive cover for the perceived inadequacy of the Romantics' relation to English. Scholarship on Romanticism has fought an uphill battle to prove the aesthetic value of its language, a battle still being fought around newly canonical figures like Mary Robinson and Felicia Hemans.

John Guillory's *Cultural Capital* has put a different spin on the failure of Romanticism by arguing that the "failure of poetry to produce a definitive new *Hochsprache* on the basis of its generic superiority . . . will ultimately make it necessary to conceptualize a category of 'literature' inclusive even of the novel" (131). According to Guillory, if only the Romantic poets had done a better job of generating a *Hochsprache*, a linguistic decorum mirroring a social decorum could have been salvaged. Yet I would argue that by the Romantic period, it was too late for any literary mode to produce a *Hochsprache*. The point of the English experts' work was that they defined good and bad English, not literary writers. If one could not have a *Hochsprache*, however, one could at least have style, though within certain generic constraints.

In the following chapters, I want to revisit the question of Romantic English from a new perspective. According to Foucault,

> At the beginning of the nineteenth century, at a time when language was burying itself within its own density as an object and allowing itself to be traversed, through and through, by knowledge, it was also reconstituting itself elsewhere, in an independent form, difficult of access, folded back upon the enigma of its own origin and existing wholly in reference to the pure act of writing. Literature is the contestation of philology (of which it is nevertheless the twin figure): it leads language back from grammar to the naked power of speech, and there it encounters the untamed, imperious being of words . . . . It breaks with the whole definition of *genres* as forms adapted to an order of representations, and becomes merely a manifestation of a language which has no other law than that of affirming—in opposition to all other forms of discourse—its own precipitous existence; and so there is nothing for it to do but to curve back in a perpetual return upon itself, as if its discourse could have no other content that the expression of its own form. (*Order of Things* 300)

Foucault's rhapsody, of which I have excerpted only a part, is a prose poem in itself, as if to challenge the conflict between philology and literature that it describes. For Foucault, philology leaves literature with no choice but "contestation" in the form of art for art's sake, the "law . . . affirming . . . its own precipitous existence." Foucault presents an idealized picture of literature which, in opposing philology, insists on "the naked power of speech."

Romantic as Foucault's history is, "contestation" is not the best word to describe the relation of the literature of the Romantic period to philology. Though Foucault refers specifically to comparative philology, the density of knowledge that he associates with it had one of its origins in the eighteenth-century English experts. Writers of the Romantic period had lost whatever contest there was to lose. Never again would literature define English, even as myth. Moreover, the naked power of speech was long gone by the Romantic period because by the early nineteenth century, literature was not literature until it was in print. Important as reading aloud might be, it usually happened only after a work had been printed (with certain prominent exceptions, as in Coleridge's performances of *Christabel*).

Rather than contesting pure English by appealing to a nostalgic orality, as Foucault suggests, Romantic literature recognized that print had changed English, what it meant to write in English, and what it meant to be a person using English. The result was an extraordinarily fertile period of innovation and experimentation with the new forms of agency available to English users. The following chapters trace both the tentativeness and uncertainty surrounding Romantic authors' relations to English and the remarkable durability of some of their results.

§ 2 Romantic Syntax

In "Resolution and Independence" (1802), English usage becomes part of Wordsworth's overt topic, since what draws Wordsworth to the Leech-Gatherer is partly his English:

> His words came feebly, from a feeble chest,
> Yet each in solemn order followed each,
> With something of a lofty utterance drest;
> Choice word, and measured phrase; above the reach
> Of ordinary men; a stately speech!
> Such as grave Livers do in Scotland use,
> Religious men, who give to God and Man their dues.   (99–107)

Wordsworth's lyric privileges the Leech-Gatherer's Scottish diction as a sign not of provincialism or vulgarity but of superiority to "ordinary men." This superiority does not come from the Leech-Gatherer alone; it is like that of Scottish "grave Livers" and therefore comes burdened with historical associations.[1] These are so powerful that the Leech-Gatherer's English overcomes his physical weakness. Though linked by assonance, the repeated "feebly"/"feeble" of the first line gives way to the solemnly repeated "each"s of the second line, as Wordsworth detaches the Leech-Gatherer's words from his solitary, weak body and relocates them (though only in his perception) as a powerful communal voice.

Yet Wordsworth's praise of the Leech-Gatherer's English only goes so far. He lets little of the "lofty utterance" appear in his poem, since he quotes the Leech-Gatherer directly for only three lines. When the Leech-

Gatherer does speak, his speech is not distinctively Scottish in terms of word choice, syntax, or phonemes:

> "Once I could meet with them on every side;
> But they have dwindled long by slow decay;
> Yet still I persevere, and find them where I may."   (131–33)

The Leech-Gatherer's actual English, powerful in its use of inversion ("dwindled long") and etymological contrast (the Latinate "persevere" stands out among words largely derived from Anglo-Saxon), does not differ obviously from Wordsworth's, despite differences in tone.[2] Wordsworth raises the expectation of historically and nationally marked speech from the Leech-Gatherer but assimilates the Leech-Gatherer's words to his own linguistic idiom.

The Leech-Gatherer's dialect is present in Wordsworth's description but absent in actual quotation. As a result, despite Wordsworth's sympathy and respect for the Leech-Gatherer, "Resolution and Independence" plays a role in the larger history of pure English by privileging Wordsworth's English over the Leech-Gatherer's. Wordsworth writes as if an accurate printed representation of the Leech-Gatherer's actual phonemes would be too vulgar for his purposes. In erasing the Leech-Gatherer's dialect, Wordsworth becomes an agent of pure English as a tool of social stratification.[3]

Yet to leave the matter there is to sidestep the more interesting theoretical challenges that Wordsworth's stanza poses to the study of Romanticism. Beneath Wordsworth's topically foregrounded contrast in language use lie other aspects of the history of English that do not rise so obviously to thematic significance or blend so tidily with familiar histories. The history of English usage is not simply an aftereffect of, or accompaniment to, more familiar histories of social stratification. For example, in the nineteenth century, "*to be* finally disappeared as a perfect auxiliary, where it had been dominant with verbs of motion," to be replaced by "to have": hence, "we are now arrived" became "we have now arrived"; in this usage, English distinguished itself from other European languages (Görlach, *English in Nineteenth-Century England* 71–72). In itself, this development has little visible connection to the achievement of middle-class hegemony, the spread of the British empire, the redefinition of sex-gender roles, the rise of industrialization, or any other of the building blocks of modern British history. To force it into such a relationship would be, to use Jakobson's terms, to confuse the history of the code with the history of the context.[4] Both histories occurred simultaneously, but the history of English usage was not driven solely by the need to sustain some other history, either literary, philosophical, or political.

The stanza thus bears out Foucault's contention that grammar has a history of its own separate from its social function: "The history of grammar is not the projection into the field of language and its problems of a history that is generally that of reason or of a particular mentality, a history in any case that it shares with medicine, mechanical sciences, or theology; but . . . it involves a type of history—a form of dispersion in time, a mode of succession, of stability, and of reactivation, a speed of deployment or rotation—that belongs to it alone" (*Archaeology of Knowledge* 127). Wordsworth's stanza demonstrates in miniature some of Foucault's claims. Grammar's "mode of succession" appears in the phrase "something of a lofty utterance." Before Wordsworth, when the phrase "something of a [noun phrase]" was used, its status as a hedge often gave it an informal, slightly comic register.[5] In Wordsworth's poem, this mildly undignified phrase undergoes reregistration by appearing in a newly serious context.[6] The Leech-Gatherer's "lofty utterance," in other words, is introduced in syntax with an unlofty history, and the result is a line whose tone is consequently difficult to gauge. "Something of a lofty utterance" can mark the speaker's slightly condescending distance from the Leech Gatherer's loftiness, a lessening paralleled by the metrical contraction of the Leech-Gatherer's "utterance" from three to two syllables; a factual recognition that the conversation was, after all, an ordinary one, and that the Leech-Gatherer's speech only rose to "lofty utterance" at certain moments; or a sign that the concept of lofty utterance is a metaphor that approximates the Leech-Gatherer's speech without quite capturing its "dress" perfectly.

The stanza's grammatical "stability" appears in its general adherence to conventional grammatical codes, including the repetition of a dominant subject-verb-object pattern and its tight appositional elaboration of "words" in the first line. Wordsworthian grammatical "reactivation" appears in the line "such as grave Livers do in Scotland use." By the early nineteenth century, the pleonastic "do" had become obsolete in terms of general practice, except in contexts "where an adverb intervened between auxiliary and lexical verb" (Denison, "Syntax" 194).[7] Coleridge, for example, was scathing about Maturin's use of the pleonastic "do."[8] Yet

Wordsworth reactivates a dated verb form and thereby creates a certain tonal ambiguity. The extra "do," which receives metrical stress and retrospective emphasis from its assonance with "use," expands and weights the verb in ways that both exemplify and possibly ironize the dignified language of the "grave Livers."

This philological analysis disintegrates Wordsworth's stanza, making it "dusty" in ways that do not point to a tidy overall thesis about Wordsworth, the poem, or even the poem's relation to English. One could potentially do such an analysis for every stanza in the poem, and end up with a jumble of unrelated linguistic facts, of varying interest. This chapter will foreground this dustiness by analyzing not authors or even works, but certain problems of usage created by the purification of English. These problems were not unique to literary works, but are found in all printed English of the period. Yet I use literary works to document not only the appearance of these problems, as traditional philology would do, but also the kinds of transactions that they made available among readers, works, and implied authors.

As I noted in the previous chapter, English experts had modeled how to analyze English: reviewers, educators, and everyday readers paid close attention to a given author's successes or failures with linguistic purity. This high cultural value put on noticing correct usage distinguishes early nineteenth-century readers from twenty-first century readers: it is rare to see correct English used as a yardstick to judge contemporary literature. Yet the evidence of reviews, marginalia, and other forms of reader response from the late eighteenth and early nineteenth centuries suggests that readers behaved differently. My point is not that readers corrected every grammatical or stylistic error in all that they read. Instead, reading took place within a cultural setting that highly valued certain forms of English usage and the ability to notice them. Rather than looking solely at what Foucault calls the "author-function," I will treat English usage as the site for uncovering the "author-work-reader" functions, the ways that local instances of usage offer multiple possible methods for readers to understand their relation to works and authors.

I take two representative case studies arising from the most notorious rules of the eighteenth-century English experts: the prohibition on double negation, and the will-shall distinction. The first case study concentrates on William Wordsworth's "Tintern Abbey"; the second, the literature of the Romantic period as a whole. These studies are the most technical in this book, in the sense that they engage most carefully the linguistic details that have given philology a bad name among literary critics. I offer them as a challenge to the assumptions that an analysis must make a "bigger point" to be considered important by confronting the history inherent in the dustiest elements of usage.

"Tintern Abbey" is a good test case because it has long been recognized as the most linguistically difficult of the 1798 *Lyrical Ballads*. As Henry Nelson Coleridge noted in 1820, "Tintern Abbey" contained lines that "speak to the wise, but for the generality need interpreters."[9] There are many sources for this difficulty, such as the ambiguous grammar described by William Empson (*Seven Types* 151–54) and the complex signals around the status of the speaker described by Anthony Easthope (*Poetry as Discourse* 125–33). Another difficult characteristic is the frequent negation: the poem's speaker is more comfortable with announcing what is not than in describing what is.

Eighteenth-century English experts loved discussing the proper treatment of negation. Since, as had been noted since Sidney's *Astrophil and Stella*, two negatives logically made a positive, they disliked the traditional use of multiple negations as intensifiers (van Ostade, "Double Negation"). Robert Lowth, for example, noted that "two negatives in English destroy one another, or are equivalent to an affirmative." His verb choice is striking, as if syntax self-destructed under the pressure of too many negations. He quoted lines from Shakespeare's *Much Ado About Nothing* with double negatives and added, "It is a relique of the antient style, abounding with negatives; which is now grown wholly obsolete" (*Short Introduction* 95). His adverb "wholly" insists on his ability to define modern usage: what is past is past, but modernity belongs to Lowth.[10]

Lindley Murray repeated Lowth's prescription and added more detail by quoting bad sentences and then correcting them:

> Some writers have improperly employed two negatives instead of one; as in the following instances. "I never did repent for doing good, nor shall not now;" "*nor shall I now.*" "Never no imitator ever grew up to his author;" "*never did any,*" &c. "I cannot by no means allow him what this argument must prove;" "I cannot *by any* means," &c. or, "I can by *no means.*" "Nor let no comforter approach me;" "nor let *any* comforter," &c. "Nor is danger ever apprehended in such a government, no more than we commonly apprehend danger from thunder or earthquakes:" It should be "*any more.*" (*EG* 121)

Lowth and Murray were not alone: the prohibition on double negatives was a firm site of consensus among the English experts. They disagreed about other, finer points, but together they created a daunting, much-repeated ban.[11]

Lowth and Murray provide a philological context for certain passages in "Tintern Abbey":

> *Nor*, perchance,
> If I were *not* thus taught, should I the more
> Suffer my genial spirits to decay.   (112–14)

> *Nor* greetings where *no* kindness is   (131)

> *Nor*, perchance,
> If I should be, where I *no more* can hear
> Thy voice, nor catch from thy wild eyes these gleams
> Of past existence . . .   (147–50; my emphasis)

None of Wordsworth's sentences breaks grammatical rules, yet his clusters of negations border on the constructions that the English experts outlawed. The poem's English skates on the brink of linguistic impropriety, coming close to a perilous edge without actually being incorrect.

William Cowper is a valuable yardstick for judging such negations because, prior to Wordsworth, Cowper had had great success in adapting Latinate style to conversational blank verse. Juxtaposing their uses of a similar form of negation ("nor less") reveals why Wordsworth seemed so much harder than Cowper:

> Nor less composure waits upon the roar
> Of distant floods, or on the softer voice
> Of neighb'ring fountain, or of rills that slip
> Through the cleft rock.   (*The Task* 1:190–93)

> Nor less, I trust,
> To them I may have owed another gift,
> Of aspect more sublime.   ("Tintern Abbey" 36–38)

Like any conjunction, "nor" is both anticipatory and retrospective. It implies that what follows will contrast with what has come before, but that there is some conceptual equivalence between the two conjoined items.[12] In Cowper, the anticipatory function of "nor less" is obvious since the phrase immediately precedes the noun it modifies, "composure." The retrospective function of "nor less composure" is equally obvious: it refers back to other forms of composure described in the preceding lines: sounds that "restore / The tone of languid Nature," such as forest winds that "lull the spirit while they fill the mind" (1.182–83, 187).

Wordsworth's "nor less" seems simple and is not. Cowper's "nor less" is adjectival; Wordsworth's "nor less" is adverbial. The problem is deciding which verb the adverbial phrase modifies. There appear to be two possibilities: "trust" and "(may have) owed." Given its proximity to "I trust," "nor less," especially out of context, appears to modify it, to mean something like, "And I do not trust the less. . . ." However, there is a problem with this reading. No previous verb resembling "I trust" exists for which "nor less" could be a conjunction. Instead, "nor less" actually looks back to the clause "I have owed to them / In hours of weariness, sensations sweet" ten lines earlier in lines 27–28, which in itself renames the "forms of beauty" identified in line 24. Put prosaically, the conjunction works like this: "I have owed to these forms of beauty sweet sensations. . . . Nor less I may have owed to them another gift." "Nor less" modifies "may have owed" rather than "trust"—but "Tintern Abbey" does not make it easy to see this construction because the syntactically related parts of speech are far apart.[13] In particular, although the syntax aligns "nor less" with "owed" rather than with "trust," Wordsworth's lineation does not. Since the phrase "Nor less, I trust," occupies its own half line and the verb "owed" does not appear until the middle of the next line, the spacing invites the reading of "nor less" as modifying "I trust." The arrival of the relevant verb "owed" in the next line may not cancel the sense that the exact scope of "nor less" remains ambiguous, especially since ten lines of poetry separate the two conjoined uses of "owed." Is the speaker uncertain about the quality of his trust ("nor less I trust"), or his debt to the "forms of beauty" ("nor less . . . I may have owed")? The first possibility is more directly personal; the second still personal, but more indirect, since it is mediated through his understanding of the effect of the "sensations sweet" on him. A further complication arises from the lack of semantic fit between adverb and verb: "nor less" promises a climax, which turns out to be the tentative verb phrase "may have owed." Although for readers used to poetry that shatters grammar, such syntax may not seem especially troubling, it marked a significant increase in difficulty for readers used to Cowperian transparency.

While I have thus far discussed "nor less" as a conjunction, Wordsworth's use of it is further complicated by its status as a double negative, though not quite of the kind denounced by eighteenth-century English

experts. They objected to the redundancy of explicitly negative free morphemes, but there are other classes of negatives, such as the negatively
coded member of pairs of scalar contraries, as in "disturb" (14, 95, 133)
(vs. "compose"), "blind" (25) (vs. "sighted"), or "trivial" (33) (vs. "important").[14] Including such implicit negatives allows us to see how often
Wordsworth in "Tintern Abbey" negates words associated with loss or absence to create lexical, if not always syntactic, double negatives: "*Nor . . .
disturb*" (14); "These forms of beauty have *not* been to me, / As is a land-
scape to a *blind* man's eye" (24–25); "As may have had *no trivial* influence" (33); "*Nor less*, I trust" (36); "That had *no* need of a *remoter* charm"
(82); "*Not* for this / *Faint* I, nor mourn nor murmur" (86–87); "*not* as in
the hour / Of *thoughtless* youth" (90–91); "*Not harsh nor grating*" (93);
"Nature *never* did *betray*" (123); "*Nor . . .* wilt thou then *forget*" (147, 150);
"*Nor* wilt thou then *forget*" (156) (emphasis added).

The rhetorical name for a double negation like "nor . . . forget"
is litotes, a rhetorical figure with a long and vexed history: writing as
Martinus Scriblerus, for example, Alexander Pope and his collaborators
had condemned it as the characteristic usage of "Ladies, Whisperers and
Backbiters" (*Peri Bathous* 203). The eighteenth-century grammar books
that condemned double negation usually did not mention litotes, but
many eighteenth-century guides to style did. In them, rhetorical figures
like litotes belonged to a fund of customary usages whose psychological affect could be defined. For example, the *Encyclopædia Britannica* explained that litotes was "a mode of speech, in which, by the denying the
contrary, more is intended than the words express." This mode "is often
used for modesty sake [*sic*] where a person is led to say any thing in his
own praise, or to soften an expression which in direct terms might sound
harsh or give offence" ("Rhetoric" 8:5700).

Although the eighteenth-century English experts treated such figures
at length, they surrounded their examinations with considerable suspicion and the sense that these were relics of a rhetorical style that modern
English could reject. For them, plainness and perspicuity were hallmarks
of good English: in their eyes, indirection of the kind described by the
Encyclopædia Britannica was a messy business that went against the soul
of plain English. Hugh Blair, for example, noted that "the strong pa-
thetic, and the pure sublime, not only have little dependence on figures
of speech, but, generally, reject them" (*LRB* 1:278–79). They were most
impatient with rhetorical schemes like litotes (as opposed to tropes like

metaphors) because they seemed dispensable, flourishes that stood in the way of communication. Even when they acknowledged the virtues of figurative language, they included strict rules for using it correctly.[15]

Cowper uses litotes in *The Task* in the way that the rhetoricians describe, as when he looks back on his boyhood experience eating wild berries: "Hard fare! but such as boyish appetite / Disdains not, nor the palate undepraved / By culinary arts unsav'ry deems" (*The Task* 1.123–25). Even as Cowper insists on the moral value of his pure boyhood experiences with nature (his palate is "undeprav'd / By culinary arts"), he plays with a gap in decorum between the ordinariness of the experiences described and the weighty periphrasis of his language ("nor . . . unsav'ry deems"). The result is an urbane indirectness of the sort detested by the English experts, who stressed the importance of simple, straightforward communication.

While the syntax of Wordsworth's litotes in "Tintern Abbey" is not obscure, its pragmatic use is. The *Encyclopædia Britannica*'s definition, in which litotes reveals that "more is intended than the words express," is put to the test in "Tintern Abbey." The figure undergoes an *ad hoc* semantic broadening in which its range of possible psychological associations dramatically increases. Critics have usually read negation in "Tintern Abbey" as evidence of Wordsworth's defensiveness and uncertainty. As Wolfson notes, "disarming a question by negative containment is visibly evasive action, however; it is not the same as putting doubt to rest" (*Questioning Presence* 64). To concentrate on one example, Wordsworth concludes his poem by twice commanding Dorothy, "Nor wilt thou then forget," presumably because he feels unable to assert more positively that Dorothy will always remember. In the traditional reading, his over-insistence on her not forgetting points to his own fears about the impermanence of her memory and, consequently, his fears about himself.

Yet attention to the history of English points to several other possible readings as well:

1. The *Encyclopædia*'s association between litotes and the need to "soften an expression which in direct terms might sound harsh" may still obtain: Wordsworth writes "Nor wilt thou then forget" to veil the potential bossiness of his commands to Dorothy.

2. As Scriblerus recognized, litotes can also slide easily into irony; Wordsworth may tell Dorothy not to forget as a gently ironic comment on how well he believes that Dorothy will remember.

3. Given the English experts' distrust of rhetorical schemes, litotes may work as archaism, denoting not hesitation or uncertainty but certainty so absolute that it can be presented lightly, as in the Homeric "not the least hero." As an archaism, Wordsworth's "nor wilt thou then forget" may declare his deep faith in the power of Dorothy's memory, one that gains seriousness by drawing on usages of English that were becoming outmoded.

4. "Nor wilt thou then forget" also acquires possible meanings internal to the poem because it revises Wordsworth's previous command "with what healing thoughts / Of tender joy wilt thou remember me." The revision may mark a desire for an increased stylistic weight: "nor wilt thou then forget" sounds more important than "wilt thou remember" because it requires more words.

5. More subtly, this revision may also suggest that "remember" is too specific a term for what Wordsworth wishes, and the vaguer "nor . . . forget" allows for a broader range of possibilities from Dorothy.

6. Within the context of the poem, this litotes contrasts the role of negation in the lives of William and Dorothy; the double negation he assigns to her counters the simple negation he assigns to himself ("Nor, perchance, / If I should be, where I no more can hear / Thy voice . . . / . . . wilt thou then forget").[16]

Although Tilottama Rajan claims that the vagueness of Wordsworth's language in "Tintern Abbey" "redefines the process of reference so that it requires a correspondence no longer based on mimesis but rather on affect" (*Supplement of Reading* 113), close attention to Wordsworthian usage throws into question just what the poem's affect is.[17]

My argument is not that reading the English experts can decode negation in "Tintern Abbey," as if one could simply map their rules onto the poem's grammar. Instead, the increased salience of English usage during the period created a novel set of relations between author, work, and audience, or at least broadened an experience of literature previously found mostly in the confined academic world of classical scholarship. In the case of Wordsworth, for all his investment in simplicity, from almost the beginning of his career, he was perceived to be obscure, as I noted in the previous chapter: his reception enacted the tension between poetry as a manifestation of usage and as an example of style. When he published his *Descriptive Sketches* and *An Evening Walk* in the early 1790s, Dorothy Wordsworth thought that "obscurity" was one of his poems' "many Faults"; the *Analytical Review* noted the style "often involves the poet's meaning in obscurity"; the *New Annual Register* commented on the "obscure expressions"; and even Coleridge called the diction "too frequently obscure."[18]

Despite Wordsworth's radical reform of his diction in the later *Lyrical Ballads*, he never lost his distinctive obscurity. Early in the nineteenth century, James Losh, for example, found Wordsworth "too often defective in elegance of language, and clearness of arrangement"; of "Nutting" John Stoddart could "make neither head nor tail"; Anna Seward thought him "turgid and obscure." This impression remained even as Wordsworth's reputation grew. For example, in a thoughtful account of Wordsworth's career, John Taylor Coleridge in 1821 wrote, "With all these advantages of a strong conceptive, and clear reasoning power, aided by an excellent diction, Wordsworth is not always so intelligible a writer, as from these circumstances might fairly be expected."[19] Such readers revealed the success of English's purification in creating an assumed common ground of clarity, an almost universal measure among educated readers in the period, including Wordsworth himself. Their reactions also reveal how difficult it was for readers to understand Wordsworth in terms of English's purification. Wordsworth's English in "Tintern Abbey," as evidenced by the use of negation, dramatically complicates, without breaking, the prescriptions of the English experts that were common ground for his readers.

If some readers expected Wordsworth to follow a set of prescriptions about clear, accessible English, another group developed a new sense of authorial agency in light of difficulties like those posed by negation in "Tintern Abbey." To look at early reactions to Wordsworth is to be struck by how often, in an age in which many people knew poetry by hearing it read aloud, Wordsworth's poems demanded new reading practices felt to be unusual or unfamiliar. In particular, his work required careful readings and rereadings, usually silent ones, to allow initial negative impressions to turn into admiration. Simply reading Wordsworth aloud was a dangerous business, as Coleridge learned when Fanny Allen greeted his reading of an early version of *Resolution and Independence* with "a convulsive fit of laughter." Instead, as Wordsworth's brother John wrote, "Most of W's poetry improves upon 2ᵈ 3 or 4ᵗʰ reading now people in general are not sufficiently interested with the first reading to induce them to try a 2ᵈ." Poems that readers liked were ones that they read often: "Sir George read part of a Poem by [Wordsworth] called 'Tintern abbey', which He thinks exquisite, & has read it 100 times."[20] Walter Pater would later enshrine this sense that Wordsworth required a new kind of literacy: Wordsworth demands "a habit of reading between the lines" because "he meets us with the promise that he has much, and something very peculiar, to give us, if we will follow a certain difficult way" ("Wordsworth" 415, 416).

These reactions demonstrate how seriously readers took the strictures of pure English and how different their responses to it could be. As English grew denser as a body of knowledge and set of rules, the experience of a literary work also grew potentially denser as well, insofar as tracking the work's relation to English became part of the reading experience. This tracking occurs at a highly local level, from moment to moment, with constantly shifting possibilities for understanding. As the responses to Wordsworth indicate, for some, the overall effect was one of frustration; others learned that they needed to become even more careful readers than they had been before. Wordsworthian English was not just about Wordsworth: it was also about what his work's relation to the code of English, as prescribed in his day, meant for his readers.

My second case study expands and concretizes the possibilities for understanding the history of such local encounters in a given literary text by concentrating on the distinction between the modal auxiliaries "will" and "shall." This distinction became a strangely intense grammatical flashpoint during the period. Tracing its history illustrates the range of functions that prescriptivism made available to Romantic works in their underinvestigated roles as transmitters of English.

Modal auxiliaries like "will" and "shall" are vexed in English because its so-called future tense is a strange hybrid: unlike the present and past tenses, it is not created with bounded morphemes but with auxiliary verbs. Moreover, this supposedly distinctive tense is dispensable, since describing the future without "will" or "shall" is easy (e.g., "I am going to go to the store"; "The train leaves tomorrow at noon").[21] Eighteenth-century English experts skirted some of these definitional challenges but not others by distinguishing two relations to the future, which contemporary linguists categorize as epistemic and deontic modalities. According to Leo Hoye, "epistemic modality is concerned with matters of knowledge or belief on which basis speakers express their judgements about states of affairs, events or actions," while "deontic modality is concerned with the possibility or necessity of acts in terms of which the speaker gives permission or lays an obligation for the performance of actions at some point in the future" (*Adverbs and Modality* 42–43). The will-shall distinction, as codified by Bishop Wallis in the seventeenth century and echoed in the eighteenth, grammaticalized these modalities, which eighteenth-century English experts often described in terms of predicting and promising. According to Leslie K. Arnovick, a speaker observing the Wallis rules "asserts his or her belief in declaratives which predict, asserts his or her intention in declaratives which promise" (*Diachronic Pragmatics* 50).[22]

In one of its most popular versions in Murray's *English Grammar*, the distinction between "will" and "shall" went as follows:

> *Will*, in the first person singular and plural, intimates resolution and promising; in the second and third person, only foretells . . . *Shall*, on the contrary, in the first person simply foretells; in the second and third persons, promises, commands, or threatens. (55–56)

A more schematic version of the distinction, using the verb "to go," would look like this:

Prediction	Promise
(Epistemic Modality)	(Deontic Modality)
I shall go. We shall go.	I will go. We will go.
Thou wilt go. You will go.	Thou shalt go. You shall go.
S/he will go. They will go.	S/he shall go. They shall go.

Although no two eighteenth-century grammar books have the same version of these rules, the most detailed study of their history concludes that "in the eighteenth century there was hardly any development in the formulation of the rules for *shall/will*" (Van Ostade, "'I Will be Drowned'" 141; see also Moody, "*Shall* and *Will*"). English experts presented a united front regarding modal auxiliaries. This unanimity lasted into the nineteenth century because eighteenth-century grammars, like Murray's, continued to be used and later English experts echoed his rule.

The tidiness of the will-shall distinction helped it succeed: it fit neatly into introductory grammar books. Furthermore, although some later critics treated the will-shall distinction as a fantasy of overzealous eighteenth-century English experts, a number of studies have demonstrated that it characterized actual written usage by the end of the seventeenth century, and that it remained common, especially in England, into the twentieth century.[23] Nevertheless, usage was never as clean as the Wallis rules mandated, for several reasons. One, pointed out by the English experts themselves, was the King James Bible. Murray noted with irritation, "The following passage is not translated according to the distinct and proper meanings of the words *shall* and *will*: 'Surely goodness and mercy shall follow me all the days of my life; and I will dwell in the house of the Lord for ever:' it ought to be, '*Will* follow me,' and 'I *shall* dwell'" (*EG* 56). Peter Walkden Fogg elevated grammar to theology by claiming that "a great many disputes in religion would perhaps be settled if it were known that *shall* is generally applied to simple futurition in that book [the King James Bible], and *will* to volition. A new translation would be the best help" (*Elementa Anglicana* 2:128). Such comments are typical of an often-overlooked aspect of the English experts: their insistence on correctness had a leveling effect, in which even the Bible could be criticized. They are so often seen as constructors of an oppressive hegemony that it is easy to forget grammar's iconoclastic edge. Nevertheless, in the case of "will–shall," the English experts were helpless in the face of the Bible's familiarity. Given its permeation, the Wallis rules could never triumph as a final authority, and, as I noted in the previous chapter, even the English experts recognized the dangers in being too prescriptive.

Yet there were other reasons, not recognized by the English experts, that also prevented the Wallis rules from ever mapping entirely onto usage. Although the rules divide prediction from promise, this separation is not absolute because no statement about the future has the same certainty as statements about the present or past. As F. R. Palmer notes, "making statements about one's future actions can be taken as a promise" (q. in Hoye, *Adverbs and Modality* 120). In systematizing different modalities in the future tense, the English experts tried to maintain as a difference in kind what was a difference in degree: how deeply language producers believed themselves to be engaged in making the described future action happen. As a result, the distinction between the two auxiliaries was inherently unstable and did not conform to an efficient, reproducible mode of correctness.

At a phonological level, distinctions between spoken and written English further unsettled the authority of the Wallis rules. The reduction of "will" to "'ll" made a locution like "I'll" a less effortful marker of futurity than either "I will" or "I shall," particularly in speaking. Moreover, certain uses of "shall" and "will" had long histories in English usage that were not accounted for in the Wallis rules. While the English experts' association of "I will" with promising seems to have had some basis in actual usage, it did not encompass the auxiliary's full range of meaning. As Kytö notes in a study of early modern English, "first-person WILL is favoured in contexts with dynamic uses of the main verb . . . while SHALL occurs mainly with stative main verbs" (*Variation and Diachrony* 352). First-person "will" had often been used to express the intention to perform an immediate action, whether or not the subject was making a promise.[24] Moreover, "shall," though supposedly used only for epistemic futurity in the first person, could be used with a more deontic sense, especially when expressing "a determination insisted on in spite of opposition."[25] Likewise, "shall" had long been used in all three persons in "hypothetical, relative, and temporal clauses denoting a future contingency."[26]

Given this complex history, one might expect that English experts would acknowledge the provisionality surrounding the will-shall distinction. Exactly the opposite happened: grammarian after grammarian enforced the supposedly obvious distinction between the auxiliaries. Nationalism fueled them: misusing "will" and "shall" became a glaring marker of foreignness. As a result, the relative historical autonomy of grammar that led to the distinction between "will" and "shall" co-existed, under the pressure of the English experts, with a heteronomous use of the distinction as a tool of nation-building. William Mitford believed that the distinction between "will" and "shall" "gives a clear superiority of precision to the English over all those languages which have the advantage, in form, of expressing the future by a single word" (379). Wallis himself and later Samuel Johnson noted that the distinction was difficult for "foreigners and provincials" (q. in Van Ostade, "'I Will be Drowned'" 129). Later English experts targeted the Scottish and Irish:

> Our fellow citizens of North-Britain and Ireland, find much difficulty in these auxiliaries. Even such writers as Lord Kaim, Dr. Goldsmith, and Dr. Blair, are not always correct in them. I would recommend a careful perusal of this article, its examples, and notes. The main point of their error seems to be putting *will* for *shall* with the first person, when futurition without or even contrary to choice is affirmed. Thus they say, "I will die. We will fall. I will be sick. We will disagree by and by. We will have ill luck". All these are the grossest paronomasias to an Englishman; as they imply a *willingness* to suffer things disagreeable. He uses *shall* in these and all similar sentences. (Fogg, *Elementa Anglicana* 2:129)[27]

The passage is packed with nationalist insults, from the misspelling of Lord Kames to the list of incorrect sentences, which has an uncomfortably threatening tinge. The smallest details of linguistic usage are laced with maledictory pitfalls, and a single misstep rises to the level of treason against the nation's soul.

Extravagant as this passage seems, the passion surrounding the will-shall distinction proved weirdly durable. In 1866 Henry Alford noted,

> I never knew an Englishman who misplaced "shall" and "will:" I hardly ever have known an Irishman or a Scotchman who did not misplace them sometimes. And it is strange to observe how incurable the propensity is. It was but the other day that I asked a person sprung of Irish blood, whether he would be at a certain house to which I was going that evening. The answer was, "*I'm afraid I won't.*" Yet my friend is a sound and accurate English scholar, and I had never before, during all the years I had known him, discovered any trace of the sister island. (*Plea* 169)

A tiny verbal detail ("won't" instead of "shan't") carries a wildly improbable weight of damaging cultural meaning. The friend's "uncurable . . . propensity" instantly levels his seemingly immaculate facade of "sound and accurate" Englishness and unmasks him as a mere colonial mimic, a pretender to the status of Englishman. Likewise, Oscar Wilde asked an English journalist to look over *The Picture of Dorian Gray* before publication: "Will you also look after my 'wills' and 'shalls' in proof. I am Celtic in my use of these words, not English" (*Complete Letters* 473). Wilde's novel upset virtually every code of late Victorian respectability, but he had to get his modal auxiliaries just right.

The sanctity of the English will-shall survived into the twentieth century through Henry Fowler's scary pronouncement in his *Dictionary of Modern English Usage*: "There is the English of the English, & there is the English of those who repudiate that national name; of the English of the English *shall & will* are the shibboleth, & the number of those who cannot 'frame to pronounce it right' . . . best reveals to us the power in the English press wielded by Scots & others who are not English" (729). Holding the nationalist line, the *Oxford English Dictionary* retains language originally published in 1926, which notes that using "shall" in place of "will" is a sign of "Scottish, Irish, provincial, or extra-British" use: the catalogue suggestively positions Scottish and Irish as equivalent to "extra-British," as if Scotland and Ireland never really had become part of the United Kingdom.[28]

The very murkiness of the will-shall distinction was part of its power. Even as the English experts repeated the Wallis rules, the crux of the distinction was that the English knew the correct usage of "will" and "shall," and the non-English did not and never would. Though English might become a global language, policing the will-shall distinction became a haven for true Englishness, a bulwark against the impurity of empire. Indeed, it seems to have become ever more precious as other, more tangible signs of Englishness faded.

The oddly galvanizing power of the will-shall distinction makes it a good case study for the relation of Romantic authors to English usage. Shakespeare, Milton, and Swift might be excused their perceived improprieties, since grammar had not yet been codified when they wrote. Authors of the Romantic period, in contrast, were more accountable since, at least in the eyes of English experts and the readers who absorbed their prescriptions, correctness had been defined. My goal is not to serve as latter-day grammarian patrolling which Romantic authors got it right or not, but to use the will-shall distinction to specify potential responses to English usage in Romantic works. A given work did not necessarily occupy a single position consistently because it was by a single author. More interestingly, a given usage did not necessarily represent a single possibility: it might float between various positions, depending on the reader's viewpoint and context.

To determine what these positions were, I performed a corpus analysis on a selected body of Romantic works, mostly by well-known authors (see Appendix). In the passage I quoted earlier in this chapter, Foucault specifies the positions "of succession, of stability, and of reactivation" as characteristic of grammatical history. My analysis expands and adapts his positions slightly to include the following categories: reproduction, transmission, archaism, supersession, and stylization. These categories are not inherent in given usages; instead, they name different sets of possible relations among reader, context, work, and projected author.

In reproduction, the work's usage follows the rules of the English experts. The author is less important as an individual genius than as a representative source for pure English. According to Austin E. Quigley, paraphrasing John Rupert Firth, "We can find systems and systemic relations in language use, but they are a function of the history of fluid and changing speech activity and not a consequence of preexisting or imposed schema that establish in advance what is possible for a language as a whole" (*Theoretical Inquiry* 60). Yet the literature of the Romantic period suggests that only once English was visible "as a whole" could "systematic relations" that were "fluid and changing" become visible.

Even works that might be expected to flout the English experts' rules often reproduce them. For example, William Blake's "Little Black Boy" from *Songs of Innocence and of Experience* exemplifies Blake's typically nonstandard punctuation; it also has marks of nonstandard grammar, as in the line "And thus I say to little English boy" (22), where the absence of an article before "little" suggests an African-English pidgin. Nevertheless, the Little Black Boy and his mother come through with flying colors in their use of epistemic "will–shall":

> For when our souls have learn'd the heat to bear
> The cloud will vanish we shall hear his voice.
>
> And then I'll stand and stroke his silver hair,
> And be like him and he will then love me.   (17–18, 27–28)

Whatever the color of the Little Black Boy's soul or his mother's geographical location, when it comes to what Fowler terms the "shibboleth" of "will–shall," they show themselves thoroughly English. Other examples of correct usage are so commonplace that listing them can seem superfluous: "Peace, who delights in solitary shade, / No more will spread for me her downy wings" (Charlotte Smith, *The Emigrants* 66–67); "We shall find / A pleasure in the dimness of the stars" (Coleridge, "The Nightingale" 10–11); "Say . . . that thou wilt be / One of the blessed—and that I shall die" (Byron, *Manfred* 2.4.124–26). These three randomly chosen quotations can stand for the many usages in Romantic literature that quietly reinforced the English experts' rules about the epistemic use of "will" and "shall." When Fredric Jameson argues that linguistics-based interpretation is "generally effective only when it visibly or even violently rewrites the surface appearance of the text, that is, when the restoration of the 'deep structure' alters our initial reception of the sentences themselves," his adjective "effective" polices a boundary between literary criticism and linguistics ("Ideology of the Text" 19–20). For an understanding of philological agency, it is equally important to recognize the "ineffective" moments in which works quietly but steadily bolster the authority of the English experts, and possibly their nationalist agendas, by reproducing their rules.

Reproduction involves not only epistemic but also deontic uses of the will-shall distinction. As in epistemic usage, the author again appears as the reinforcer of the English experts' rules. Yet these moments do not disappear into a neutral background quite so easily because promises and threats typically mark key moments in the emotional states of characters or poetic narrators. For readers tracking the emotional arc of a piece of writing, the deontic use of "will" and "shall" may contribute to an ability to recognize and understand emotional tone and intention:

> I will provide for myself and child. I leave as free as I am determined to be myself—he shall be answerable for no debts of mine. (Mary Wollstonecraft, *Wrongs of Woman* 162)

> Strange fits of passion I have known
> And I will dare to tell   (Wordsworth, "Strange Fits of Passion" 1–2)

> I will advance a terrible right arm
> Shall scare that infant thunderer, rebel Jove (John Keats, *Hyperion* 1.248–49)

> A man cannot say: "I will compose poetry."
>   (Percy Bysshe Shelley *Defence of Poetry* [Wright 242])

> And I awoke in struggles, and cried aloud—"I will sleep no more!"
>   (De Quincey, *Confessions* 113)

In such cases, in accordance with the rules of the English experts, "I will" carries a stronger sense of first-person agency and investment than "I shall." Often, Romantic works manifest the third-person deontic future in climactic prayers or promises: "Therefore all seasons shall be sweet to thee" (Coleridge, "Frost at Midnight" 65); "So haply shall thy days / Be many, and a blessing to mankind" (Wordsworth, *Prelude* [1805], 2.483–4); "But success *shall* crown my endeavours" (M. Shelley, *Frankenstein* 23); "This shall not be thy lot, my blessed child!" (Hemans, *Forest Sanctuary* 1.10). In such moments, the new rules of grammar heightened emotion.

In transmission, Romantic works follow long-established patterns of grammatical usage not explicitly acknowledged by the English experts. Here, works and authors appear less as the followers of the English experts than as custodians of traditional English. For readers expecting works to follow only the stated rules of the English experts, such usages might have been confusing, although I have found no historical evidence that they were. Rather, transmission let readers gain an intuitive sense of usages that had the sanction of custom, though they were not named as such by the English experts.

For example, as I noted above, "shall" has a long history of use in "hypo-thetical, relative, and temporal clauses denoting a future contingency" (*OED*), as in Wordsworth's "Preface to *Lyrical Ballads*": "If the time should ever come when what is now called science . . . shall be ready to put on, as it were, a form of flesh and blood, the Poet will lend his divine spirit to aid the transfiguration" (456) or De Quincey's "I will terrify all readers of mine from ever again questioning any postulate that I shall think fit to make" (*Confessions* 87). Also, first-person "will" often appears in contexts less of promising than of marking an intention to perform an immediate action, as in Christabel's "But we will move as if in stealth" (120). In my corpus, I found that writers used first-person "will" frequently (though not consistently) in metatextual moments about their own activity: "I will not tell you how I was buffeted about" (Wollstonecraft, *Wrongs of Woman* 178); "In the second place I will speak of my views" (Keats, letter to Wood-house, 27 Oct. 1818 [Wright 58]); "I will, however, candidly acknowledge that I have met with one person who bore evidence to its intoxicating power" (De Quincey, *Confessions* 75). Lastly, although the Wallis rules specify "I shall" only for predictions, it also had long been used for espe-cially strong promises: "I accepted of office at the obvious inclination of this House: I shall not hold it a moment after the least hint from them to resume a private station" (C. J. Fox [Wright 109]); "I deemed, and ever shall deem, myself free" (Wollstonecraft, *Wrongs of Woman* 197); "What-ever fate / Befall thee, I shall love thee to the last" (Wordsworth, *Michael* 425–26); "Make me happy, and I shall again be virtuous" (M. Shelley, *Frankenstein* 100). Rather than modeling the correct English of the En-glish experts, Romantic works at such moments transmit the continuity of educated English usage by preserving often-used forms.[29]

In what I call archaism, the work emerges as an inheritor of an elevated literary tradition that, for readers familiar with the English experts' prescrip-tions, it continues in the teeth of their disapproval: the usage of the King James Bible. This usage typically appears in third-person "shall" to mark predictions of future events where the Wallis rules would insist on "will":

He shall follow his sheep all the day
And his tongue shall be filled with praise.   (Blake, "The Shepherd" 3–4)

"And soon," I said, "shall Wisdom teach her lore
In the low huts of them that toil and groan!"
                              (Coleridge, "France: An Ode" 59–60)

His soul shall taste the sadness of her might,
And be among her cloudy trophies hung.

(Keats, "Ode on Melancholy" 29–30)

All plants . . . shall take
And interchange sweet nutriment; to me
Shall they become like sister-antelopes. . . .
The dewmists of my sunless sleep shall float
Under the stars like balm; night-folded flowers
Shall suck unwithering hues in their repose.

(Shelley, *Prometheus Unbound* 3.3.91, 95–97, 100–102)

"All the powers of darkness," added he, "shall never be able to pluck you again out of your Redeemer's hand. And now, my son, be strong and steadfast in the truth. Set your face against sin, and sinful men, and resist even to blood, as many of the faithful of this land have done, and your reward shall be double." (Hogg, *Private Memoirs* [Wright 206])

While the closeness to Biblical language may be most obvious in the passages that have Biblical themes, so pervasive is the association of the third-person "shall" with prophecy that it appears even in fully secularized moments like the ending of Keats's "Ode on Melancholy."

In supersession, the work of the Romantic period makes little meaningful distinction between "will" and "shall." It consequently prefigures what later philologists agree is the general weakening of the distinction between the two during the nineteenth century, despite the English experts' continued insistence upon it (Denison, "Syntax" 167–68; Görlach, *English in Nineteenth-Century England* 84). This category presumes either a reader familiar enough with the rules of the English experts to register the weakening distinction or a reader looking to works for models of usage and discovering that no consistent rules can be found. The author in this category appears, once more, less as an individual creator than as a representative of general trends in the language, but here the trends are not those of the English experts, but of common usage. In the corpus that I examined, this fading seems to be more characteristic of the writings of the second-generation Romantics, especially in the Keats-Shelley circle, as in this excerpt from Keats's *Endymion*:

A hermit young, I'll live in mossy cave,
Where thou alone shalt come to me, and lave
Thy spirit in the wonders I shall tell.

Through me the shepherd realm shall prosper well;
For to thy tongue will I all health confide.   (4.860–65)

Neither the rules of the English experts nor the traditional usages of English would provide an obvious grammatical reason for Keats to use "shall" in line 863 and "will" in line 865. Most of the passage uses the familiar prophetic "shalls" of Romantic visionary passages, so that the "will" seems out of place.[30]

Byron and the Shelleys also move easily between the two auxiliaries. In one stanza of *Childe Harold's Pilgrimage,* Byron uses the prophetic "shall" to lament the dead, who are "ere evening to be trodden like the grass / Which now beneath them, but above shall grow / In its next verdure, when this fiery mass . . . shall moulder cold and low" (3.27). A few stanzas later, in an equally prophetic passage, he uses "will": "The tree will wither long before it fall . . . / And thus the heart will break, yet brokenly live on" (3.32). Percy Shelley's "Ode to the West Wind" imagines a time when the wind's "azure sister of the Spring shall blow / Her clarion" (9–10), but then describes the storm from the west wind, "from whose solid atmosphere / Black rain and fire and hail will burst" (27–28). In Mary Shelley's *Frankenstein,* the monster, having killed William Frankenstein, exults in the murder's effect on Victor: "This death will carry despair to him, and thousand other miseries shall torment and destroy him" (143); the point of the change from "will" to "shall" seems to be largely to vary the sound. In a particularly odd example from *Frankenstein,* the monster promises Victor, "I shall be with you on your wedding-night," which Victor promptly misremembers as *"I will be with you on your wedding-night"* (168); several pages later, he again misremembers the threat as *"I will be with you on your wedding-night!"* (this time with an exclamation point) (188), only to recall it, finally, in its correct form: "I shall be with you on your wedding-night" (191).

The last mode of agency with regard to grammar is stylization. This usage represents the most substantial rearrangement of relations between author, reader, work, and code. It presumes authors and readers who know the English experts' rules. But whereas in reproduction and the other categories, the author functions largely as a relayer of linguistic trends determined elsewhere, in stylization, the author appears as the manipulator of linguistic detail for thematic ends. The set of relations belonging to stylization may be the most comfortable for literary critics because it grants authors and readers the most potential for agency. Authors, rather than appearing as neutral products of grammar, emerge as creative responders to potential in the rules of grammar. Readers, rather than appearing as the passive recognizers of grammar, emerge as skilled interpreters of grammatical subtleties. Stylization is not "in" the work, but in kinds of reading that the work's relation to the English experts' code makes possible.

At its most virtuosic, stylization occurs when writers switch "correctly" between "will" and "shall" within a relatively short space, as in this interchange between Fanny, Edmund, and Lady Bertram in *Mansfield Park*:

> "If you cannot do without me, ma'am—" said Fanny, in a self-denying tone.
> "But my mother will have my father with her all the evening."
> "To be sure, so I shall."
> "Suppose you take my father's opinion, ma'am."
> "That's well thought of. So I will, Edmund. I will ask Sir Thomas, as soon as he comes in, whether I can do without her." (Wright 180)

Lady Bertram does not do very much in *Mansfield Park*, but, when roused by Edmund's advice, she is capable of shifting auxiliary verbs. In response to Edmund's first comment, she musters a vaguely epistemic "I shall," but at the thought of listening to Sir Thomas, she is roused to a comparatively more vigorous, and twice repeated, deontic "I will." Austen's joke, of course, is that Lady Bertram arouses herself to her semi-enthusiastic assertion of agency only in the service of having her will decided by someone else.

In the opening of *Prometheus Unbound*, Shelley uses the will-shall distinction to make the opposite point. Despite his dismissive remarks about grammar in his *Defence of Poetry* and his indifference to the will-shall distinction elsewhere, his poems allow for the recognition of a careful use of English. Prometheus envisions the downfall of Jupiter, and eagerly awaits the approach of the hour of his downfall:

> One [Hour] among whom
> —As some dark Priest hales the reluctant victim—
> Shall drag thee, cruel King, to kiss the blood
> From these pale feet, which then might trample thee
> If they disdained not such a prostrate slave.
> Disdain? Ah no! I pity thee.—What Ruin
> Will hunt thee undefended through wide Heaven!
> How will thy soul, cloven to its depth with terror,

Gape like a Hell within! I speak in grief,
Not exultation, for I hate no more.   (1.48–57)

In Prometheus' lurid vision of Jupiter's extinction, he uses a "shall" construction ("Shall drag thee, cruel King") that moves between the prom-
ise/threat of the English experts and the more generalized prophetic
"shall" of the Bible. The difference between the two is that, in the "correct" use of third-person "shall," the speaker took direct responsibility
for bringing about the promise or threat, but Prometheus does not seem
to care.[31] He has so identified his desires with the inevitability of future
events that his vengeance is assured.

Yet, suddenly, his disdain evaporates and he is left with pity. With
the emotional change comes a new sense of Jupiter's future, one marked
not by "shall" but by epistemic "will" constructions: "What Ruin / Will
hunt thee undefended through wide Heaven! / How will thy soul . . . /
Gape like a Hell within!" No longer a vindictive participant in Jupiter's
downfall, Prometheus, by switching modal auxiliaries, becomes a horri-
fied, pitying witness. The critical dramatic action of Shelley's entire drama
occurs through a minute shift in grammar. Jupiter's downfall remains certain, whether Prometheus disdains or pities him: it belongs to the realm
of necessity. Yet Shelley uses the seemingly impersonal rules of grammar
to mark the realm of freedom. If the future is fixed, the human attitude
toward it is not, and the movement from "shall" to "will" marks the possibilities for change.

Of all Romantic poets, Wordsworth may be the most precise in his
handling of stylization; at least with regard to "will" and "shall," he thoroughly earns Coleridge's praise of his good grammar.[32] In "Three Years
She Grew in Sun and Shower," for example, the voice of Nature speaks
consistently in a deontic modality of the wonders that Lucy will experience: Lucy "shall feel an overseeing power" (11); "She shall be sportive
as the fawn" (13); "Hers shall be the breathing balm" (16); "The stars of
midnight shall be dear / To her, and she shall lean her ear / In many a
secret place" (25–27). The euphony of the alliterations in the many repetitions of "she shall" allows grammar and sound to work together to
create a heightened solemnity and sense of ritual around the future held
out to Lucy. After the rapturous promises of Nature, the poem saves for
the crushing conclusion a bleak switch into the epistemic future: "The
memory of what has been, / And never more will be" (41–42). Gram-

mar carries all the tragedy of Lucy's loss in the seemingly insignificant movement from the visionary "shall" to the blunt ordinariness of "will." The deontic third-person "shalls" that in many Romantic poems mark the climactic moment of vision give way instead to a conclusion in which grammar heightens collapse.

In a remarkable passage from *Michael,* Wordsworth dramatizes the conflict between Michael and commerce as a clash between the archaic third-person "shall" of prophecy and the epistemic "will":

> Our Luke shall leave us, Isabel; the land
> Shall not go from us, and it shall be free,
> He shall possess it free as is the wind
> That passes over it. We have, thou knowest,
> Another kinsman, he will be our friend
> In this distress. He is a prosperous man,
> Thriving in trade, and Luke to him shall go
> And with his Kinsman's help and his own thrift
> He quickly will repair this loss, and then
> May come again to us.   (254–63)

In the passage, "will" is associated with temporary, worldly solutions: the kinsman "will be" a friend until the "distress" is relieved; Luke "quickly will repair" the loss that Michael has suffered. The relative smallness of the "will" actions is set against the grand aspirations of Michael's "shall" statements: "The land / Shall not go from us, and it shall be free, / He shall possess it." The continuity of this auxiliary verb between such statements and Michael's actual descriptions of Luke's fate ("Our Luke shall leave us"; "Luke to him shall go") raise a grubby and embarrassing business (the need for Luke to earn back the money that Michael lost) to the status of a biblical journey: Michael's "shalls" make it seem as if Luke is departing to enter Zion rather than to do low-level drudgery in London. The grammar captures the appalling pathos of Michael's attempts to retain his family's dignity in the face of circumstances that tear it from them.

I have stressed the relationality of these categories. The same work might fit into different categories, depending on the reader's perspective. For literary critics, the disciplinary insistence on the literary object's uniqueness is so ingrained that the thought that an author may be "merely" reproducing standard usage, or that variation in word choice may be insignificant, is a challenge ripe for refutation. Literary criticism is frightened by the prospect of *not* seeing stylization in literary language use; it demands language saturated with meaning. For example, it might be argued that it is hardly coincidental that the mother of Blake's Little Black Boy shows her mastery of the "will–shall" distinction at exactly the moment when she imagines being free from color; other readers might find Victor Frankenstein's waffling memory of the wording of the monster's threat an important element in Shelley's characterization of him.[33]

My goal is not to deny these readings, but to emphasize that they belong to one subset of possible relations among author, work, and audience that the new English of the eighteenth century made available. The ability to reproduce the English experts' usage, transmit older usages, maintain the language of the King James Bible, or erode old distinctions were all equally available, though they do not fit as interestingly within the confines of conventional literary criticism. Instead, they suggest, like the work of negation in "Tintern Abbey," that the purification of English gave literary works a variety of secret ministries, depending on the sensitivity of readers to local instances of usage.

Concentrating on such localism frustrates the desire to create a sweeping argument about the function of pure English in Romantic literature as either a source of guidance or of rebellion. Neither metaphor is adequate to gauge the proliferation of possibilities set in motion by the transformation of the code by the eighteenth-century English experts. I prefer to think of them in terms proposed by a computer programmer, Joel Spolsky, the Law of Leaky Abstractions: "All non-trivial abstractions, to some degree, are leaky. Abstractions fail" (q. in Rosenberg 282). In reading, to find meaning in a work involves a process of abstraction, of moving from the literal signs on the page to the more abstract level of mental representation of concepts and emotions. In this process of abstraction, the rules of English usage usually are invisible because they are taken for granted. Yet English's purification increased the likelihood that the smooth process of abstraction might hit a snag over specific moments of usage, places at which a lower level of the code disrupted a more familiar reading process. To use the metaphor of Scott Rosenberg, a lower "layer of abstraction" erupts "like a slanted layer of bedrock poking up through more recent geological strata and into the sunlight" (281).

In software, the Law of Leaky Abstractions is a problem; in everyday terms, it is often the sign of a computer crash. In literature, however, the sudden visibility of English as a code can be either a problem (a sign of incorrect usage) or an opportunity (a moment of what I have termed stylization). Moreover, whereas a leaky abstraction in software is immediately visible as such, in literature, it depends on the goals and knowledge of the reader to recognize and interpret. One of philology's challenges to traditional literary criticism is to make such sudden shifts in the status of the code visible. The task that remains is to understand how in the early nineteenth century these shifts became organized into perceptions of authorial styles and careers, the topic of the following chapter.

Appendix

Austen, Jane. *Sanditon.* In *Northanger Abbey, Lady Susan, The Watsons, and Sanditon.* Ed. John Davie. Oxford: Oxford University Press, 1980. 321–79.

Blake, William. *The Book of Thel, Songs of Innocence and of Experience,* and *Visions of the Daughters of Albion.* In *The Complete Poetry and Prose of William Blake.* Ed. David V. Erdman. Rev. ed. Garden City, NJ: Anchor, 1982. 3–6, 7–32, 45–51.

Burke, Edmund. *A Letter to a Noble Lord.* In *Eighteenth-Century English Literature.* Eds. Geoffrey Tillotson, Paul Fussell, Jr., and Marshall Waingrow. New York: Harcourt Brace Jovanovich, 1969. 1288–1309.

Butler, Marilyn, ed. *Burke, Paine, Godwin, and the Revolution Controversy.* Cambridge: Cambridge University Press, 1984.

Byron, George Gordon Lord. *Childe Harold's Pilgrimage, Cantos III and IV,* and *Manfred.* In *Selected Poems.* Eds. Susan J. Wolfson and Peter J. Manning. Harmondsworth, Middlesex: Penguin, 1996. 415–55, 508–69, and 463–506.

Coleridge, Samuel Taylor. "Ode to the Departing Year," *Christabel,* "Frost at Midnight," "France: An Ode," "Fears in Solitude," "The Nightingale," and "Dejection: An Ode." *Samuel Taylor Coleridge: The Major Works.* Ed. H. J. Jackson. Oxford: Oxford University Press, 1985. 31–36, 68–87, 87–89, 89–92, 92–98, 99–101, and 114–18.

Cowper, William. *The Task, Book 3.* In *Eighteenth-Century English Literature.* Eds. Geoffrey Tillotson, Paul Fussell, Jr., and Marshall Waingrow. New York: Harcourt Brace Jovanovich, 1969. 1317–26.

De Quincey, Thomas. *Confessions of an English Opium Eater.* Ed. Alethea Hayter. Harmondsworth, Middlesex: Penguin, 1971.

Hemans, Felicia. *The Forest Sanctuary. Felicia Hemans: Selected Poems, Letters, Reception Materials.* Ed. Susan J. Wolfson. Princeton: Princeton University Press, 2000. 268–322.

Keats, John. *Endymion,* "Ode to a Nightingale," "Ode on a Grecian Urn," "Ode to Psyche," "Ode on Melancholy," and *Hyperion. Complete Poems and Selected*

Letters of John Keats. Ed. Edward Hirsch. New York: Modern Library, 2001. 59–182, 236–38, 238–40, 240–42, 250–51, 251–76.

Lamb, Charles. "On the Tragedies of Shakespeare," "On the Acting of Munden," and "On the Artificial Comedy of the Last Century." In *Romantic Critical Essays.* Ed. David Bromwich. Cambridge: Cambridge University Press, 1987. 56–70, 71–72, 72–79.

More, Hannah. "Slavery: A Poem." *British Literature, 1780–1830.* Eds. Anne K. Mellor and Richard Matlak. Fort Worth, TX: Harcourt Brace, 1996. 206–9.

Scott, Walter. *The Black Dwarf.* New York: Hovendon, n.d.

Shelley, Mary. *Frankenstein, or The Modern Prometheus.* Ed. M. K. Joseph. Oxford: Oxford University Press, 1969.

Shelley, Percy Bysshe. *Prometheus Unbound,* "Ode to the West Wind," and *The Cenci.* In *Shelley's Poetry and Prose.* Eds. Donald H. Reiman and Sharon Powers. New York: Norton, 1977. 132–210, 221–23, and 237–301.

Smith, Charlotte. "The Emigrants," "Beachy Head," and "The Truant Dove from Pilpay." In *British Literature, 1780–1830.* Eds. Anne K. Mellor and Richard Matlak. Fort Worth, TX: Harcourt Brace, 1996. 231–44, 244–56, and 257–60.

Wollstonecraft, Mary. *The Wrongs of Woman.* In *Mary and The Wrongs of Woman.* Ed. Gary Kelly. Oxford: Oxford University Press, 1984. 69–204.

Wordsworth, William. "Essay Supplementary to the Preface [of 1815]." In *Romantic Critical Essays.* Ed. David Bromwich. Cambridge: Cambridge University Press, 1987. 29–51.

———. "Preface to the Second Edition of *Lyrical Ballads* [1800; includes 1802 additions]." In *Selected Poems and Prefaces.* Ed. Jack Stillinger. Boston: Houghton Mifflin, 1965. 445–64.

———. *The Prelude, 1799, 1805, 1850.* Eds. Jonathan Wordsworth, M. H. Abrams, and Stephen Gill. New York: Norton, 1979. 28–151.

———. "Simon Lee," "Strange Fits of Passion I Have Known," "Lucy Gray," "The Fountain," "Three Years She Grew in Sun and Shower," *Michael,* and "Ode: Intimations of Immortality." In *British Literature, 1780–1830.* Eds. Anne K. Mellor and Richard Matlak. Fort Worth, TX: Harcourt Brace, 1996. 564–66, 582, 583, 584–85, 586, 586–92, and 603–5.

Wright, Raymond, ed. *Prose of the Romantic Period, 1780–1830.* Harmondsworth, Middlesex: Penguin, 1956.

§ 3 Bad Englishes

The previous chapter took seriously the claim that language has its own history and is not the aftereffect of some other, supposedly prior history. Looking at tiny details of usage opened up textual relations invisible in literary studies, ones not easily fit into usual models of British history. Yet, as the discussions of the social valences of double negation and the national ones of the will-shall distinction demonstrated, confining the effects of purification solely to formal grammar overlooks that during the Romantic period, "grammar, virtue, and class were so interconnected that rules were justified or explained not in terms of how language was used but in terms of reflecting a desired type of behaviour, thought process, or social status" (Smith, *Politics of Language* 9).

A starting point for linking literature to this context is Donald Davie's key insight in *Purity of Diction in English Verse*: "Discussion of diction becomes discussion of the poet's place in the national community, or, under modern conditions (where true community exists only in pockets), his place in the state" (17). For Davie, late Augustan poets like Oliver Goldsmith and William Cowper lived in an ideal moment when "taste and judgment . . . went with power and wealth" (25). The connection tied literature to the "common tongue" because both poetry and prose could draw on common ideals of polite speech. Unfortunately, according to Davie, this commonality collapsed abruptly at the century's end, leading to the disaster of Romanticism: "The diction of the Romantic poets is extremely impure" (26). The language of Romantic poetry was no longer that of common culture and therefore lost its role in the state.

This chapter adopts several of Davie's key concepts (the idea of a common tongue and the purity of English) but treats what he takes as a given, the ideal community of the eighteenth century, as a fantasy enabled by print's spread. Purity of English was less a serene cultural consensus than a massive, decentralized goal on the part of educators, lexicographers, politicians, orthoepists, clergymen, actors, and grammarians. From its first appearance, pure English was shadowed by its dark twin, impure English, both because standardizers enjoyed creating bad English to criticize and because novelists, dramatists, and poets worried that too much purification might be a problem.

Although the flood of grammar books that dominated the mid-eighteenth century focused on vocabulary, syntax, and semantics, far less work was done by the English experts on pronunciation until the last decades of the century. As late as 1799, James Adams could note that no "comprehensive theory . . . of Pronunciation" had appeared, even though "no literary subject" had been so frequently "distinguished by the exertions of learning, wit, and ingenuity, as grammatical systems of the English language" (*Pronunciation* 3). But if English experts had not sufficiently engaged problems of English pronunciation, eighteenth-century plays, poems, and novels were obsessed with them.

At first glance, this focus on pronunciation seems odd. Benedict Anderson maintains that a "national print-language" creates a sense of community precisely because it is not spoken (*Imagined Communities* 41–9). If printed English was supposed to rise above distinctions created by pronunciation, then it seems illogical that the initial literary response to purification was all about how people spoke. Contrary to Anderson, purifying English as a print language made pronunciation more, not less, important than it had ever been. In the "Grammar of the English Tongue" that prefaced his *Dictionary*, Johnson revealed good pronunciation as an aftereffect of print. He claimed that in English, as in "all living tongues, there is a double pronunciation, one cursory and colloquial, the other regular and solemn. The cursory pronunciation is always vague and uncertain, being made different in different mouths by negligence, unskilfulness, or affectation. The solemn pronunciation, though by no means immutable and permanent, is yet always less remote from the orthography, and less liable to capricious innovation" (294). Johnson assumed that print had standardized orthography, which therefore provided a firmer source for judging pronunciation than unstandardized orthography. As such, he justified the role of his *Dictionary* in fixing English pronunciation.

Nevertheless, as Johnson well knew, sanctifying orthography as a guide to pronunciation looked better in theory than in practice. Real English spelling offered poor cues to pronunciation. In the *Dictionary*, Johnson marked lexical stress but felt that the phonemes were so variable as to be immune to purifying. But his treatment of spelling inspired his followers to find ways to show good pronunciation in print, even if doing so meant enlarging the graphemic repertoire: Sheridan, Walker, and other late eighteenth-century orthoepists, for example, used number schemes to identify vowels. For "chameleon," Walker gives the pronunciation, "ka^4-me$^{1\prime}$le^1-u^{2}n" (in the dictionary, the numbers appear directly on top of the vowels); the pronunciation guide, repeated at the top of each page, notes that a^4 stands for the vowel sound in "fat"; e^1 stands for the vowel sound in "me"; and u^2 stands for the vowel sound in "tub"; the "$\prime$" follows the word's primary stress. The guide thus indicates a pronunciation of "chameleon" that is close to, but slightly different from, that of current standard American English.[1]

Useful as these graphemic systems were for the English experts, the real challenge was how to disseminate good pronunciation. The answer was the stage. As Aaron Hill noted in 1735, the stage should be where "the Delicacies of *Good-breeding*, might be *learnt*, in their sublimest Purity; and the Elegancies of LANGUAGE, in its most refin'd, and absolute, Perfection" (q. in Goring, *Rhetoric of Sensibility* 128).[2] Grammar could be learned from a book, but, in an era before sound reproduction, mastering good pronunciation needed live models. Eighteenth-century Britons had actors' voices as a medium for reproducing good pronunciation. Audiences listened carefully: quality of pronunciation was usually the first thing that critics noticed about any new actor. George III congratulated Sarah Siddons because, while listening to her, he "had endeavored, vainly, to detect . . . a false emphasis" (q. in Michaelson, *Speaking Volumes* 108); the high point of Joshua Steele's "rational prosody" was his preservation of some exact inflections of David Garrick's version of Hamlet's "To be or not to be" (*Prosodia Rationalis* 47–48); John Philip Kemble became notorious for the fussy precision of his attempts to promote the best pronunciation of the day (Michaelson 110–11). In Thomas Skinner Surr's *Richmond* (1827), the hero, describing his childhood, noted that his teacher entertained "a very high opinion of the theatre—not as a school for morals, but as affording a standard for correct pronunciation and gesture, and an admirable auxiliary to his two great authorities, Walker's Dictionary, and Enfield's Speaker" (1:44).

While Johnson believed that good and bad pronunciations were universal, his *Dictionary*, by standardizing spelling, changed the printed sign. Print now projected a powerful fantasy: standardized graphemes stood for a pre-existing aural universe of uniform phonemes. After this semiotic transformation, dialect could appear only as a series of corrupted graphemes, a secondary and imperfect representation rather than as legitimate English. As such, dialect became a powerful marker of otherness, one easily seized upon for purposes of national or imperial self-assertion. While dialect pronunciation could be found in literary works before the eighteenth century, it exploded after Johnson because, until the standardization of orthography, spelling variation made it difficult to tell dialect apart from the prestige language variety. As Paula Blank notes about the early modern period, "While the notion of linguistic authority was already current in the sixteenth and early seventeenth centuries, writers were not yet constrained by any established system of rules" (*Broken English* 4). With orthographic standardization, dialect became audible as dialect because it became visible as bad English.

To bolster the theater's authority as a site for disseminating good pronunciation, playwrights typically created an in-group of characters who used correct English and an out-group who did not. No explicit pronunciation rules for the characters within the in-group were ever announced: their speeches simply appeared in standard spelling. In performance, actors taking the parts of the in-group characters, or private readers performing their English, did not need absolutely uniform pronunciation. They needed only to produce phonemes close enough to each other so that their relation to those of the out-group formed what linguists call "minimal pairs": small phonemic differences that produce differences in meaning, as in the difference between the first consonant in "sip" and "zip." For English speakers, there are many allophones that count as /s/ and are different enough from /z/ to be recognized as a different phone, although such recognition may vary depending on individual listeners. As such, a fact about language perception became an unexpectedly powerful model for national identity: "Phonemic categories construct similarities across allophones but differences from one phoneme to another" (Jay, *Psychology of Language* 62). Just as all pronunciations of a given phoneme do not need to be identical, all within the nation were not required to be identical, only similar enough to mark their difference from outsiders.

Dialect pronunciation changed not just the role of the performer, but also that of the audience. It projected an implied audience for whom standard pronunciation was easier to understand than spoken dialect. Although in the theater, certain listeners may have found dialect pronunciation easier to understand if it was closer to their own English, the plays assume an audience already subject to linguistic purification. For printed dialect, the situation was slightly different: orthographic standardization almost automatically made understanding dialect harder because it disrupted automatic recognition of word forms. The implied reader had to recognize an aural or visual sign as a "misrepresentation" and translate it back into its unmarked form for it to become comprehensible.

One reason that characters who speak in dialect may have been attractive to readers and hearers was that, quite apart from their personalities, the extra effort that their language required to be understood may have made them more memorable. Characters who did not speak pure English needed more focus; characters who did, had to say something interesting to command attention. Such focus could become a satisfying proof of mastery: if you were a good reader or listener, you knew standard English well enough to comprehend even its deformations. At the same time, nonstandard language could go only so far. If typographic deformations were too extreme, then even those well-versed in a language would be unable to decode them. Literary dialect walked a fine line between marking otherness and marking too much otherness.[3]

For the most part, eighteenth-century writers managed dialect by relying on a tiny cadre of substitutions to mark bad English: /b/>/p/, /w/>/v/, /s/>/ʃ/, /θ/>/d/, and /ð/>/d/. Given the immense power attributed to English pronunciation as a vehicle for Englishness, it is striking that so few phonemes separated in- and out-groups. Many foreigners sound alike: "Dat be ven Singer oppen vide de troat" (Italian; Wolcott, "Lord Brudenell and the Eunuch" 155); "Dere caps all your varriors a feather vear in" (Jewish; Dibdin, "Jew Volunteer" 124); "Such joy I at her sight vould show / Dat she vould think it must be me" (African; Opie, "Negro Boy's Tale" 57). In some cases, these graphemic mistakes involve simple one-to-one substitution, as when /v/, represented by "v," is substituted for /w/, represented by "w." Others are slightly more complicated, as when /d/, represented by "d," substitutes for /θ/, represented by the digraph "th": in this case, a single grapheme takes the place of two. Such bad sounds and letters encode generalized foreignness; specific identities (French, Dutch, Italian, Irish, Scottish) are indicated by additional lexical accessories, such as "massa" or "buckra" in slave speech.[4]

Since the sheer amount of nonstandard pronunciation in eighteenth-century and Romantic era literature is overwhelming, I select two case studies: the speech of Jews and slaves. I choose them partly because considerable work has already been done on better-known dialects, especially Scottish and Irish, and because these two posed a special challenge to eighteenth-century writers.[5] Few Britons would have ever heard slaves or Jews speak.[6] If they had, they would have gained no coherent sense of distinctive pronunciation because members of these groups came from varying backgrounds. Print gave slaves and Jews a recognizable dialect, a typographical and aural hallucination through which they acquired concreteness as a familiar, much-repeated set of deviations from a Johnsonian standard.[7]

While slave and Jewish dialect had precedents in earlier British literature, in both cases a popular play marked a watershed moment for their suddenly increased salience: for slaves, Isaac Bickerstaffe's *The Padlock* (1768); for Jews, Samuel Foote's *The Nabob* (1772).[8] These works sparked numerous comic representations of African servants and grasping Jewish moneylenders in plays, songs excerpted from the plays, and books of stories, jests, and riddles. Typical of comic representations of African speech are two anecdotes from joke books about Africans about to be flogged:

> A negro in Jamaica was tried for theft, and ordered to be flogged. He begged to be heard, which being granted, he asked, "If white man buy stolen goods, why he no be flogged too?"—"Well," said the judge, "so he would."—"Dere den," replied Mungo, "is my massa, he buy tolen goods; he know me tolen, and yet he buy me." (*New Joe Miller* 204)

> When Lord Howe was captain of the Magnanime, a negro sailor on board was ordered to be flogged: every thing being prepared, and the ship's company assembled to see the punishment inflicted, captain Howe made a long address to the culprit, on the enormity of his offense, poor Mungo, tired of the harangue, exclaimed, "Massa, if you floggee, floggee; or if you preachee, preachee; but not floggee and preachee too." (*Festival of Humour* 32–33)

The anecdotes rush to a punch line that reflects badly on the white supervisors. The jokes project an audience that will enjoy resistance to authority at a point when authority is being violently imposed. While one can imagine contexts in which such stories might lead to explicit abolitionist sentiments, they do not do so here: nothing suggests real outrage at the treatment of the Africans. Instead, the stories take a frequent trope of abolitionist rhetoric, the flogged African, and erase its politics in favor of the presumed pleasure of fleeting amusement at a snappy response.[9]

Mispronunciations heighten the Africans' resistance to authority. In the first anecdote, Mungo's pronunciation is proof that he was indeed "tolen," because his language shows that he is not English. In the second anecdote, the "-ee" inflection that Mungo adds to "preach" and "flog" make these two non-rhyming words into near rhymes. These actions sound interchangeable, to provide an aural metaphor for Mungo's view that being flogged and being preached at are double punishment. In both anecdotes, deformations of standard pronunciation acquire a stylistic life of their own that underscores the Africans' resistance to authority.

The opening stanza of an untitled anti-Semitic song offers a similar association between mispronunciation and resistant roguery:

Vatsh te matter, goot folks,
    Dat you pass your jokes,
On dish new fashion goots what I cry?
  Dant you know very well,
  Dat a Jew ought to shell,
Vatever a Christian will buy:
    If itsh a long tail'd pig,
    Or a short tail'd pig—
Or a pig without never a tail,
    A Jew pig,
    Or a true pig—
Or a pig wid a curling tail.   ("[The Pig-Selling Jew]" 212)

In this anti-Semitic rewrite of an older, traditional song about pigs' tails, the Jew's dialect is inconsistent; he uses /s/ in "folks" and "jokes" but mysteriously mispronounces it in "vatsh" and "itsh"; likewise, /w/ becomes /v/ in "vatsh" and "vatever," but remains /w/ in "well," "will," "without," and "wid." This inconsistency has no obvious practical function, and, in performance, a particular reciter may have made the dialect more uniform. But, at least in print, the Jewish speaker conforms to and departs from pure English with weird unpredictability. In this song, such slipperiness at the level of code coexists with the Jew's roguishness at the level of theme: anyone free from pure English might be free from the usual forms of respectability, yet still be respectable enough to sell pigs to eager Christians.[10]

For both the Africans and the Jew, nonstandard pronunciation marks simultaneous debasement and license. Outside of literature, dialects could have a range of uses, from common ground for in-group communication to a potential resource for code switching; although there was no uniform Jewish or slave dialect in the eighteenth century, there may have been local adaptations of pronunciation within particular communities. Yet within literature, this rich range of uses contracted to what Stallybrass and White term "phobic enchantment": the ability of a dominant culture to form selected images of marginalized groups and endow them with alluring attractiveness (*Politics and Poetics of Transgression* 124). They are not permanent role modes but sets of behaviors (including bad English) available for possible short-term imitation or at least daydreaming. Africans and Jews in these works may not speak good English, but they have cheek, a slangy vitality that makes respectable people and English look a little dull in contrast. Forms of behavior exiled from politeness can be projected onto despised others with all the ambivalence of a repressed alternative.

Not all eighteenth-century slave and Jewish speech is in dialect. More politically engaged eighteenth-century writers also generated numerous idealized representations of speech by sympathetic slaves and Jews. These works invite a condescending pity that works less as the opposite of phobic enchantment than as a continuation of it. Most of these works have a similar endpoint: slaves or Jews who speak pure English are probably about to die. Bad pronunciation does not guarantee a long life, but good pronunciation has a high mortality rate. Pure English marks characters as too pure for England: having risen so far above the supposed taint of their origins, they have nowhere to go but up.

This high mortality rate literalizes the metaphoric deathiness that already surrounded pure English. Eighteenth-century writers responded to this perceived impoverishment with a powerful fantasy. In it, they organized the hidden fears surrounding the purification of English into a masterplot that transformed the metaphoric loss of power springing from too much purification into a literal death for certain Others (formerly despised but now sympathetic) as a reward for attaining good English and good English values.

For Africans who speak good English, the choice seems to be to die with the hope of a better life after death (Thomas Day's "The Dying Negro," Samuel Whitchurch's "The Negro Convert," or Hannah More's Yamba in "The Sorrows of Yamba") or to die in abject despair (Mary Robinson's Zelma in "The Negro Girl"); the first is the preferred alternative.[11] The relation of the most famous of such poems, William Blake's "The Little Black Boy," to abolitionist rhetoric is complex, but the poem nevertheless follows a well-worn formula by imagining an African who speaks standard English (with the possible exception of one line, "And thus I say to little English boy") and anticipates an afterlife better than his life on earth. The most distressingly "innocent" aspect of Blake's poem is that its speaker imagines no adult future: instead, he skips to heaven, and his relationship there to God and to the little white boy. For Blake's speaker, as for so many others, good English seems incompatible with long life.

The situation is slightly more complex for Jewish characters. Sander Gilman has described the anti-Semitic tradition, dating back to the Gospels, of the "'hidden' language of the Jew . . . which mirrors the perverse or peculiar nature of the Jew" (*Jew's Body* 12). British writers develop their own strange twist on this tradition by representing and not representing the supposed otherness of the Jewish voice, so that the Jews' language is so secret that it defies typographic print. In novels, for example, narrators comment in passing on the perceived strangeness of Jewish talk, but do not represent it graphemically. In Maria Edgeworth's *Harrington* (1817), at the first appearance of the model Jew, Mr. Montenero, the narrator notes that he "spoke English with a foreign accent, and something of a foreign idiom; but his ideas and feelings forced their way regardless of grammatical precision, and I thought his foreign accent agreeable" (143). Despite this description, his "foreign accent" and "foreign idiom," except possibly for his first speech, are invisible when he talks, like the perceived semi-Scottishness of Wordsworth's Leech Gatherer. On the contrary, Montenero's "grammatical precision" is usually better than that of the British characters, so that no "force" is needed.

Possibly influenced by Edgeworth, Scott manifests a similar embarrassment around the Jewish voice in *Ivanhoe*'s Rebecca (1820):

"What country art thou of?—a Saracen? or an Egyptian?—Why dost not answer?—thou can'st weep, can'st thou not speak?"

"Be not angry, good mother," said Rebecca.

"Thou need'st say no more," replied Urfried; "men know a fox by the train, and a Jewess by her tongue." (194)

Rebecca utters seven syllables, and Urfried immediately knows the female Jewish voice, even though the narrator has not explained how men know a "Jewess by her tongue," or even how a fox's tail is like Jewish speech. The reader seems meant retrospectively to project a foreign pronunciation onto Rebecca's speech after Urfried's comment, even though nothing in Rebecca's graphemes warrants it. Rebecca is a linguistic virtuoso in *Ivanhoe*: she moves easily between Saxon, French, or Hebrew, depending on her interlocutors. But her actual speech floats between pure English graphemes and creepy hints from a character like Urfried that the hidden language of the Jews is not so hidden in Rebecca's case. The reader is left with several interpretive possibilities: Scott, like Edgeworth, creates an impression of foreignness countered by the characters' actual language, in order to make foreignness less salient; the Jewish characters' speech is meant to be imagined as being spoken with an accent, although Edgeworth and Scott do not represent it graphemically; or the supposed foreignness of the Jewish characters' speech says more about those who hear them than about the Jews themselves.

The uncertainty about the Jewish voice in English opens into uncertainties about Jews in England: do Jews have to prove that they can belong to the nation because their voice is foreign, or does the nation have to prove that it can accept Jews because their vocal foreignness is not obvious, can be overlooked, or is noticed only by bad characters? For both Edgeworth and Scott, the key seems to be how much otherness can be represented without alienating potential sympathy. Hints of nonstandard pronunciation mark the Jewish voice as other, but such hints, in the context of the novel as a whole, are relatively perfunctory. Jews may sound different from Christians, but only for a short textual moment.[12]

Different though the Jewish voice may be from the Africans', Jews who use pure English are as doomed as slaves are. In Scott and Edgeworth, good Jewish characters do not die off *per se*; instead, what dies is the Jewish future. In *Harrington*, Mr. Montenero's daughter Beatrice turns out to be not ethnically Jewish at all but the baptized daughter of a Protestant: she safely marries Harrington with no fear of tainting the British nation. In *Ivanhoe*, Rebecca becomes a Jewish nun, one of those women who "have devoted their thoughts to Heaven, and their actions to works of kindness to men" (401). In dying, slaves and Jews purify the nation by showing that pure English is really not exportable: the others who use it will eventually be eliminated.

The most interesting representations of slave and Jewish voices hybrid-ize the two categories I have discussed by presenting sympathetic represen-tations of impure English. These are especially remarkable because they have virtually no precedent before the 1790s. For centuries, dialect meant ridicule. In Adam Smith's *Theory of Moral Sentiments* (1759), sympathy with others required them to moderate their feelings so that we would not have to work too hard to imagine ourselves in their shoes (16–19). Speak-ers of dialect would presumably put up too many barriers to sympathy because linguistic difference blocked the effort to imagine ourselves as them. Yet much literature of the 1790s wanted to remove such barriers, and the change reveals the growing establishment of pure English as a norm so accepted that violations of it no longer looked threatening. The ability to create sympathy across linguistic difference was a critical mo-ment in the history of British toleration, and possibly even a precondition for major shifts that would lead to the abolition of the slave trade and, decades later, the removal of Jewish "disabilities."

Writers avoided making their sympathetic dialects too alienating, as the contrast between Charles Dibdin's satiric song from *In the Wags* and Thomas Russell's abolitionist text, "The African's Complaint on Board a Slave Ship," reveals:

One Negro, wi my banjer,
    Me from Jenny come,
        Wid cunning yiei
      Me savez spy
    De buckra world one hum
As troo a street a stranger
    Me my banjer strum.   (Dibdin, "One Negro" 88)

Trembling, naked, wounded, sighing,
    On dis winged house I stand,
Dat with poor black-man is flying
    Far away from their own land!   ("African's Complaint" 2:162)[13]

Dibdin uses unusual words ("banjer," "savez," "buckra") and complex deformations of standard typography: in changing "through" to "troo," the initial /θ/, represented by "th," becomes /t/ represented by "t"; /uw/,

represented by "ough," is condensed into the digraph "oo," even though
the phoneme is the same. In Russell's "African's Complaint," however,
vocabulary is standard and typographic deformations limited to using "d"
for /θ/, and making small syntactic errors (no article before "poor black-
man" and "their" for "his"). Russell gambles that the reader who sympathizes with this African will feel superior to a reader who sympathizes
only with Africans speaking pure English. Yet this gamble is low-risk because the linguistic barrier is small. Moreover, despite his nonstandard
pronunciation, the complaining African follows the lead of the slaves who
speak good English: he looks forward to imminent death. He still will
undergo "purification," even if his English is not as good as that in some
other African speech from the period.

Other writers foregrounded purification in a different way by having
Africans' speech improve in the course of a work, as if their English refined itself the closer they came to heaven. In Legh Richmond's much-
reprinted "The Negro Servant" (1814), the story of his encounter with an
American slave, the slave William speaks nonstandard English for most
of Richmond's conversation with him: "'My friend,' said I, 'I will now
pray with you for your own soul, and for those of your parents also.' 'Do,
Massa, dat is very goot and kind, do pray for poor Negro souls here and
every where'" (*Annals of the Poor* 185). By the end of their conversation,
William, having proved his Christian orthodoxy, abandons his nonstandard pronunciation, except for the obligatory marker of white superiority:
"'God bless you, my dear Massa.' 'And you, my fellow Christian, for ever
and ever'" (186). Yet this improvement is not enough. Richmond appends
a poem to the tale, "The Negro's Prayer," spoken by an imaginary slave
whose pure English is even better than William's. Although Richmond
does not know what happened to the real William, his imaginary Negro
anticipates glory:

> In heaven the land of glory lies:
>   If I should enter there,
> I'll tell the saints and angels too,
>   Thou heardst a Negro's prayer.   (202)

Richmond's text organizes the purification of English into a symbolic
masterplot, whereby an admirable real African who speaks imperfect
English is followed by an even better imaginary African who speaks perfect English.

For Jewish speakers, this plot of purification is even more prominent. In Richard Cumberland's hugely successful *The Jew* (1795), the Jewish moneylender Sheva first appears speaking with the usual signs of a Jewish accent: "The goot day to you, my young master! How is it with your health, I pray? Is your fader, Sir Stephen Bertram, and my very good patron, to be spoken with?" (1:2). By the end of the play Sheva's seeming miserliness has been revealed as a ruse enabling him to give away large sums to the needy, especially, in this case, the poor Christian heroine Eliza. Sheva concludes the play by praising his own beneficence: "I do not bury it [his money] in a synagogue, or any other pile; I do not waste it upon vanity, or public works; I leave it to a charitable heir, and build my hospital in the human heart" (1:16).[14] Having given away his Jewish money to nice young Christians, he abandons his bad phonemes as well. His reward is metaphoric death, which, as in *Harrington* and *Ivanhoe*, is the death of Judaism: the childless Sheva leaves his money not to synagogues or to public works that help Jews, but to a Christian couple.

For both slaves and Jews, the masterplot of purification is a linguistic correlative of conversion. From the point of view of the dominant culture, conversion is easily seen as a myth: it involves not a true change of heart, but merely throwing off a disguise that masked what was there all along. Admitting the possibility of change in conversion would involve admitting the possibility of otherness; the more comforting possibility is that the other is always actually the same, and conversion is merely peeling away an outer skin. Although Clifford Siskin has claimed that development becomes a guiding mastertrope for the Romantic period, the masterplot of purification does not allow for development.[15] Instead, such works follow the fantasy of standard orthography: all appearances to the contrary, everyone speaks standard English, and the closer that others come to espousing good British values (especially Protestant ones), the more they reveal their true selves as their phonemic mistakes fall away.

According to Papillon, the pseudo-French footman in Samuel Foote's *The Lyar* (1794), "Whoever speaks pure English is an Englishman: I speak pure English; ergo, I am an Englishman" (9). In the works that I have discussed, slaves and Jews get to be Englishmen, just not for long. They are Englishmen "lite," allowed to join the linguistic community for the space of the work to enable the audience's sympathy and even respect, but finally cast out in order to be received into the heaven of blessed phonemes.

While these representations of slave and Jewish speech have considerable interest on their own, they enable larger generalizations about the place of pure English in the eighteenth century. I want to read Romantic poetry in an unusual light by considering it in relation to the dialect English of eighteenth-century drama and popular song. The tension whereby pure English could become so pure that it became a metaphoric death, while impure English easily became associated with fraudulence, moved beyond the boundaries of explicit dialect representation to dominate poetic English in the late eighteenth century. It did so by modeling the power of usage over that of style: in light of English's purification, authorship became an aftereffect of the exemplification of standard or nonstandard Englishes.

Many of the most widely admired poets of the second half of the eighteenth century took purification seriously, and did so to mark poetry's continuing relevance to the nation. The most successful was William Cowper. Although he disagreed loudly with Samuel Johnson's condemnation of Milton, he nevertheless believed strongly in the value of Johnson as an English expert: "They are just going to publish a new Edition of Johnson's Dictionary revised by himself and much improved . . . It is a work that ev'ry Writer should be possessed of" (*Selected Letters* 116). His approval of Johnson's *Dictionary* was not a throwaway compliment, but a firm positioning of himself within a heated debate over appropriate poetic diction. In praising the *Dictionary*, Cowper located himself on the side of Johnson, the English experts, and pure English.

In *The Task*, Cowper developed an English blank verse that provided at least a partial acknowledgement that prose norms had become the dominant stylistic models, as opposed to the Popean couplet. Cowper worked so hard to create an image of cozy Protestant domesticity in *The Task* that it is easy to overlook just how innovative a poet he actually was. Not surprisingly, he serves as one of Davie's prime examples of purity of diction in his poetry. This purity marks not Cowper's comfortable place within an existing tradition, but his poetry's success in meeting the demands of pure English, in which printed prose was the distinctively modern medium of communication.

In Cowper, English bolsters Englishness: *The Task* insists on Cowper's loyalty to England, not Britain, in spite of what Cowper perceives to be the nation's faults. His poetry ties together modernity, Christianity, patriotism, and pure English—or at least strives to. Where Davie sees smooth tonal transitions, others have seen uncomfortable and even irritating uncertainties about just what kind of tone and diction are appropriate for a modern long poem.[16] But Cowper uses his patriotic invocations of national pride to ground the hope that poetry, rescued from the suspicions of English experts, can embody the national imagination.

If Cowper represents modernity, nationalism, and pure English, many other eighteenth-century poets, most famously Thomas Chatterton and Robert Burns, chose archaism, anti-nationalism, and impure English. Hugh Blair had raised the stakes for such archaisms by claiming, in his *Lectures on Rhetoric and Belles Lettres*, that modernity was the age of prose. The early bard sang "indeed in wild and disorderly strains; but they were the native effusions of his heart"; however, in "after ages," poets "composing coolly in their closets . . . endeavoured to imitate passion, rather than to express it" (2:322–23). The prospects for modern poets seemed dim if they were doomed to produce tepid pseudo-emotion in pure English. Late eighteenth-century poets responded by inventing Englishes that were meant to be perceived as antedating its eighteenth-century codification. Archaic English could be seen as reviving the "wild and disorderly" language of true poets, reaching back to more genuine, though less polished, expression.

As such, poets who experimented with English, like comic writers of slave and Jewish speech, found vitality in bad English. The difference between the two was that poets located impurity as much at the level of style as of pronunciation. In their hands, it was not merely a few orthographic deformations that indicated a deviant relation to English, but more systematic iconoclasm. In dialect representations, an out-group speaker was usually put in the context of a dominant in-group who spoke pure English; this context made the others seem especially un-English. In the hands of eighteenth-century poets, however, experimental diction became the dominant context, so that pure English was exiled to the world outside the text, or at least to paratexts like prefaces and footnotes.

Moreover, these writers did not develop their experimental idioms to mark groups supposedly outside of Britishness, like Jews and slaves, but ones already part of Britain who refused the dominance of London English. For them, nonstandard English stood for local pride, not embarrassment. If the purifiers were inventing a cosmopolitan, transnational version of English that could unite England, Scotland, Wales, Ireland, and North America, archaic poetic English refused the union by privileging the individual nations in Great Britain and local areas within them. It set pure English, Great Britain, and oppression against pseudo-archaic English, provincial culture, and liberty. For these writers, their dialects would not need purification: they stand unapologetically on their own.

The most famous impure English came from Thomas Chatterton, a poor seamstress's son from Bristol. He invented for himself an identity as a fifteenth-century Bristol poet, Thomas Rowley, along with a fantasy of Rowley's English, as in the opening of this "Mynstrelle's Song" from *Aella: A Tragycal Enterlude* (1777):

> O! synge untoe mie roundelaie,
> O! droppe the brynie teare wythe mee,
> Daunce ne moe atte hallie daie,
> Lycke a reynynge ryver bee;
>> Mie love ys dedde,
>> Gon to hys death-bedde,
> Al under the wyllowe tree.   (961–67)

Especially striking in Chatterton's "Bristol" English is its etymological art: most of his words have roots in Anglo-Saxon or Norman French, unlike the more Latinate diction of Chaucer. The fictional Rowley's etymological relation to Chaucer was a cover for the real Chatterton's relation to Pope, the English experts' model of pure English in poetry. This etymological battle had a political edge because the diction of poets like Pope stood for the supposed entrenched power of a poetic establishment nurtured on the classics and on the elite educational system (though Pope himself had had an oblique relation to this system because, as a Catholic, he could not attend Oxbridge). The aggressive Englishness of Chatterton's vocabulary created the fantasy of a more pure, original mode of English. Hence, John Keats would later write that Chatterton "is the purest writer in the English Language. He has no French idiom, or particles like Chaucer— 'tis genuine English Idiom in English words" (*JK* 266). For Keats, who, like Chatterton, was rebelling against the class implications of the standardizers' cosmopolitan English, Chatterton, far more than Chaucer, was the well of English undefiled.

Yet, as many critics have noted, this "genuine English Idiom" was a fraud: Chatterton was an ambitious nobody, not a fifteenth-century poet.[17] If the fear haunting pure English was that it created instant ossification, the fear haunting rebellions against it was that they were all flash and no substance, attention-getting ploys. As such, a writer like Chatterton appears as a more sophisticated version of the author of the pig-selling Jew song. In both cases, dialect is linked to fraud. The song's author concocts a mock-Jewish voice for a character who boasts of his own fraudulence; Chatterton concocts a mock-medieval voice for an author who does not exist. For Chatterton as for the authors using slave and Jewish dialect, this ploy reinforced the purification it seemed to contest. In Chatterton's case, Rowley's magic lies almost solely at the level of the grapheme. If one ignores his pseudo-medieval spelling and reads the poems aloud, the actual phonemes follow the strictures of eighteenth-century orthoepists exactly; Rowley's pronunciation is arguably far more standard than Pope's. As William Hazlitt noted in 1818, "the poems read as smooth as any modern poems, if you read them as modern compositions; and . . . you cannot read them, or make verse of them at all, if you pronounce the words as they were spoken at the time when the poems were pretended to have been written" (q. in Russett, *Fictions and Fakes* 58–59). Whereas the eighteenth-century dialect speakers purified their English as they went to heaven, Chatterton's poetry is dialect superimposed on pure English, even as it looks back to a historical moment before a print standard.

Another influential form of localism involved fleeing England altogether for the Celtic fringe. While Chatterton located his Rowleyan language far in the past, the Scots of Robert Burns insisted on the continuing vitality of non-standard language varieties.[18] In 1786, he published *Poems, Chiefly in the Scottish Dialect*, which demonstrated his mastery both of pure English and of Scots, though it was the poems in "the Scottish Dialect" for which he became famous. If English experts agreed on the need to preserve some "liberty" in usage, they also, as I have noted, agreed that this liberty did not include Scottish or Irish. Even as the Scottish intelligentsia were proud of their academic and scientific eminence, they were nevertheless eager to erase Scottishness from their speech, as is indicated by Thomas Sheridan's enormous success giving elocution lessons in Edinburgh.

Burns, however, transformed the despised Scottish dialect from bad English to nature's pure voice. There had been peasant poets before Burns, like Stephen Duck, but they did not write in dialect; there were dialect poets, like Lady Nairne, but they did not claim to be unlettered peasants.[19] Burns linked dialect to a peasant persona (though his actual class position was far more complex than this phrase implies), and, in so doing, provided another alternative to pure English. Burns's early reviewers regretted his use of Scottish; Henry Mackenzie noted that in Scotland, his dialect "is now read with a difficulty which greatly damps the pleasure of the reader" and that in England "it cannot be read at all" (q. in Low, ed., *Burns: Critical Heritage* 69). Tellingly, Mackenzie responds to Burns's poetry primarily as graphemes: while a spoken version of Burns's poetry might have been quite comprehensible to many eighteenth-century Scottish ears, the written version is not because, after purification, it can appear only as a weird deformation of good English.

Yet Burns's dialect (actually a hybrid of standard English and several Scottish language varieties) quickly became one of his prime attractions. James Currie, publisher of the first collected Burns, noted that Burns's Scots "excels . . . in the copiousness and exactness of its terms for natural objects; and in pastoral or rural songs, it gives a Doric simplicity, which is very generally approved" (q. in Low, ed., *Burns: Critical Heritage* 152). Elizabeth Hamilton similarly maintained that "the simplicity of the Scottish dialect is, surely, infinitely better adapted to such descriptions [of emotion] than the cold refinement of modern language" (q. in Benger, *Memoirs* 2:19–20); her comment is a good example of the fear that pure English, far from being a source of vitality, could be merely "cold refinement." For such readers, only those insecure about their English would be threatened by Burns; more sophisticated readers could recognize his poetry's aesthetic value, so that, as in the case of Ossian, Scottish cultural nationalism could co-exist (albeit uneasily) with Britishness.

The valorization of Burns's Scottish poetry may have been an important precedent for the sympathetic representation of slave and Jewish dialect that I discussed earlier. In both cases, admiring poetry written in non-standard English allowed readers who already spoke good English to congratulate themselves both on their education, which could not be threatened by non-standard English, and on their flexible sympathies, which extended across the supposedly superficial differences of language to find the human essence beneath. As I have noted, purification transformed semiosis by its supposed ability to represent all phonemic qualities graphemically and to treat dialect as corruption. But it had a second potential effect: to draw attention to printed English as signs governed by a self-contained set of rules; the more visible language became as a system, the less adequate it potentially seemed as a vehicle for expressing thoughts and emotions not part of such a system. The sympathetic representation of dialect projected a pure thought and intention prior to language that a reader could recover from its imperfect realization in print.

Blake's poetry best exemplifies the double movement whereby departures from pure English draw attention to themselves as a deliberate remaking of English and simultaneously question how important the surface code of language may be. His work avoids pure English and the assumption that any community based on a national print standard is worth joining. He became a printer to produce his own illuminated poems that broke down the distinction between words and pictures. A side benefit was that he eliminated any editorial eye disapproving of his English. Given his deep mistrust of his country's governing institutions, it was not surprising that English liberty appears in Blake's work through the liberties he takes with English. Whereas Chatterton and Burns linked their patriotism to a particular place, William Blake's takes the form of radical individualism: he stands for England by being himself. As a result, he bypasses conventions of grammar, spelling, and punctuation to develop his own peculiar idiolect, a dialect that never needs purification.

For example, in "The CLOD & the PEBBLE" in *Songs of Innocence and of Experience* (1794), he writes,

> Love seeketh not Itself to please,
> Nor for itself hath any care;
> But for another gives its ease,
> And builds a Heaven in Hells despair. (1–4)

As "Hells despair" indicates, Blake has little time for the niceties of standard punctuation; like John Clare, he found rules of punctuation silly. Less noticeably but perhaps more strangely, Blake suddenly modernizes his verb conjugations in mid-stanza. The Clod begins in lines 1–2 with archaic forms of the third-person singular verbs ("seeketh," "hath") yet by lines 3–4, it suddenly updates them ("gives," "builds," instead of "giveth," "buildeth").

This philological moment resembles what I called "stylization" in the previous chapter, in which, for knowing readers, authors seem to play with the results of purification for local effects, so that the figure of the interpretable author briefly emerges from the anonymity of usage. Blake contests the dialect masterplot of purification because his poem moves from older to newer forms of the verb, but, unlike in the dialect treatments of slave and Jewish speech, this movement has no thematic significance. Instead, the change from older to newer verb forms asserts not progress but indifference. In the Blakean context, new verbs are not new; archaic verbs are not archaic: they just coexist. Newer, purer English is not obviously better or more meaningful than older verb forms.

A similar effect occurs in *The Marriage of Heaven and Hell* (1793):

> An Angel came to me and said. O pitiable foolish young man! O horrible! O dreadful state! consider the hot burning dungeon thou art preparing for thyself to all eternity, to which thou art going in such career. I said. perhaps you will be willing to shew me my eternal lot & we will contemplate together upon it and see whether your lot or mine is most desirable. (Plate 17)

The tone of this dialogue hinges on a tiny, easily missed detail: second-person pronouns. The Angel addresses Blake with "thou" and "thyself," while Blake addresses the angel with "you" and "your." In earlier centuries, "thou" and its derivatives had marked the second-person singular; "you," the second-person plural and the formal second-person singular. Yet by Blake's day, "thou" and its derivatives had fallen out of common usage except in exalted poetic language and in debased language for inferiors. A 1754 grammar, for example, described using "thou" as an "ungenteel and rude" form of address (*DENG* 221).

Blake's dialogue teeters between the different associations of the second-person pronoun. Initially, it may seem that the angel employs a formal tone by using "thou." But Blake's response, in which he uses "you," may suggest retrospectively that he, at least, has heard the angel's "thou" as an insult, so that his "you" appears exquisitely polite. At the same time, his "you" could also be a refusal of the angel's formality, an insistence on taking the dialogue down a notch. Here, rather than reinforcing the emergence of the author, knowledge of usage unsettles it by posing two equally correct but divergent possibilities. One could recuperate this unsettling as itself the product of an author effect: the uncertainty of tone around the second-person pronoun resembles what Blake calls the marriage of heaven and hell, the coexistence of contraries that refuses absolute resolutions. Yet, as I suggested in the previous chapter, such a recuperation is a possible but not necessary means of recognizing the agency of English. The passage also raises the possibility that the purification of English stymied an author effect by defining precisely just why a passage might escape univocal intention.

Traces of late eighteenth-century experiments with English can be found throughout Romantic poetry. Coleridge in *The Rime of the Ancient Mariner* (1798, 1817), Scott in *The Lay of the Last Minstrel* (1805), Byron in the first canto of *Childe Harold's Pilgrimage* (1812), and Keats in *The*

Eve of St. Agnes, and *La Belle Dame Sans Merci* (1820) all employ moments of pseudo-medieval English that recall Chatterton and, more generally, sympathetic dialect representation. Wordsworth and Coleridge's decision to entitle their joint volume "Lyrical Ballads" was in part a nod to the English of Percy's *Reliques*, although the results were quite different from anything that Percy had written; Coleridge also took the name "Christabel" from Percy's collection. Scott followed Burns's lead by collecting Scottish ballads in his *Minstrelsy of the Scottish Border* (1802–03); James Hogg wrote poetry in Scots; and Hemans adapted Welsh ballads in her *Selection of Welsh Melodies* (1822).[20]

Yet scholars tend to leave the matter there, simply noting these connections. What remains unexplained is a peculiar fact: Romantic poets consistently abandoned the more flagrant oddities of eighteenth-century dialect experiments. The plot of purification that I traced in relation to slave and Jewish speech describes not only the relationship of Romantic poetry to late eighteenth-century poetry, but also the relation for certain Romantic poets of their late careers to their earlier ones. Faced with the remarkable range and variety of Englishes produced by eighteenth-century poets and the wealth of information about alternatives to pure English in the form of dictionaries, glossaries, and antiquarian works, Romantic poets stage a mass desertion of overt dialect. Although Donald Davie believed that the language of Romanticism was impure when compared with that of eighteenth-century poetry, exactly the reverse is true: next to Chatterton, Burns, and Blake, Coleridge, Wordsworth, and even Shelley and Byron, are models of good English. William Keach has described the "Romantic resistance to the vulgar, . . . the desire to be above or beyond vulgarity," which he finds to be "various and pervasive" even among writers with republican sympathies (*Arbitrary Power* 72). I would extend his observation to locate this resistance in terms of a reaction against the earlier "vulgarity" of late eighteenth-century alternatives to pure English.

To take one of the most famous examples of such desertion, Coleridge rewrote *The Rime of the Ancyent Marinere* as *The Rime of the Ancient Mariner* to omit many of its most obvious archaisms, as in the altered title. His changes to the following stanza reveal the results:

> She doth not tack from side to side—
>   Hither to work us weal
> Withouten wind, withouten tide
>   She steddies with upright keel.   (159–62)

See! see! (I cried) she tacks no more!
Hither to work us weal;
Without a breeze, without a tide,
She steadies with upright keel!   (167–70)

Removing the quaintness of the earlier version boosts the stanza's emotional temperature, as if the veil of archaism keeping the poem's events at a safe distance had suddenly vanished. The neutral formality of "She doth not tack from side to side" becomes the more immediate, personal, and urgent, "See! see! (I cried) she tacks no more," urgency so great that Coleridge even sacrifices to it the "side / tide" rhyme in his first version. He modernizes the faux-archaic "withouten wind, withouten tide" to the more pointed and concrete "without a breeze, without a tide." Whereas for a writer like Chatterton, poetry's excitement came from sustaining his weird fake Middle English, for Coleridge, excitement increases when pseudo-Gothic vocabulary falls away. The revision underscores the potential sense of fraudulence always lurking in literary dialect. In the long run, Romantic authors recognize that dialect is just a disguise, to be discarded in order to reveal the supposedly more authentic poem, and more standardized English, that lurked beneath.

Yet rejecting dialect is not the same as embracing pure English. Instead, Romantic poets experimented both with new sociolects that did not depend so explicitly on "mispronunciation," as well as with the plot of purification as a metaphor for development. They shift from explicit to implicit dialects, ones that are less amenable to simple translation into standards of pure English. I turn to Wordsworth, Keats, Byron, and Hemans to describe not their English in particular poems but the authorial identity that accrues from their encounters with eighteenth-century dialect representation. If English's purification had unsettled authorial identity at local levels of usage, these poets suggested that it could be reasserted at the macrostructural level of a career, understood as an alternative history of linguistic development.

William Wordsworth, in the "Advertisement" to the 1798 *Lyrical Ballads*, frets about the purity of his English; he fears that readers might believe he had "sometimes descended too low, and that many of his expressions are too familiar, and not of sufficient dignity" (739). Given the shape of late eighteenth-century poetry, this is an odd claim. Wordsworth worries about an issue that should have been old hat by the time he wrote, since much literature before 1798 had gone far lower than any-

thing in *Lyrical Ballads*. Although *Lyrical Ballads* features rural characters, it firmly avoids dialect representation. Even Johnny the "idiot boy,"
in the little snippet Wordsworth gives of his speech, produces perfectly
good English: "The cocks did crow to-whoo, to-whoo, / And the sun
did shine so cold" (460–61). Although, as Stephen Land notes, much of
Wordsworth allows "the unspeakable poetry of the contemplative experience of nature to remain unspoken," we learn about unspoken experience through well-written English ("Silent Poet" 167).

Early critics of Wordsworth's diction reacted less to his English's supposed lowness than to the fact that it was not low enough. If Wordsworth's rural characters really had spoken in dialect, then they would have
seemed hardly different from the sympathetic Africans or Jews of 1790s
literature. But Wordsworth made his characters occupy an unnerving
middle ground because they came from "low and rustic life" but were not
represented as speaking as if they did. Instead, his poems disrupted the
myth that pure English worked as nation-building common ground. The
breakdowns in communication in his poems seem all the more infuriat-
ing because both speaker and interlocutor share the same language, which
(according to the myth of pure English) should guarantee mutual comprehensibility. An eight-year old child who has mastered her grammar as
perfectly as the girl of "We Are Seven" ought to be able to understand
death; a shepherd whose English is as refined as that of the speaker of
"The Last of the Flock" ought to have managed his sheep better. If these
characters had had the decency to speak bad English or at least some form
of dialect, their problems might be more sympathetic, but to have mastered good English without having mastered good sense was an outrage.
Likewise, if they had spoken in the high-flown, elaborate English of slaves
in some abolitionist poetry, their English could have been understood
as an obvious fiction, a sentimental ploy to gain readerly sympathy. But
in Wordsworth, English is neither low nor high enough to belong to an
obviously marginalized group. *Lyrical Ballads* shatters the easy bond between English and England by questioning the ability of pure English to
form any community, real or imagined.

Nevertheless, the progress of the 1798 *Lyrical Ballads* as a whole encap-
sulates a familiar plot: in moving from Coleridge's *The Rime of the Ancyent
Marinere* through experimental poems like "The Thorn" and "The Idiot
Boy" and ending with *Tintern Abbey*, it presents a fantasy mini-history
of English. Coleridge's poem, like Chatterton's, begins the volume with

a pseudo-archaic English; Wordsworth's experimental poems are in modern English with a deliberately restricted syntax and vocabulary; the concluding *Tintern Abbey* presents grown-up English of exceptional syntactic complexity. This maturation of English recalls the masterplot of eighteenth-century dialect, in which slaves and Jews became more respectable as their English became more pure, until they were good for nothing except heaven. In *Lyrical Ballad*'s myth, the rural characters help English to hone itself, but they can eventually be abandoned for Wordsworth's transcendentally hard diction. At the volume's end, Wordsworth belongs not to a larger Christian community, like the purified slaves and Jews of eighteenth-century representation; instead, he earns a darker, more tentative knowledge of the "still, sad music of humanity," which, depending on your point of view, epitomizes or erases the rural poor in the earlier poems. Like so many eighteenth-century texts, *Tintern Abbey* links linguistic maturity with a vision of the afterlife, but for Wordsworth, this vision is not Christian glory but his possible reincarnation in Dorothy.

The macrostructure of Wordsworth's career likewise recapitulates the microstructure of the *Lyrical Ballads*. It, too, moves from experimental to pure English: by the time of *The Excursion* (1814), Wordsworth's blank verse accommodates pure English to poetry even better than Cowper's *Task* did. Wordsworth's notes even include a quotation from "one of the finest passages of modern English prose," as if to demonstrate how closely he had modeled his poetry after it (n. to 3.931); far more than in the *Lyrical Ballads*, Wordsworth in *The Excursion* could claim to have followed "prose when it is well written." Moreover, this accommodation had a political purpose: pure English accompanies a celebration of England and its potential as a global power. For Wordsworth, as for Cowper, writing in pure English placed the poet in the nation.[21]

The English of the rural poor in *The Excursion* consequently sounds quite different from their English in *Lyrical Ballads*:

> He was a peasant of the lowest class:
>
> . . .
>
> And he returned our greeting with a smile.
> When he had passed, the Solitary spake;
> "A Man he seems of cheerful yesterdays
> And confident to-morrows; with a face
> Not worldly-minded, for it bears too much
> Of Nature's impress,—gaiety and health,

Freedom and hope; but keen, withal, and shrewd.
His gestures note,—and hark! his tones of voice
Are all vivacious as his mien and looks."   (7.550, 555–63)

None of the peasant's words actually appears; Wordsworth skips the rural
speech so central to *Lyrical Ballads*. The peasant returned a "greeting with
a smile," a line that leaves open the possibility that he did not speak at
all, but only smiled back at the poem's band of talkers, a possibility made
more likely by his lack of any actual English. Only at the end of the
Solitary's speech do we learn that the peasant might have said something
because the Solitary finds his "tones of voice . . . vivacious as his mien and
looks." Any meaning in the peasant's English fades before the physicality
of his voice and face: his unrepresented English matters only as a vehicle
for his general bodily vivaciousness.

The darker suggestion that the poem makes, possibly in spite of itself, is that those who speak about the peasant lack his vivacious tones of
voice, mien, and looks. The praise of his qualities points to their lack in
the observers. The band of thinkers whose English is represented at length
in the poem trade vitality for what Elizabeth Hamilton called the "cold
refinement" of good English. If all the life goes to those whose English is
so impure that it cannot be represented, then the characters who are left
risk a posthumous linguistic existence.

The English of all the later Romantic poets reacts against the plot of
purification represented by Wordsworth's career: how could vitality be
relocated in the language of poetry without using explicit dialect? The
Cockney style of the Hunt circle, exemplified most famously in Keats, was
the most controversial of such responses. Keats consistently and self-con-
sciously associated himself with English and Englishness, as in his famous
statement: "I think I shall be among the English Poets after my death"
(*JK* 209). The sentence's multiple meanings are rarely noted: Keats longed
to be among the poets who wrote in English; to be among the poets of a
particular nation, England; and to be among the poets prestigious enough
to be collected in large anthologies like Alexander Chalmers's *The Works
of the English Poets*. Most striking is the unspoken implicature of Keats's
phrase, which is that an adjective like "great" or "memorable" necessarily
modifies "English." One can imagine other writers for whom the phrase
"English Poets" would be a letdown: to be merely an "English Poet" is
not to be a poet of the world, one for all times and places. But for Keats,

creative ambition is welded to the specificities of language and nation, English and England.

The sting of the "Cockney" label was that it denied Keats a place among the English poets by denying his ability to write English. Keats's poetry does not really represent Cockney dialect by providing an accurate graphemic representation of London pronunciation. If it had, early reviewers would have found it far less threatening, since it could be assimilated easily to familiar forms of poetry that I have discussed. Keats's outrageousness, like Wordsworth's in *Lyrical Ballads*, was that he did not use dialect. Instead, he seemed to be aiming for respectable English, only to reveal that it was full of (carefully contrived) "mistakes."

Keats's English, as his reviewers recognized, belonged to a particular socio-political group: men of lower middle-class origins with radical political sympathies who explored an aesthetics of pleasure and liberation from Evangelical mores.[22] Whereas Chatterton and Burns developed Englishes that stood for particular (pseudo)sociolects, Keats's Cockneyisms did not even have the respectability of representing a substantial marginalized group. Like Chatterton, the Hunt circle created a pseudo-English for poetry, but one that represented not an actual sector of English society, but only a coterie, a small group of ambitious young men with questionable backgrounds.[23] It was outrageously arbitrary, substituting the affectations of suburban puppies for Burns's peasant persona.

A long tradition in Keats criticism reads his career as if it moved away from an embarrassing early style associated with Hunt to a purer, more mature one, epitomized by "To Autumn." This story of purification allows Keats's career to repeat Wordsworth's in a finer tone: a development from an earlier, experimental English to a later, purer one, free from the supposedly deadening effects of purification on *The Excursion*.[24] Yet Keats's actual poetry refuses to conform to this narrative of progress because of the sheer variety of his styles. The result could be an English that, while not dialect, traveled as far as possible from Wordsworthian prosaicism, as in this passage from the "Ode to Psyche" (1820):

> 'Mid hush'd, cool-rooted flowers, fragrant-eyed,
>   Blue, silver-white, and budded Tyrian,
> They lay calm-breathing on the bedded grass;
>   Their arms embraced, and their pinions too;
>   Their lips touch'd not, but had not bade adieu,
> As if disjoined by soft-handed slumber,

> And ready still past kisses to outnumber
>> At tender eye-dawn of aurorean love. (13–20)

If Keats wanted to be "among the English poets," this was certainly a strange way of showing it.[25] As Thomas Pfau argues, "the ultimate antagonist in the early Keats's radical reconceptualization of literary authority . . . was less a Coleridgean idea of complex inwardness than the cultural authority of the English language" (*Romantic Moods* 370).[26] Although nothing in the passage counters the rules for English grammar, spelling, or punctuation, everything in it counters the rules for what made a good English style or what Wordsworth meant by well-written prose. Lindley Murray's *English Grammar*, for example, included detailed advice about "promoting perspicuity in speaking and writing." It advised students to strive for "purity" by avoiding words and phrases that were "*obsolete*, or *new-coined*, or *ungrammatical*, or *not English*." He advocated a clean, unfussy style that promoted sentences characterized by "1. *Clearness*. 2. *Unity*. 3. *Strength*" (*EG* 191).

For clearness, Keats substitutes lush sensuality; for unity, a pile-up of choice phrases; for strength, a post-orgasmic laxity. He writes as if Murray's rules about stylistic purity supported the same repression as the aristocratic use of the classics. If avoiding "*obsolete* and *new-coined*" words produced "pure" English, then Keats's English does the opposite. The "Ode to Psyche" packs its lines with such novelties as "cool-rooted," "fragrant-eyed," "silver-white," "eye-dawn," "aurorean," and "soft-handed." Whereas Murray warned against obsolete words, Keats preserves the full pronunciation of the "-ed" suffix in words where this suffix had long ceased to be a separate syllable, as in "embraced" and "disjoined." Keats's style gleefully effeminizes the implicit sexual politics of Murray's rules.

Nevertheless, Keats seems to have felt the danger of disappearing into a style, as Chatterton had. He famously writes to Reynolds that "English ought to be kept up" to explain abandoning *Hyperion*, as if writing in a Miltonic style was not keeping up English (*JK* 267). Having abandoned his Miltonisms, Keats plans to give himself "up to other sensations," including those of less artificial English. Yet the beginning of *The Fall of Hyperion* suggests how difficult it is to know what such an English might be:

> Who alive can say,
> "Thou art no Poet; mayst not tell thy dreams?"
> Since every man whose soul is not a clod

Hath visions, and would speak, if he had lov'd
And been well nurtured in his mother tongue.
Whether the dream now purposed to rehearse
Be poet's or fanatic's will be known
When this warm scribe my hand is in the grave.   (11–18)

Keats begins by democratizing poetry (albeit in gender-exclusive terms), since "every man . . . hath visions, and would speak." Yet he adds a crucial qualification: a poet can be only a man who has "lov'd / And been well nurtured in his mother tongue." Keats insists on vernacularity and rejects the classics as a precondition for poetry. Yet considerable uncertainty surrounds what counts as being "well nurtured": it can mean to know the grammatical and orthoepical tenets of pure English, to know language's history, or to have imbibed the great works of literature written in it. The "mother tongue" as a value is central to poetry, but, as is typical of Keats's career, just how it realizes itself remains uncertain. Strikingly in this passage, Keats has abandoned the stylistic extravagance of works like the "Ode to Psyche" in favor of a more prosaic blank verse, as if respect for the "mother tongue" involved a chastening of his earlier English.

This chastening accompanies a thematic movement from orality to writing, as if turning "dreams" into written signs demonstrated the fact of being "well nurtured" in English. Yet being too well-nurtured in English is fatal, since the scribe's "warm hand" is destined for the grave. While the invocation of the grave has a strong biographical resonance for Keats, it also has implications for his English. Keats's anticipation of death presents a grimly secular version of the masterplot of dialect purification I traced earlier in this chapter, whereby the purification of English is presented as a stepping-stone to heaven.

As if to escape this fate, the stylistic restlessness of Keats's late poetry (*The Fall of Hyperion*, the odes to Fanny Brawne, *Lamia*, *Otho the Great*, and *The Cap and Bells*) looks as if Keats were trying to run through as many different versions of English as possible in a short time. To be well-nurtured in the mother tongue turns out to require generating constant new possibilities for realizing it: a "camelion poet" needs "camelion" English (*JK* 214). "Camelion" English is Keats's guarantee that his English becomes neither a rigid dialect, a frozen style, nor an exemplar of pure usage. Keats's career uncovers a new flexibility for the author in relation to English that provides a model for freeing authors from the strictures of usage and the precedents set by their earlier poems: it is always possible to reinvent oneself and one's English.

Yet it would not be as a "camelion" experimenter with English that Keats (or Blake, Shelley, or Wordsworth) eventually acquired a place in nineteenth-century literary history. Instead, their reception and the visibility of their Englishes were shaped by the twin influences of poets who sold much better in their own day, Byron and Hemans. So powerful were their answers to the challenges of pure English that they eventually scripted the reception of other poets whose work did not become widely known until later. The core of their success was making the Englishness of poetry marketable.

Byron did so by revising the masterplot of purification in terms of the mystique of genius.[27] His early bad English in works like *Childe Harold's Pilgrimage* and the Eastern Tales, as represented by his notorious indifference to grammar, sprang from a more cosmopolitan outlook than that of writers who identified their language with particular locales, like Chatterton and Burns. To seem too English would be, for Byron, to seem too like the middle classes, too willing to abdicate the aristocracy's traditional superiority to national boundaries. Byron's solecisms are a continual reminder that his English is not tethered to England, as if he were developing a strange global English that showed itself above prescriptivism.

For example, Byron's most notorious solecism appears in his address to the ocean concluding Canto 4 of *Childe Harold's Pilgrimage* (1818). He accuses the ocean of toying with the shipwrecked mariner:

> The vile strength he wields
> For earth's destruction thou dost all despise,
> Spurning him from thy bosom to the skies,
> And send'st him shivering in thy playful spray
> And howling, to his Gods, where haply lies
> His petty hope in some near port or bay,
> And dashest him again to earth:—there let him lay.   (4.180)

The final verb should be "lie." Eighteenth-century standardizers had clarified the difference between "lie" and "lay" (*DENG* 223), and Byron's passage became a much-quoted warning that famous literature was no guide to good usage.

Yet, to be fair to Byron, in the poem's context, the solecism is much less glaring than it is often supposed to be. The Spenserian rhyme scheme *ababbcbcc* sets the reader up for a word that will rhyme with "spray" and "bay," so that "lay" has a felt inevitability that moderates its grammatical wrongness; in addition, the alliteration of "let" and "lay" makes the error less prominent. The fact that Byron's publisher, John Murray, allowed the mistake to slip by means that Byron's supposedly glaring errors may have been less troublesome than later readers have sometimes claimed. Usually, Byron adheres to standard English; his slips feel less like programmatic rebellions than the result of putting grammatical perfection low on his list of poetic priorities. What counts for him is the vivid emotional climax; if pure English needs to be sacrificed, so be it. This emotionalism, rather than the purity of his English, became his poetry's selling-point. Byron's non-standard English becomes a metaphor for international English be-cause it insists that not every rule needs to be followed in order to write acceptably. Rather than seeing English grammar as a guide to perfection, he takes a "good enough" approach to grammar: an error here or there will hardly disrupt the overall sweep of his poetry.

Yet by the time of *Don Juan*, Byron famously praised his poem to Douglas Kinnaird by praising his English: "As to 'Don Juan'—confess—confess—you dog—and be candid—that it is the sublime of *that there* sort of writing—it may be bawdy—but is it not good English?—it may be profligate—but is it not *life*, is it not the *thing*?—Could any man have written it—who has not lived in the world?" (*Letters and Journals* 6:232). This letter's syntax sets up "good English" as a compensation for bawdiness, as if the second made up for any problems created by the first. Yet exactly what Byron means by "good English" is as uncertain as what Keats means by being "well nurtured" in the mother tongue. *Don Juan* is never happier than when foregrounding bad English:

> Our friends the Turks, who with loud 'Allah's' now
>   Began to signalise the Russ retreat,
> Were damnably mistaken; few are slow
>   In thinking that their enemy is beat,
> (Or *beaten*, if *you* insist on grammar, though
>   I never think about it in a heat)
> But here I say the Turks were much mistaken,
> Who hating hogs, yet wish'd to save their bacon.   (7.42)

Byron's stanza has it both ways: he can produce bad English, but immedi-ately apologize for it in a way that stresses that he does indeed think about grammar. Whereas in *Childe Harold*, his solecisms manifested a cosmo-politan indifference to the rules of pure English, the language of *Don Juan* has become good English because Byron acknowledges the rules even as he breaks them.

Don Juan does more than just break grammatical rules: it is flagrantly promiscuous in its linguistic choices, borrowing from numerous languages as well as a range of contemporary argots. Gary Dyer cautions against see-ing Byron's linguistic virtuosity in too celebratory a mode because the poem's codes link it to multiple groups in Byron's Britain who found themselves forced to use codes because of legal prohibitions ("Thieves, Boxers, Sodomites, Poets" 573–74). Yet when these codes enter Byron's poem, their nature changes, just as the nature of his linguistic solecisms changes: they are deracinated from a social context of communication and put into a linguistic context in which they appear as part of the narra-tor's voice. They are dissolved as sociolects to be reborn as style. The result is a new kind of purification: any kind of English—good, bad, coded, slang, high, low—can appear in *Don Juan* because it has lost its status as a representation of usage and gained status as a marker of Byronic genius. *Don Juan* purifies its English by severing its links to national identity. Byron writes English that has nothing to do with being a good English-man, or even that makes a bid to place him "among the English poets." Instead, good English equals Byron's own personal stamp on language: it has become an aftereffect of Byron's marketable style.

Style was hardly a new concept in literary criticism: it had long been a yardstick for distinguishing between modes of writing, as in the difference between high and low.[28] The proverb that "the style was the man" had also had a long life, but it had little purchase as a tool of critical analysis until Byron changed what it meant to be a man with style. Byron had style in a new way because Byron had "Byron" in a new way. His career broke style's connection to the nation and communal norms of propriety and reinvented it as the unique, mysterious mark that a great writer's genius left on language: it could be imitated, but never truly reproduced.

Style has usually been thought of in terms of a collection of linguistic features, but style as created by Byron means far more once it has been welded to personality. It comes closer to what Eve Kosofsky Sedgwick has described as "texture," which she believes is "a promising level of attention for shifting the emphasis of some interdisciplinary conversa-tions away from the recent fixation on epistemology . . . by asking new questions about phenomenology and affect" (*Touching Feeling* 17). To move from style to texture involves viewing the language of a work not solely as a collection of linguistic devices but as an opportunity for taking the author-reader-functions that I discussed in the previous chapter in a particular direction: the reader's ability to create, from the language of the text, a memory representation during and after reading of the "feel" of what it means to read the work in relation to a projected vision of the author's personality. For *Don Juan*, this texture involves the combination of a kaleidoscopic range of events, an outrageous tonal instability, a free-floating narrative wit and sophistication, and the undergirding steadiness of the repeated *ottava rima* format. Such a conception of style makes the minute questions that I asked in the introduction about responsibility for content words versus function words seem to be irrelevant because style is not perceived at such a minute level: it is an overall impression arising from large sweeps of text, not word-by-word processing. Particular linguistic devices in *Don Juan* can be imitated, but its texture cannot (or at least is experienced as inimitable).

With Byron, the unique texture of genius replaces purity of diction once poetic diction abdicates its place in the state. While the shift is implicit in the work of many of the first-generation Romantics, the break happens when Byron writes *Don Juan*. In his revision of the eighteenth-century plot of dialect purification, none of his solecisms is a real solecism anymore because he no longer belongs to a linguistic community that could define them as such, unlike Wordsworth or even Keats. His English has become subject to his rules, at the cost of no longer standing for England or the English: sociolect has become marketable idiolect.

If Byron's English became influential because, as the aftereffect of his genius, it could not be imitated, Hemans's English became influential because it could. Of all the Romantic poets, she was the most successful in creating what John Guillory believed the Romantics failed to create, a new *Hochsprache* that defined "poeticity" (*Cultural Capital* 131). Yet, in light of the success of the English experts, her work could never define good usage in general, only good poetry in particular. She did what Wordsworth, Keats, and Byron did not, create a distinctive English that stood for the language of poetry, yet that was not a dialect.

This success fell to Hemans not solely because she was a powerful poet but also because she was a woman writer. Traditionally, men had targeted women for using bad or vulgar English, since their educational opportunities were far more restricted than those for men.[29] The grammatical slips that in Byron would be treated as mere carelessness were signs of incompetence in a woman writer. As Carol Percy has noted, eighteenth-century critics had developed a repertoire of subtly damning adjectives—"modest," "easy," "sprightly"—to dismiss women's English as less serious and substantial than men's ("'Easy Women'"). It might seem, therefore, that a writer like Hemans would be particularly eager to adhere to all the prescriptions of the standardizers and write in perfectly pure English; her letters give ample evidence that she paid careful attention to her proofsheets.

Yet Hemans's work was not quite so simple, since, as I have noted, the standardizers had emphasized that the model of perfect English was Addisonian prose, not poetry. Wordsworth's prosaicism had been treated as an odd experiment; Keats's demolition of standard English style had been widely scorned. Hemans's solution was to return to the initial site of dialect's deviation from pure English: pronunciation. She recognized that pronunciation was a potential weapon for linguistic distinctiveness, but took it in a direction quite different from eighteenth-century dialect literature. Rather than deforming words in accordance with a perception of ethnic or regional usage, she made poetry a sanctuary for certain kinds of highly emotional prosody that were being exiled from respectable prose, as in this excerpt from "Evening Prayer at a Girls' School" (1826):

> Gaze on, 'tis lovely! childhood's lip and cheek,
>   Mantling beneath its earnest brow of thought!
> Gaze, yet what seest thou in those fair and meek
>   And fragile things, as but for sunshine wrought?
> —Thou seest what grief must nurture for the sky,
> What death must fashion for eternity!   (7–12)

Eighteenth-century purification of English had focused not only on grammar, spelling, and pronunciation, but also on punctuation. Hemans's poetry loudly exploited this new resource to give poetry a distinctive sound. This relatively short stanza from "Evening Prayer at a Girls' School" contains three exclamation points, two dashes, and one question mark. About exclamation points and question marks, Lindley Murray noted that they were "indeterminate as to their quantity of time, and may be equivalent in that respect to a semicolon, a colon, or a period, as the sense may require" (*EG* 170). Their indeterminacy stood for freedom within the strictures of purification because the reader could decide how much time each needed, and what tone each created. A similar indeterminacy surrounds the dash before "Thou seest." Dashes typically marked an abrupt break within a sentence; one between sentences was odd because terminal punctuation, like the question mark in the previous line, should be enough to indicate a pause. Hemans, however, signals a further pause with the dash, as if to make sure that it is not passed over. Such marks insist on the presence of the real or imagined reading voice, as if the poetry could be fully realized only through oral performance.[30]

This vivid use of punctuation allows Hemans to carve out a particular kind of English characterized by its close connection with vocal signals of strong emotion.[31] While not offending against any rules of the puri-fiers, it nevertheless insists on poetry's special relation to English as a site for emotion, sound, and voice, without turning to dialect. Through her insistent exploration of themes and motifs associated with femininity, she gendered this special English as a peculiarly feminine one. This was a risky strategy, since, as I have noted, any uses of English that seemed par-ticularly feminine had been traditionally despised. Hemans successfully re-invented poetic English not as non-standard English but as a hybrid of archaisms, standard grammar, and, above all, a foregrounded use of standard punctuation insisting on the power of voice.

Yet Hemans's success had a cost: stylistic stasis. Unlike the restless ex-perimentation of Wordsworth, Byron, and Keats, the style that Hemans perfected in her *Tales, and Historic Scenes, in Verse* (1819) and *The Siege of Valencia* (1823) locked into place and changed little until her death in 1835. In part, this sameness was the product of Hemans's circumstances: as one of the very few women able to make money from poetry and as a single mother of five children, she had less room to experiment than an inde-pendently wealthy aristocrat like Byron. He could afford to be "Byron"; she had to be "Poetry." Near the end of her life, she admitted, "The con-stant necessity of providing sums of money to meet the exigencies of the boys' education, has obliged me to waste my mind in what I consider mere desultory effusions" (q. in *Felicia Hemans*, ed. Wolfson, 521). Yet the popularity of her "desultory effusions" indicates a critical aspect of her success as a poet: her poeticity was most in demand in the form of short lyrics that could be easily reproduced and anthologized, rather than in the form of long tales, of the kind popularized by Moore, Scott, and Byron. What mattered was a crystallized bit of poetical English, an occasion not to model good usage but to foreground the expressive voice. This prettiness could be commodified, reproduced, imitated, and taught. To copy Byron was to be an obvious failure, to be caught in an absurd attempt to reproduce his inimitable genius. To copy Hemans, however, was to write poetry.

The two possibilities created by Byron and Hemans script the progress of poetry to the present day. Byron's brazen contortions of English throughout *Don Juan* marked the poet as genius, capable of remaking English in his own image. Hemans's poeticity marked off the realm of polite poetry, a region of heightened but accessible diction addressed to supposedly universal emotions. Byron's precedent becomes the marker of genius and prestige; Hemans's, the English of popular poetry. Nineteenth-century publishers and literary critics remade much of literary history in terms of Byronic and Hemansian strands: Shelley, for example, could appear both as a brilliant innovator and as the author of pretty lyrics. Some of Byron's poetry fit into the Hemansian model; some recent critics read Hemans's style Byronically.

The inadequacies of language as a medium of expression have long been a theme in the study of Romanticism. Yet language's inadequacies are the triumphs of standardized English: the failures of language as rhetoric are undergirded by the successes of English as grammar, spelling, and punctuation. The poetry of the Romantic period marks the emergence of English literature fundamentally as literature in English, with English no longer serving as a second-order reflection of the supposedly higher languages of Greek and Latin or as the strawman against which the provincial poet had to rebel. Yet this emergence occurred at the moment that the language of literature lost its ability to stand for the language of the nation. The result was a major re-organization of literary authority around its relation to English and Englishness in terms of a rejection of earlier dialect representation. Poetry gained new authority not from its mythic link to national print culture, but from its status as a particular kind of commodity that could be valued either as a marker of genius or as a heightened language of emotion.

§ 4 Sounding Meaning

Where the previous chapter examined Romantic poetry and various modes of "bad English" in eighteenth-century drama and experimental writing, this chapter examines poetry's increasing separation from novelistic English. To do so, it turns from dialect representation to eighteenth-century rhetoric and from concerns about vulgarity to ones about comprehensibility. Rhetoricians faced the challenge of relocating common ground on the domain of printed English. This was an uphill battle: print can outlast its author and travel far in time and place from its first compositional context. While concerns about comprehensibility are as old as writing itself, problems of comprehension became more urgent in the eighteenth century. The power of print to open up gaps between reader and writer had been held in comparative abeyance by the tight controls on the book trade, which guaranteed that most books, especially new ones, had a small circulation.[1]

At the beginning of the eighteenth century, however, the specter of uncomprehending readers haunted novelists. As scholars of the early novel have often noted, its authors fret about whether or not readers will understand quite basic aspects of what it means to read fiction. The development described by Catherine Gallagher, whereby readers of novels learned to sympathize with characters who did not exist, required considerable assistance from authors.[2] After a novel of many hundreds of pages, Samuel Richardson includes a postscript to explain that Lovelace has been punished for being bad and Clarissa rewarded for being good; he continued to revise *Clarissa* (1748) as if these points were seriously in doubt. Mary Manly includes a preface to *The Secret History of Queen Zarah* (1705) to explain, in part, that the novel's opening would explain where and when the action took place and who the main characters were; Henry Fielding in *Tom Jones* (1749), Eliza Haywood in *The History of Miss Betsy Thoughtless* (1751), and Charlotte Lennox in *The Female Quixote* (1752) spend considerable time guiding readers' reactions; and Smollet's preface to *Roderick Random* (1748) explains satire as if readers had never heard of it.

These writers shape narratives, paratexts, or both with explicit directions, as if they could guarantee understanding only by belaboring what now seems obvious. Such directions are often understood to mark what J. Paul Hunter terms a "nostalgia for community," as if they could compensate for the loss of face-to-face talk, which supposedly gave more clues to comprehension (*Before Novels* 156–61). This compensation masks the accommodation of fiction to a print culture characterized by uncertain common ground between author and audience. The point is not so much that early novelists miss an older form of intimacy but that, by simulating orality, they make it obsolete. Their techniques both recognize a gap across which only partial communication might occur and teach readers how to bridge it.

Such techniques, while not invisible, are far less common in early eighteenth-century poets. Poets are hardly indifferent to readers, but modes such as the verse epistle and practices such as publication by subscription assume the common ground that novelists could not. Only the most skeletal outlines preface works like Alexander Pope's *Moral Essays* (1731–35) or James Thomson's *Seasons* (1730); Edward Young's vast *Night Thoughts* (1745) has a perfunctory introduction; Samuel Johnson gives readers of "The Vanity of Human Wishes" (1749) no help with the poem's topicality. When Pope does provide detailed interpretive material, as in his *New Dunciad* (1742, later the fourth book of the *Dunciad*), it's a joke: a good poem should need no explanation. The haunting self-consciousness of early novelists that they are confronting readers with a profoundly unfamiliar experience is not present, at least not to the same degree, among poets.

By the beginning of the nineteenth century, novel and poem have switched. Romantic poems take on the fears of incomprehension associated with the early eighteenth-century novel, while the novel has acquired the relative confidence of early eighteenth-century poetry. If Fielding, Richardson, Haywood, and Lennox assume what looks like an elementary reader, William Godwin in *Caleb Williams* (1794), Maria Edgeworth in *Belinda* (1801), Jane Austen in *Emma* (1816), and Charles Maturin in *Melmoth the Wanderer* (1820) assume advanced ones. Scott is a partial exception; the odd introductory materials he sometimes uses to preface his novels show considerable discomfort at having to explain forms that most readers should already have mastered. Throughout the Romantic novel, implied readers receive scant paratextual help from authors. They are expected to handle, unaided, unreliable first-person or engaged narrators, the absence of allegorical names or omniscient moral judgments, and bewildering amalgamations of genre. The scathing criticism that early nineteenth-century writers often bestowed on novels for being brainless entertainment ignored just how complex many of them were.

Romantic poems, on the other hand, come with lengthy instruction manuals (elaborate prefaces, epigraphs, and prose accompaniments) and online help features as well (footnotes). Works as different as Blake's *Jerusalem* (1804–20), Mary Tighe's *Psyche* (1805), Coleridge's "Kubla Khan" (1816), Byron's *Childe Harold's Pilgrimage* (1812–18), and Hemans's *The Siege of Valencia* (1823) all have extras designed to help the presumably struggling or at least underinformed reader.[3] Nor is this extra material always marked off typographically by a distinct place on the page. It is just as common, as in Wordsworth's *Prelude* (1850) or Byron's *Don Juan* (1819–24), for poems to absorb their own paratexts, as if writing commentaries on poetry had become more poetical than poetry itself.

To judge by the contemporary reception of Romantic poetry, these paratextual aids failed badly. While much recent historicist criticism has assumed early nineteenth-century readers attuned to subtle ideological nuances in poetry, actual responses from readers often come closer to cluelessness. Incomprehension (non-understanding, as opposed to misunderstanding) emerges as a major issue in reviews of Romantic poetry. While comments about not understanding the poetry under review often have a political edge, they also point to genuine bafflement. It is no surprise that no one understood Blake, but other poets fared not much better. I discussed in my first chapter the difficulties that Wordsworth's first readers found with his work. Coleridge's *Christabel* was "the standing enigma which puzzles the curiosity of literary circles. What is it all about?" ("Rev. of *Christabel*" 166), while another reviewer asked about Shelley, "What, in the name of wonder on one side, and of common sense on the other, is the meaning of this metaphysical rhapsody about the unbinding of Prometheus?" ("Rev. of *Prometheus Unbound*" 168). Even Keats was condemned for "his frequent obscurity and confusion of language" (John Scott, "Rev. of *Lamia*" 321) and his "unintelligible quaintness" ("Rev. of *Lamia*" 485). Byron, never to be outdone, boasted in *Don Juan* that not only did he not understand many of his fellow poets, he did not understand himself either: "I don't pretend that I quite understand / My own meaning when I would be very fine" (4.5). While female poets seem to have done better with readers, their longer, more intellectually challenging works rarely acquired the reputation of their shorter, simpler lyrics.

Evidently, in the movement from the early eighteenth to the early nineteenth century, reading novels became easier and reading poems became harder, and the puzzle is why. Critics like Gallagher and Deidre Shauna Lynch have developed part of the answer by describing large-scale changes in reading habits encouraged by the novel, such as the rise of sympathetic reading and the emergence of new understandings of character.[4] In terms of poetry, critics like Walter J. Ong, Friedrich A. Kittler, Celeste Langan, and Kevis Goodman have looked to media studies to understand poetry's peculiar position at the beginning of the nineteenth century.[5] I, too, find this a compelling approach, but want to complicate how media has usually been understood. First, the very different influences of Marshall McLuhan, Ong, and Jacques Derrida have led to an occasional overvaluation of the literacy/orality binary, which had lost most of its explanatory power by the Romantic period. The conflict was no longer between orality and print, but between different technologies and possibilities for realizing print. The focus on the materiality of media has also led some critics to attribute too much causal agency to the sheer proliferation of books during the period (Siskin, "More is Different"). Print had been around for a long time by the Romantic period, and the mere fact of its increased prevalence cannot fully explain the changes I have noted.

My argument is not that by the beginning of the nineteenth century, novel readers had progressed and poetry readers had regressed, but that the nature of comprehending these modes had changed. Literature increasingly responded to contemporary developments in rhetoric that explained how to use the code of pure English. The Romantic period inherited two key interfaces for disseminating it: the elocutionary voice, as developed by Thomas Sheridan and John Walker; and expository prose, as developed by Adam Smith, Hugh Blair, George Campbell, and other Scottish academics. In describing voice and prose as new interfaces, my point is not that nobody before the second half of the eighteenth century ever used a voice or wrote in prose. Instead, voice and prose changed in light of printed English, and these changes in turn changed literature. Although writers within these movements differed significantly from one another, these differences played a smaller role in the social reception of elocution and expository prose than did their similarities; my discussion is selective in that it focuses on the aspects of these movements that had the greatest effect on Romantic literature.

The London-based elocutionary project replaced the older mode of speech with a newer mode, the voice. The elocutionary voice subordinated phonetic sounds of English, extra-linguistic properties of human sounds, and bodily gesture to perceived demands of textual comprehension. As described by William Cockin,

> *Reading* IS THE ART OF DELIVERING WRITTEN LANGUAGE WITH *propriety, force,* AND *elegance.* WHERE (AS IN SPEAKING) THE PRONUNCIATION OF THE WORDS IS COPIED AFTER THE POLITE AND LEARNED OF OUR COUNTRY, AND THE EMPHASIS OF SENSE, THE PAUSES, and SIGNIFICANT CADENCES ARE DETERMINED BY THE MEANING OF WHAT IS BEFORE US: WHERE THE MODULATION IS BORROWED FROM FASHIONABLE SPEECH, BUT A LITTLE IMPROVED AND HEIGHTENED IN PROPORTION TO THE BEAUTY AND HARMONY OF THE COMPOSITION: WHERE ALL THE SIGNS OF THE EMOTIONS ARE IN *quality* THE SAME AS THEY WOULD FLOW SPONTANEOUSLY FROM NATURE, BUT ABATED SOMETHING IN *quantity.* (*Art of Delivering Written Language* 140–41)

Cockin's description is a virtuosic example of the art of the page, and is typical of the elocutionists' writing in using typography to master the voice. His definition uses terms from a variety of discourses. Elocution is a mode of hermeneutics: it modulates the voice in accordance with "THE MEANING OF WHAT IS BEFORE US." It also acknowledges social emulation; those who study elocution will learn to speak "AFTER THE POLITE AND LEARNED OF OUR COUNTRY." Yet it also corrects that speech as well, since an elocutionist's voice is "A LITTLE IMPROVED" next to fashionable speech. Lastly, elocution modifies emotions to make them appropriate for an audience by keeping the signs of emotion the same in "*quality*" but lesser in "*quantity.*" Elocution was far more than simply learning to talk with a good accent: it was a wide-ranging, ambitious intellectual program.

During the Romantic period, elocution made the physiological capacities of the human larynx arguably more important than they had ever been before because of their functionality as a mode of comprehending print. Whereas classical oratory involved the "oral creation of an oration with the help of the topics or 'places' and of thematic and formulaic memory . . . in the existential situation" in which speakers found themselves when they rose to their feet (Ong, "[Rev. of Howell]" 640), elocution stressed reading and often the verbatim memorization of a previously written text, sometimes by the speaker, but more often by someone else.[6] Even when the speaker transmitted his or her own writing, the script had an inherent otherness because the speaker no longer produced it spontaneously. Rather than being a site to realize the formulae of rhetoric through the individual's cognitive, vocal, and gestural capacities, elocution became a technology of transmission, an interface for translating one medium (print) into another (voice) for the benefit of an audience.

At the heart of the movement was a revision of the central doctrine of Protestant literacy, "The letter killeth, but the spirit giveth life," which I have discussed in connection with the purification of English. In the elocutionary revision, writing became the killing letter; the voice, the life-giving spirit. As the movement's founder, Thomas Sheridan, noted, it was pointless to attempt "to produce effects by the dead letter, which can never be produced but by the living voice" (*Course of Lectures* xii).[7] For Sheridan, only through translation into audible phonemes and visible gestures could print be truly understood. Elocution superseded older practices of comprehension, such as translation and exegesis, by insisting on a meaningful relation between sound and sense. While the particular phonemes of a given word might be arbitrary (though this arbitrariness in itself was debated during the period), as soon as the word appeared in a communicative context, the tones in which it was pronounced were no longer arbitrary: they had to be supercharged with meaning. For the elocutionists, the cognitive, semantic, syntactic, motoric, prosodic, and phonetic properties of language would unite as a perfect medium between performer and audience, all in the service of the author. It is easy to read elocution's privileging of sound as the idealization of speech that Derrida deconstructs in *On Grammatology*. But for the elocutionists, the opposition between speech and writing was beside the point. As Cockin's description reveals, mere speech was of little interest to them: the trained voice was, because of its supposedly unique capacities for realizing print.

Typically, elocutionists admitted that silent reading could produce comprehension, but they usually went on to brand that comprehension as imperfect, flawed, or merely cerebral, an understanding of the head rather than the heart. For Sheridan, "the written language is in a sufficient state of perfection, as any one who is once master of it, can read an author who writes clearly, so as fully to comprehend his meaning." Yet when he actually describes silent reading, comprehension turns out to be a confrontation with uncertainty: "The man who has learned to read, has been taught to connect or separate his words, by arbitrary rules of stopping, which are not taken from the natural train of our ideas. He has no mark to point out the most important word, which is therefore often neglected." If "the most important word" is "often neglected," then written language is not transparent. Only with the elocutionary voice do readers encounter "the language of emotions, tones, looks, and gestures" that creates full comprehension (*General Dictionary* 46). Likewise, Walker notes that reading aloud "not only expresses the sense of an author, so as barely to be understood, but . . . at the same time, gives it all that force, beauty, and variety, of which it is susceptible." A silent reader may have "barely . . . understood" the sense, but oral reading realizes its full "force, beauty, and variety" (*Rhetorical Grammar* 29).[8] To create such effects, the elocutionists developed detailed rules for pause, emphasis, climax, cadence, and inflection that would be sure to convey the true meaning of the words.

They also experimented with typographic markers to represent these prosodic cues, from italics to accent marks to variations in spacing and typesetting. Sheridan, for example, created a much-discussed version of the Church Service: "But″, if we confe`ss our sins, ″He″ is fa`ithful, and ju`st, to forgi`ve us our sins, and to clea`nse us, from āll unrighteousness" (*Course of Lectures* 64). Walker experimented with word spacing and emphasis to make appropriate meaning groups apparent:

Britons, attend! beworth likethis approv'd,
Andshow youhave the virtue tobemov'd.
Withhonest *scorn* the*first*fam'd Catoview'd
Rome learningarts from Greece, whomshesubdu'd. (*Rhetorical Grammar* 111)

In Sheridan, unfamiliar accent marks break up familiar words to make them visible as mere signifiers, while Walker produces blobs of what look like nonce words, such as "beworth" or "learningarts." These visual techniques, while intended to heighten communication, defamiliarize English into strange new forms. Print manifests its control over the elocutionary voice even at the cost of easy decoding.

An example of the pervasiveness of elocutionary concerns about pronunciation and comprehension appears in Mary Shelley's *Frankenstein* (1818), when the creature worries about his voice: "My organs were indeed harsh, but supple; and although my voice was very unlike the soft music of their [the De Laceys'] tones, yet I pronounced such words as I understood with tolerable ease" (143). The creature is intensely self-conscious about the melody of his voice because he realizes that it represents him. While his raw acoustic sounds are only moderately promising ("harsh, but supple"), comprehension comes to his rescue: "I pronounced such words as I understood with tolerable ease." The creature connects his ability to pronounce words "with tolerable ease" to his prior comprehension of them, as if he could only pronounce well words that he already understood. On the surface, this is a strange statement, since no necessary connection exists between comprehension and pronunciation. We can pronounce words we do not understand, and understand words we cannot pronounce. The creature, however, like the elocutionists, treats them as causally linked: good pronunciation requires prior comprehension. He thus manifests the dream of elocutionary English, that the physiological and acoustic qualities of speech could become completely subordinate to the cognitive ones of the voice.

Elocution became a much-desired job qualification for the upwardly mobile young gentleman in eighteenth-century Britain. Although it is often associated with the middle classes, elocution spread across the social spectrum.[9] At elite public schools like Harrow, students were trained in proper speaking; the fact that they may have imbibed fashionable English pronunciation from their parents and friends did not exempt them from the rigors of elocution in Latin.[10] Although John Walker's textbooks in elocution became especially valued in the new schools focusing on English education, he also lectured at Oxford and tutored the sons of several Parliamentarians.[11]

The advertisement of Henry Smeathman for his elocutionary services indicates the prospective audience for his lessons. Elocution deserves

the attention of all those who wish to have the pleasure of reading the English classic authors with grace and propriety, or to write and speak correctly; of those Gentlemen, who are intended for the Navy, the Army, the Public-office or the Counting-house; or whose juvenile studies may have been obliterated by an early introduction into those situations; and of all those who may have been deprived of the advantages of a liberal education. They are effectually cured of any defects in pronunciation, which do not arise from an imperfection in the organs of speech; and instead of provincial, disagreeable or absurd habits, they acquire an energetic, a persuasive and a graceful manner of speaking, reading and reciting. Above all, the younger pupils receive this singular and important advantage, that their minds are opened more early, their reason is assisted in its exertions, and directed to such objects as naturally promote the perfection, and the happiness of human beings. ("Elocution and Polite Literature" 2)

Smeathman's advertisement blends several justifications for elocution. He begins with the usual stress on realizing print correctly through oral performance, and then moves to what may have been the more bankable lure of a correct accent. Yet to see social climbing alone in Smeathman's advertisement would miss the cognitive and hermeneutic ambitions of eighteenth-century elocution. Smeathman insists that elocution makes his pupils smarter: it is not merely a surface accomplishment, but one able to open the mind and assist the reason.

The memoirs of William Herringham reveal just how meaningful elocution could be. Born in 1757 to a poor family, he was orphaned when young. Largely self-educated, he planned on a career in the church. A turning-point in his education occurred when he read Sheridan:

I immediately set myself to the practice of reading aloud. . . . I found myself labouring under a wretched monotony, and possessing a voice so weak, that I could not read aloud in an ordinary-sized room for ten minutes without coughing. By great perseverance and frequent practice I was enabled to surmount both these habits, and another equally unfortunate, of using the *v* for the *w*, and the *w* for the *v*.[12]

Herringham did not regard elocution as an alien set of practices forced upon him but welcome means to acquire basic skills he needed as a clergyman. His account underscores the variety of skills that elocution offered. It helped him with the expressivity of his voice by enabling him to abandon his "wretched monotony." It also aided his physical vocal prowess by guiding him to practice sustained vocal production at a volume appropriate to a clergyman. Only at the end does Herringham mention correct pronunciation: standardizing his use of /v/ and /w/ removed the most glaring marker of impure English from his speech. What may be most remarkable about Herringham's account is that he seems to have learned all this just by reading Sheridan and practicing on his own. Although

Sheridan and elocutionists like Smeathman offered classes, knowledge of elocution was not confined to their schools. In a manner characteristic of the dissemination of pure English, anyone who could read and could buy or borrow the relevant works had access to this valuable knowledge.

In Scotland, academics developed a different interface to respond to the same issues confronting the elocutionists: expository English. Rather than offering the "living voice," they theorized a new form of English that would render the vocal props described by the elocutionists unnecessary.[13] Whereas elocutionists focused on print's reception, Scottish academics focused on its production. Previous theories of prose had arisen from rhetorical traditions of oral delivery and adaptations of it. As Jill Marie Bradbury has argued, "the Scottish writers took the notable step of articulating a philosophical context for the analysis of prose writing" as a distinctive interface designed for silent reading, rapid comprehension, and neutral transmission of information ("New Science" 45). The importance of their work for the history of prose has sometimes been misunderstood because they frequently write as if their chief interest is spoken argument: they write much about oratory, for example. Yet even when they discuss oratory, their advice avoids physical voice. Instead, it assumes that all contemporary discourse originates as writing, and that significant improvements should occur in writing, not speaking. Blair, for example, notes that for sermons, "it is proper to begin . . . with writing as accurately as possible" (*LRB* 2:118). Voice is appended as a secondary effect, and it receives only one short chapter in Blair's lectures: writing matters, not voice.

Yet it is not any kind of writing that they advocate: an implicit set of oppositions governs these works that pits rhetoric, speech, emotion, and premodernity against exposition, prose, information, and the modern. As Blair notes,

> A Book that is to be read, requires one sort of Style; a man that is to speak, must use another. In books, we look for correctness, precision, all redundancies pruned, all repetitions avoided, Language completely polished. Speaking admits a more easy copious Style, and less fettered by rule; repetitions may often be necessary, parentheses may sometimes be graceful; the same thought must often be placed in different views. (2:237)

What Blair treats as a stylistic distinction between speech and print is really a distinction between an older style of writing indebted to rhetoric and the new expository style that Blair wishes to promulgate. Blair's book became particularly known for the many passages that pick apart the work of older writers. The faults that he notes repeatedly come back to what he treats here as aspects of speech (copiousness, repetition, and parenthesis) but are actually figures of rhetoric. He devalues these figures by associating them with the lesser mode of speech, which suffers next to clean, correct print.

Adam Smith's *Lectures on Rhetoric and Belles Lettres* (1748–51) goes so far as to divide prose into the "Didactick and the Rhetoricall." The first "proposes to put before us the arguments on both sides of the question in their true light, giving each its proper degree of influence," while the second "magnifies all the arguments on the one side and diminishes or conceals those that might be brought on the side contrary to that which it is designed that we should favour" (62). While Smith throughout his lectures acknowledges both modes, his phrasing loudly favors the first over the second. Didactic writing presents truth; rhetoric, lies. Modern eloquence, for Smith, does not need rhetoric: "The Eloquence which is now in greatest esteem is a plain, distinct, and perspicuous Stile without any of the Floridity or other ornamentall parts of the Old Eloquence" (196). As Bryan Short notes, the Scottish New Rhetoric manifests "a pervasive respect for clarity and directness of language" ("Figurative Language in the Scottish New Rhetoric" 252).

Plainness, clarity, and conciseness serve not only as stylistic markers but as implicit metaphors for the silence of print, a medium that, in silencing and invisibilizing itself, enables the production of modern knowledge. Expository English makes what Sheridan calls the "living voice" superfluous by separating knowledge from voice, especially affective voice. Prose gains antitheatrical authority by appearing as a disappearing mediator: "Perfection of stile consists in Express<ing> in the most concise, proper and precise manner the thought of the author" (Smith, *Lectures on Rhetoric and Belles Lettres* 55). In expository prose, Schleiermacher's hermeneutic distinction between grammatical and authorial sense disappears, because the two have fused.[14] At its best, prose presents thought through an efficient, frictionless medium for direct communication. Expository English made prose prosaic, a powerful but deliberately unexciting medium that could supposedly compel comprehension by clearing away all distractions, such as authorial subjectivity and emotional rhetoric; such rhetoric could come to seem fundamentally foreign to plain English (Langford, *Englishness Identified* 90–91).

Echoes of such formulations quickly became widespread, as in William Godwin's claim that a good style is "free from unnecessary parts and excrescencies" and communicates "our ideas with the smallest degree of prolixity and circuitousness" (*Enquirer* 370). They could even be applied to poetry, as when Anna Seward informed Richard Polwhele that "all which belongs to a didactic poem should be instantly obvious to the understanding, at least amongst readers who are used to poetry" (q. in Polwhele, *Traditions and Recollections* 1:168). Indeed, even the elocutionists spread expository prose because their treatises were fine examples of it, in every way opposed to the emotional expression they were designed to teach. Hence, the opposition between poetry and prose could acquire virtually allegorical significance, as when Edward Ferrars in *Sense and Sensibility* (1811) fails in his reading of poetry, but, as Mrs. Dashwood notes, "would certainly have done more justice to simple and elegant prose" (20)—a distinction that would have meant little in previous centuries, but that had acquired new force.

Although both elocutionary and expository English were originally created for the traditional professional classes, they fortuitously gained much more influence than their creators might have planned. They emerged just before the pivotal date of 1774, when copyright laws changed to allow an explosion of school textbooks and anthologies.[15] Paul Edwards has written about colonial America that "elocution books would belong in the libraries of American revolutionaries as much as the books on net surfing, webpage construction, and 'Windows for Dummies' belong in the libraries of communication-savvy politicians" (*Unstoried* 46). The same was true of British politicians, and their libraries included the Scottish academics as well. Hugh Blair's *Lectures* pervaded the curriculum in Britain and North America; even at Oxford and Cambridge, still bastions of the classical curriculum, undergraduate essays in English reveal extensive knowledge of Scottish writings on belles-lettres.[16] John Walker's prescriptions on elocution became a standard feature of nineteenth-century anthologies for oral recitation. Although expository and elocutionary English were quite different, they coexisted for most of the nineteenth century to provide powerful interfaces for the newly standardized English.

Literature used these interfaces to sharpen the distinction between the novel and poetry. In relation to elocutionary and expository English, the novel developed a particular division of labor. Elocutionary English went to characters; expository English, to narrators, especially third-person omniscient ones. Characters could be understood through how they spoke; narrators, through the clarity of their prose.[17] The novel eagerly swallowed the entire vocabulary of elocutionary pauses, emphases, tones, accents, climaxes, and cadences to describe how characters talked. Narrators pronounced on events and characters, but did not pronounce words. In novels, characters have mouths; narrators do not. The silent reader can imagine the narrator speaking with whatever pronunciation the reader believes to be appropriate, thus making the narrator of a novel (unlike the narrator of an orally recited poem) incapable of uncertain or dubious pronunciations.

This difference produces a hierarchy: silent narrators are more believable than speaking characters. The prose of the omniscient fictional narrator was paradoxically more credible than such non-fictional modes as journalism or natural philosophy because it provided a better model for accurately transmitting information. Inside the fictional contract, everything the narrator wrote was true. Even the most neutral piece of writing in natural philosophy could not aspire to the absolute knowledge possessed by a fictional narrator. The result was a powerful boost to novelistic authority insofar as novelists themselves could become associated with their narrators' voices. Even though novelists as writers compose the words of narrator and character, the link between the omniscient narrator and expository prose enabled the narrator to seem to readers to be the voice of the "real" author.

Once assigned to characters, elocutionary voice lost the broad power to translate print associated with it by Cockin, Smeathman, and others. Instead, elocutionary inflections described how a character realized not pre-existing print, but a pre-existing emotional state. When novelistic speech is described in elocutionary terms, it is as if a character has externalized an internal script. Such an externalization carries the danger of returning elocution to its theatrical origins. If a character's speech has too many elocutionary inflections, it looks not spontaneous, as in the elocutionary manuals, but stilted and insincere.[18]

Not surprisingly, given the long history of misogynistic stereotypes around female speech, the speech of female characters becomes a lightning rod for the novelistic adaptation and implicit degradation of elocution. Only once the novel has absorbed markers of elocution does the representation of female speech begin to acquire stereotypical marks of "feminine voice." Two moments from *The Female Quixote* (1752) and *Sense and Sen-*

sibility (1811) can represent the novelistic emergence of elocutionary voice. In the first, the heroine Arabella responds to her maid's account of her lover; in the second, Elinor Dashwood listens to her enemy, Lucy Steele:

> What! interrupted *Arabella*: And didst thou not observe the Tears trickle from his Eyes, which, haply, he strove to conceal? Did he not strike his Bosom with the Vehemence of his Grief; and cast his accusing and despairing Eyes to heaven, which had permitted such a Misfortune to befal me? (109)

> "I should have been quite disappointed if I had not found you here *still*," said she [Lucy Steele] repeatedly, with a strong emphasis on the word. "But I always thought I *should*. I was almost sure you would not leave London yet awhile; though you *told* me, you know, at Barton, that you should not stay above a *month* . . . I am amazingly glad you did not keep to *your word*."

> Elinor perfectly understood her, and was forced to use all her self-command to make it appear that she did *not*. (247)

Arabella indulges in her usual histrionics, but we learn little about the physical facts of her vocal delivery. While her bombast seems to invite similarly puffed-up tones, nothing in Lennox's work directs the reader about how to realize this voice. By the time of *Sense and Sensibility*, however, Austen treats Lucy's voice quite differently. "Emphasis" had been a major term of elocutionary treatises; William Cockin, quoted above, discusses it at length, and John Walker's *Elements of Elocution* spent over one hundred pages on it, with chapters including "Introduction to the Theory of Emphasis," "Theory of Emphatic Inflexion," "Practical System of Emphasis," "Single Emphasis," "Double Emphasis," "Treble Emphasis," and "General Emphasis" (*Elements of Elocution* 1:15–107). While I am not claiming that Austen's use of the word "emphasis" specifically alludes to Walker's rules, her treatment of Lucy's voice shows that she knows all about the rules of elocution.[19]

Yet Austen does more than simply take over elocutionary vocabulary and rules. She also creates a hierarchy of value. Lucy's voice is insincere; the narrator's non-voice is not. For the elocutionists, vocal inflections like pauses and emphases bolstered the perceived naturalness of reading.[20] In Austen's passage, they do the opposite. Lucy's speech pits the sociolect of polite speech against the prosodic system of the elocutionists in ways that threaten Elinor's "self-command." Elinor's ability to understand Lucy "perfectly" depends less on her ability to register the semantic content of Lucy's speech than to distinguish between the words and the effect of

Lucy's voice. The effect is revealing because Austen does not have Lucy emphasize the words we might expect, her characteristic adverbial modifiers ("*quite* disappointed," "*always* thought," "*almost* sure," "*you know*," "*amazingly* glad"). Instead, for the most part, she waits until the ends of sentences, where, according to the elocutionists, the voice was supposed to drop with what Walker calls a "falling inflexion": Elinor's aural cue is that Lucy uses stress to raise her voice where it "should" drop, thus signaling the gap between what she intends and what she says.

After Lucy's speech, the engaged narrator underscores that, for Elinor, Lucy's elocution has indeed produced comprehension; Elinor "perfectly understood her." Her understanding is so complete that the narrator even echoes Lucy's characteristic final emphasis in a description of Elinor's reaction ("was forced to use all her self-command to make it appear that she did *not*"). Yet whereas Lucy's emphases were ironic, undercutting her words' ostensive meanings, Elinor's mental emphasis does the opposite, highlighting the difficulty of retaining her composure. Since Austen does not include the actual words of Elinor's response, she protects Elinor from the rocky shoals of elocutionary voice and puts her closer to the lofty distance of narrative silence. The reader is invited only to infer the words and tones of Elinor's strained response to Lucy. Elinor handles elocution by internalization: her mental processes speak louder than spoken words.

As in the case of dialect, printed English creates a standard against which all deviations could be measured. Because, as the elocutionists realized, printed English does not help much with prosodic cues, extra features, such as italicization, are needed to indicate them. Yet the presence of such typographic indicators, which the elocutionists hoped would make print easier to comprehend, simultaneously made sentences with them seem suspicious because they deviated from a perceived norm. As Austen recognizes, the harder print works to represent the tones of an actual voice, the less authoritative that voice becomes. The standardization of typography emerges as a powerful metaphor for moral judgment: deviations from it exact a high price.

Even in passages without typographic cues, the vocabulary of elocution could still be a sign of women's subordinate status, as in this moment from *Waverley* (1814):

> "I bring you an adopted son of Ivor," said Fergus.
> "And I receive him as a second brother," replied Flora.

There was a slight emphasis on the word which would have escaped every ear but one that was feverish with apprehension. It was however distinctly marked, and, combined with her whole tone and manner, plainly intimated, "I will never think of Mr. Waverley as a more intimate connection." (207)

Since Scott's novel, unlike Austen's, does not include a typographical representation of Flora's emphasis, the reader's knowledge of it depends solely on information provided by the narrator. Indeed, like the passage from *Ivanhoe* discussed in the previous chapter, we do not learn about the emphasis until after the printed words of Flora's reply. After reading "There was a slight emphasis on the word," the silent reader needs to puzzle out exactly which word "the word" is; an oral reciter who has not read ahead faces a mini-quandary about how to handle this passage.

Our sense of Flora's voice gets stranger as the passage goes along, since the first impression of her "slight emphasis" changes when we reach the phrase "distinctly marked." Flora's voice is marked by paradox. Her emphasis is simultaneously hers and not hers; both audible and inaudible, plain and barely perceptible. In Scott's odd pun, Flora can only give her opinion of an "intimate connection" through the near oxymoron of a plain intimation. The point of the pun is the most peculiar paradox of all. Interpreting the prosody of Flora's voice, understanding her "intimation," requires decoding her unspoken thoughts in a way that presumes an intimate connection with her that her words' meaning forestalls. Vocal emphasis, indirectness, and femininity replace the elocutionists' association of prosodic emphasis with sincerity and authenticity.

Masculine pronunciation tends to be less tortured. In a famous dialogue in *Mansfield Park* (1814), Henry and Edmund lament "the want of management of the voice, of proper modulation and emphasis" (392) among many clergymen, but Austen's novel suggests that the silent narrator has taken over the authority of even the best male speaker. The concern in the period is less with the male voice's truth than with its location, as if speaking, once technologized as voice, might be removed from the body. As Jonathan Rée notes about sound, "If your first visual impressions do not tally with your later investigations, they can be discounted and attributed to your imagination instead. But sounds are not amenable to that kind of reality-testing and cross-checking, since they do not make any such definite claims to spatial location" (*I See a Voice* 47). In Romantic literature, male voices tend to go wandering, as Rée suggests they might. While

the most famous example is Brockden Brown's *Wieland* (1798), Radcliffe's
Italian (1796) may be even more remarkable, as in the episode when an
invisible monk's voice mysteriously interrupts the Inquisition:

> The monk's voice was heard again.
> "I will declare thus much," it said, addressing Vivaldi; "I am not father
> Schedoni."
> The peculiar tone and emphasis, with which this was delivered, more than
> the assertion itself, persuaded Vivaldi that the stranger spoke truth. (315–16)

For Vivaldi, like Elinor, survival demands elocutionary interpretation:
prosody says what words do not. Yet even as Radcliffe asserts this importance of tone and emphasis, she distances them from the reader because
she, like Scott, uses no distinctive typography to indicate either what they
are or what makes them "peculiar." Scott at least tells us that Flora emphasized a particular word; Radcliffe does not even provide that much
information. It is as if she wants to protect the monk's voice from too
specific an association with elocutionary inflection, as Austen does with
Elinor: doing so might diminish its authority. Instead, the narrator tells
us simply that the "tone and emphasis" were believable.

This narrative division of labor between narrators and characters allowed the novel to profit from the eighteenth-century revision of English.
Readers did not need the elaborate paratextual apparatus of earlier novels
because elocutionary vocabulary provided a powerful means to understand characters; norms of expository prose, a background against which
the narrator's words, reliable or not, could be comprehended. The novel
assumes that readers know that voices reveal motives, but narrators reveal truth. Early reviewers of novels rarely complain that they have not
understood a work, though they do comment on perceived immorality,
improbabilities, or awkward narrative construction. The novel reinforced
the strictures of elocution and the ideals of expository English so as to fit
snugly into contemporary models of communication.

Poetry had a harder time. Elocution clashed with an already-existing
poetic system for guiding oral recitation: meter. Expository prose was,
obviously, prose, and seemed to spell the obsolescence of poetry. The result was a series of restless experiments during the late eighteenth century,
paralleling but not replicating those with impure English traced in the
previous chapter. The elocutionist John Rice's *An Introduction to the Art
of Reading with Energy and Propriety* (1765) had noted that "the Observa-

tions contained in this Work, may be of some Service also to Writers, by inducing them to pay Attention to the Manner in which their Works may be recited" (6). By the 1780s, one particular school of poets, the Della Cruscans, or at least their typesetters, superimposed the new system of elocution on the older system of poetic meter, as in this characteristic moment from Mary Robinson's "A Fragment, Supposed to be Written near the Temple, at Paris, on the Night Before the Execution of Louis XVI":

> The Owl shrieks from the tott'ring Tow'r,
> Dread *watch-bird* of the *witching hour*!
> Spectres, from their charnel cells,
> Cleave the air with hideous yells!
> Not a GLOW-WORM ventures forth
> To *gild* his little *speck* of earth!
> In wild despair Creation seems to wait,
> While Horror stalks abroad, to deal the shafts of Fate!   (5–12)

Like the elocutionists, Robinson stretches the capacity of print to indicate appropriate inflections; Robinson's poetry resembles William Cockin's prose definition of reading in its typographic variety. She avoids the danger described by Sheridan, that a reader might have "no mark to point out the most important word," so that the appropriate emphasis was "often neglected." These lines that are "Supposed to be Written" are really supposed to be printed. Robinson gives the reader poetry in typographical neon, in a way that should guarantee comprehensibility when voiced. Like the open microphone at poetry slams, the typography marks the technological manipulation of the voice that justifies altering the style of pronunciation. Whatever we may think the most important words are, Robinson leaves no doubt about what she thinks they are. Elocution, like expository prose, strives to control the reader's response, as if holding to the fantasy that ambiguity will disappear if typography were insistent enough. Robinson's poem presents a voice that realizes itself through printed indications of inflection.

In Austen's work, italics in Lucy Steele's speech signaled its inauthenticity and staginess; they contrasted with the morally valued non-voice of the narrator, to whose prosaic equilibrium Elinor aspired. In Robinson, no narrator exists, so the speaking subject does not lose out next to an explicitly represented prosaic other, although the marked typography implies that the reader recognizes a more neutral mode of print as the poem's assumed background. Yet Robinson's relation to elocution is more complex than it first appears. A concern haunting the elocutionists' development of textual signals for voice was that, however impressive these looked on the page, they were so complicated that they were useless. Samuel Johnson, for example, maintained no one could learn elocution just from reading Walker's books, even though Herringham's example suggests otherwise (Osborn, *Contrary Converts* 16–17). Robinson's poem absorbs the potential arbitrariness of elocutionary typography by giving no guides about how to realize its typography. We have no sure signs about how to differentiate orally among words in italics ("*watch-bird*," "*witching hour*," "*gild*," "*speck*"), with initial capitals ("Creation"), in small capitals ("GLOW-WORM"), and with initial capitals followed by small capitals ("OWL," "TOW'R," "HORROR," "FATE"). Instead, typography takes over as an end in itself, playfully indifferent to how its variations might be realized. The visual variety of the printed page becomes a metaphor for an unsounded voice, an unheard melody that cannot quite realize itself in actual sound, independent of human acoustic capacities. As such, Robinson's poem preserves a certain freedom from the discipline of elocutionary English, as if refusing to let it have too complete a say in how poetry might sound.

By the time of Felicia Hemans, the persistent novelistic association between female voice and foregrounding pronunciation led to the development of a new form of interface, which Eric Griffiths has termed "the printed voice," as represented in the dramatic monologue:

I see one shadow, stateliest there of all,—
Thine!—What does *thou* amidst the bright and fair,
Whispering light words, and mocking my despair?
It is not well of thee!					("Arabella Stuart" 191–94)

In the previous chapter, I discussed Hemans's redirection of pronunciation from eighteenth-century dialect poetry. Her use of pronunciation also marks a critical turn on eighteenth-century elocution. At first glance, it seems that Hemans is just continuing the elocutionary English of the Della Cruscans, and so she is, but with a critical difference. In Robinson, markers of inflection were in the mouth of a non-character, the anonymous "fragment, supposed to be written" of elocutionary English. In Hemans, elocutionary markers no longer belong to a general printed voice but to a particular character, Arabella Stuart. Aided by the work of the novel, Hemans adapts a print interface as a sign of forceful personal expression. Whereas Robinson's italicization of "speck," for example, seemed generated by an abstract need to mark emphasis, Hemans's italicization of "*Thine*" signals Stuart's surprised anger when she believes her lover to have abandoned her. In Hemans's dramatic monologues, the "printed voice" comes into its own through its alienation from the lyric "I."

Whereas the novel counterposed such voices to a narrator's silence, Hemans claims a different authority for poems: the ability to represent voices without a narrator's judgmental silence. The lack of contrast between narrator and voice is vital for the "poeticity" that Hemans perfected: it allows the poem to stand on its own as a unique crystallization of emotional voice. As Yopie Prins notes, dramatic monologues circulated "as 'acoustic devices' for the mediation of voice, preceding and perhaps even predicting the sound reproduction technologies that emerged" ("Voice Inverse" 44). Only in poetry, Hemans suggests, can the voice truly be represented in print because only there is it free from the perceived superiority of prosaic, genderless, silent narrators.

Hemans's brilliant adaptation of elocution produced a flowering of the dramatic monologue in the Victorian period. In most cases, these monologues take over elocutionary voice from the novel but omit the expository narrator. Nevertheless, the presence of print means that the ideals usually ascribed to such narrators have not entirely disappeared; they have been relocated to the level of the unmarked code rather than of the message. The tension between sympathy and judgment that Robert Langbaum famously found in the dramatic monologue can be re-described as an effect of the monologue's peculiar relationship to print (*Poetry of Experience* 75–108). Sympathy is an aftereffect of absorbing elocutionary voice into printed signals; judgment, the moral analogue of the silent norms of print that are manipulated and deformed by representing the printed voice.

In sharp contrast to this appropriation of elocutionary English, certain other late eighteenth-century poets experimented with using blank verse to see how closely poetry could come to contemporary norms of prose while still remaining poetry. In the previous chapter, I examined Cowper and Wordsworth in relation to this prosaicism; it is useful to remember that other possibilities were also present, as in this excerpt from Hugh Downman's *Infancy* (1803):

> The crude or sluggish juice
> Which vegetables yield, with toil perspired,
> Weakens the stomach, whose contraction fails,

Not justly stimulated; while the skin
Its pores block'd up, or e'en its texture changed,
Is cover'd o'er with incrustations foul,
Scarcely, if ever, by the abstersive wave
Of tepid bath removed.   (2.438–45)

While Robinson's poetry is elocutionary ejaculation, Downman's is a ver-
sified medical tract, an awkward example of Wordsworth's insistence that
no essential distinction existed between the language of poetry and of
prose. Unlike Robinson's poem, Downman's does not represent a blueprint for voice, but for impersonal, scientific truths that need no voice
for their realization. Downman's few inversions are uncomfortable con-
cessions to meter, a faint vestige of sound in a text that otherwise avoids
the elocutionary emphases so characteristic of Robinson. Although there
is no reason to believe that Downman consciously wrote to illustrate the
dictates of expository English, he realizes a mode of English that subju-
gates its capacity for aural and visual interest to information transfer.

Yet, just as Robinson's poem complicated the rules of the elocutionists,
so Downman's poem complicates those of expository English. Prosaic his
language may be, but the clarity of his English is at war with what John
Guillory has described as "technicity." According to Guillory, expository
prose has a tension at its core: the battle between ideals of clarity (simple
and transparent language) and technicity (jargons of professions that use
expository prose) ("Memo and Modernity" 129–32). Clarity assumes universal readability; technicity, disciplinary specialization. This battle tends
to have an etymological edge: clarity is Anglo-Saxon; technicity, Latinate.
The language of information is never as comprehensible as the Scottish
academics liked to believe: it is quickly infiltrated by baffling techspeak.
In Downman's case, traditional Latinity of georgic diction melds weirdly
with the Latinate diction of eighteenth-century medicine.

Robinson and Downman represent extremes against which to measure the response of Romantic poets to changes in interfaces available for
English. These can be represented in miniature by Wordsworth's manuscript draft of *Michael,* now known as Dove Cottage MS. 30. What makes
this draft revealing is that Wordsworth wrote it partly on the pages of
Coleridge's *Poems on Various Subjects* (1796).[21] The competition between
Wordsworth's handwriting and Coleridge's print on the same page points to
larger competitions about directions for modernity and poetry. Coleridge's
rhymed, stanzaic poems, heavily influenced by the Della Cruscans, resem-

ble Robinson's in their plentiful manipulation of typography to indicate vocal inflections that the elocutionists prized. Wordsworth's blank verse could not look more different. His handwritten lines run to the end of the right margin, have virtually no marks of punctuation, and often do not scan. The only visible sign that they are indeed poetry is the capitalization of letters at the beginning of each line. Paradoxically, Coleridge's print is the hotter, more emotionally charged medium next to the cool steadiness of Wordsworth's handwritten blank verse.

In one fragment, "No doubt if you in terms direct had ask'd," Wordsworth's narrator describes a conversation that might be had with Michael. Initially, the conversation goes badly; when the narrator asks Michael if he loves the mountains, he gets only puzzlement from Michael and a statement that they were "frightful to behold." Yet, after probing more deeply, the narrator receives a better answer from Michael, who reveals "his thoughts" in which are found "obscurities / Wonders & admirations."[22] Wordsworth drafted several versions of this fragment on blank pages, but it did not flower until he redrafted it horizontally and vertically on top of a page containing Coleridge's "Absence: A Farewell Ode." It is as if Wordsworth needed the inspiration of actually writing over Coleridgean Della Cruscan print.

In Coleridge's poem, the power of the expressive voice, guided by typographic signals, compensates for absences mourned. Wordsworth, overwriting Coleridge's poem, rejects elocution both in the form of his writing, by eliminating its characteristic vocal markers, and in content, by having Michael reveal himself not through his speech but through his "thoughts." Wordsworth's draft looks much closer to the prose ideals of the Scottish academics—as Coleridge would later complain in the *Biographia* when he noted Wordsworth's habit of writing in a style "which is only proper in prose" (388).

Yet, just as Wordsworth implicitly criticizes elocutionary English, so he, like Downman, is not entirely at home with expository English. Technicity intrudes to upset the privileged clearness and simplicity of English; in Downman's case, the jargon was medical; in Wordsworth's, aesthetic. In particular, the narrator describes the content of Michael's thoughts in the technical language of the sublime: "obscurities / Wonders and admirations." The sublime counters the clarity of English both at the level of message and of code, with the intrusion of Latinate "obscurities" and "admirations." Indeed, it may have done so too well: Wordsworth cut this passage from the poem's final text, possibly because it made the narrator's professional interest in Michael as sublime icon too obvious.

Byron's *Don Juan* commented tartly on such poetic prosaicism:

> But here is one prescription out of many:
>   "Sodae-Sulphat. 3. vi. 3. s. Mannae optim.
> Aq. fervent. F.3. ifs. 3ij. tinct. Sennae
>   Haustus." (And here the surgeon came and cupped him)
> "*R.* Pulv. Com gr. iii. Ipecacuanhae"
>   (With more beside if Juan had not stopp'd 'em.)
> "Bolus Potassae Sulphuret. sumendus,
> Et Haustus ter in die capiendus."   (10.41)

In this mock sublime, Byron yokes incommunicability to technicity by turning his stanza into a Latin prescription for two emetics. His plentiful abbreviations parody the Scottish academics' insistence on brevity and conciseness. Like the Romantic sublime, Byron's stanza is unspeakable, either because unfamiliar abbreviations make it unpronounceable or (for those who do know the abbreviations) because it ends up sounding like a random spew of phonemes, an aural vomit mirroring the doctor's emetic.[23] This exercise in Romantic prosaicism mocks the Romantic sublime as insider jargon: straining beyond linguistic mediation leads to a quasi-professionalized, unpronounceable code.

These passages from Wordsworth and Byron point to the twin threats of eighteenth-century interfaces: elocution threatens to reduce poetry to a technologized display of voice; expository prose, to render poetry a professional jargon. If, as I suggested at the opening, poetry increasingly retreated into perceived incomprehensibility, it did so not simply because authors became more distant from audiences but because the interfaces that promised to guarantee comprehensibility resisted poetic practice. One result was the familiar Romantic assumption of a hostile audience, and the hope for a more favorable reception in the future, often after the poet's death.[24] The other was the negotiation with the aesthetics of obscurity, though, as I have suggested, its proximity to professional jargon made this option less compelling than it might have been. But Romantic poetry also confronted these new modes of English more directly.

Whereas the novel absorbed new interfaces of English, Romantic poetry found a chiastic relation to them: Romantic poetry silences elocution and gives voice to exposition. I will focus first on elocution, which has received little attention from Romanticists except in connection with John Thelwall, a fascinating figure but a far less influential elocutionist than Thomas Sheridan or John Walker.[25] Some elocutionists had hoped that poetry might solve a major challenge, the development of standard pronunciation. Rhyme's ability to link phonemes and meter's alignment of metrical and lexical stress made poetry look like a proto-technological medium for sound reproduction. As "Ausonius" wrote to the *Gentleman's Magazine,* poetry would "undoubtedly afford the best rule to direct our judgement" in matters of pronunciation because of its "measured compositions," which were "built upon established principles of sound, and the analogies of language" ("Poetry or Prose" 290).[26]

In the event, Romantic poetry failed spectacularly to help the elocutionists by standardizing pronunciation.[27] Rather than providing what Ausonius called "the best rule," Romantic poets thrilled to words that, in the new atmosphere of orthoepical correctness, no one knew exactly how to pronounce. To look at Romantic poetry and English orthoepics is to find a mass of inconsistencies. Wordsworth writes "obdúrate" ("Was a dependant on the obdurate heart" [*Vaudracour and Julia* 235]); Shelley, "óbdurate" ("But custom maketh blind and obdurate" [*Revolt of Islam* 4.9]). Coleridge gives "fealty" three syllables ("They shall swear fealty to us, because" [*Death of Wallenstein* 1.4.12]); Keats, only two ("Which bards in fealty to Apollo hold" ["On First Looking Into Chapman's Homer" 4]). Wordsworth writes "ácceptable" ("Some acceptable lesson to their minds" [*Excursion* 4.1237]); Byron, "accéptable" ("His sacrifices are acceptable" [*Cain* 2.2.353]). Coleridge stresses "oblique" on the second syllable ("With beam oblique, or perpendicular" [*Piccolomini* 4.1.16]); Wordsworth, the first ("Then would be closed the restless oblique eye" ["Humanity" 49].[28] Byron made a specialty out of having it both ways by shuttling between pronunciations, stressing "confessor," "contemplate," and "contents" on varying syllables in different contexts.[29]

Rhymes are even more of a quagmire, so that it often becomes impossible to distinguish between what correct English would have designated as perfect or imperfect rhymes. Byron's "Rome" rhymes both with "tomb" and with "home": both were acceptable, according to the orthoepists.[30] Keats rhymes "break" with "shriek" and with "cake."[31] Shelley rhymes "break" with "snake-shake" and with "weak-cheek."[32] Blake rhymes "woe-begone" with "moan"; Keats, with "done."[33] Even more baffling is the difficulty of realizing phonemes in words that, according to the orthoepists, were under significant debate, including "nature," "empire," "satire," "drama," "knowledge," "privacy," "humble," "chamber," "gold," "legend," "hospital," "legislator," "sublime," and "horizon."[34]

Such moments return us to another version of the slippage that I discussed in the first chapter because standardizing English increases rather than limits the possibilities for what literature can do. In this analysis, I have assumed that differences in pronunciation among poets can be judged from meter and rhyme, an assumption that holds true only if strict iambic pentameter and perfect rhyme are default settings. The examples above illustrate differences in pronunciation that have the support of contemporary dictionaries, which indicate, for example, both "ácceptable" and "accéptable" as possible pronunciations. Yet the possibility that prosody of the Romantic period is flexible enough to incorporate a range of deviations both in meter and rhyme means that one can never be absolutely certain as to how to pronounce such words. Such moments are another example of English as a system of leaky abstraction, in which levels of the code that are often bypassed in interpretation emerge inconveniently to disrupt the smooth processing of a surface code.

This tendency toward leaky abstraction also extends the concern of the previous chapter with the Romantic rejection of dialect: rejecting vulgarity also meant rejecting too-standardized audibility. As a sociolect, although Romantic poetry steered away from wholesale dialect, it preserves at the micro-level unpredictable flashes of independence from pure English, brief reassertions of poetry's lost power over phonemes. A familiar example is the maintenance of archaisms, such as the [aj] vowel in the noun "wind," as in Shelley's "wind-behind" rhyme in the "Ode to the West Wind."[35] The revolutionary wind of Shelley's poem will bring about a new order, but breathes through a markedly archaic rhyme that fantasizes the ability of poems to guide pronunciation. Similarly, the longstanding rhyme exemplified by Wordsworth's "by-majesty" rhyme in the Westminster Bridge sonnet preserved the contract between poets and readers to pretend that certain rhymes were better than they actually were, in the face of elocutionary standardization.

More generally, archaism licensed novelties, as in the post-Chattertonian experiments of Coleridge, Scott, and others with pseudo-Gothic English. Such experiments could have a ripple effect, as writers could briefly toy with a pseudo-Gothic moment of pronunciation in a poem for the most part written in a different mode. For example, Keats produces the following outrageous couplet in "I Stood Tip-Toe": "And as she leaves me may she often turn / Her fair eyes looking through her locks aubùrne" (105–06). William Keach has analyzed this couplet as a typical moment of Cockney rhyming, demonstrating Keats's insouciant disregard for the proprieties of accentuation (*Arbitrary Power* 53–55).[36] I would add to Keach's account that Keats's daring is part not just of an individual idiolect, but of a poetic sociolect linked to the pseudo-Gothic. Keats's precedent in "aubùrne" is the non-standard stresses of Coleridge's "That come from a far Countrée" (*Rime of the Ancyent Marinere* 551) or Scott's "Was but lightly held of his gaye ladye" (*Lay of the Last Minstrel* 4.7). Like Keats, these authors stress line-final disyllabic words on the second syllable rather than the first. What makes Keats's example outrageous is that he takes an orthoepical device out of its medievalizing context and puts it in a modern one, using a word with less claim to such accentuation than the choices of the older poets. "Keats" emerges here as a source less of improper accentuation than of a distinctive twist on a convention. He thumbs his nose not only at the prescriptions of pure English but also at the timidity of those who rebel against these prescriptions only in the guise of the pseudo-Gothic. Nevertheless, this moment is short within the context of the entire poem; as I argued in the previous chapter, Keats's work is typical of the sociolect of Romantic poets in waging not a full-scale war against standardized English, only mini-skirmishes of leaky levels of abstraction.

Even more unsettling examples of philology's relation to authorship occur when poetry seems to play with contemporary uncertainties about pronunciation, as in Coleridge's "Kubla Khan":

> But oh! that deep romantic chasm, which slanted
> Down the green hill athwart a cedarn cover!
> A savage place! as holy and enchanted
> As e'er beneath a waning moon was haunted
> By woman wailing for her demon-lover! (12–16)

Just what kind of a rhyme is "slanted—enchanted—haunted"? Eighteenth-century orthoepists indicated that "haunt" had three possible pronunciations: [æ] as in "cat"; [ɑ] as in "father"; and [ɔ] as in "ought." Sheridan and the author of *Vocabulary* preferred the first version; Walker preferred the second and treated the third with scorn (McMahon, "Phonology" 437). If pronounced with the [æ] vowel, "haunted" rhymes perfectly with "slanted" and "enchanted," but it simultaneously loses the trace of difference visible in the "au" vowel spelling. Like Robinson's typography, Coleridge's poem realizes itself, paradoxically, only in the absence of voice, as another unheard melody. It refuses full presence in elocutionary English; only in the silence of the phonological mind can the informed, invested reader entertain the fantasy of simultaneous but alternate realizations, each with its shades of possible meaning or non-meaning. The philological moment is characterized by the undecidable sources for agency in relation to language that occur the closer one gets to particular phonologies.

Another convention of poetic sound in the period is the mania for odd, often foreign proper names. As if recognizing that elocution had made English strangely unpronounceable, Romantic poets respond as if it had not become unpronounceable enough. Familiar as Blake's names are in this respect (Urizen, Los, Enitharmon, Enion, etc.), it is probably Southey who has the most to answer for (*Thalaba the Destroyer*, *The Curse of Kehama*) and the Shelley circle who perfected the art (Shelley's *Laon and Cythna*; Byron's *Sardanapalus* and *Don Juan*, with its riot of foreign names; Mary Shelley's *Frankenstein*). As Jane Austen suggested when she poked fun at Byron's unpronounceable Giaour (though, having written *Northanger Abbey*, she knew about such names herself), these names often belong to characters who have a strong charge of erotic mystery, as if the love that dare not pronounce its name had to belong to a lover whose name could not be pronounced.[37]

Keats provides a particularly vivid example of what Deleuze describes as the writer's ability to carve "out a nonpreexistent foreign language *within* his own language" ("He Stuttered" 110):

> I saw pale kings, and princes too,
>   Pale warriors, death-pale were they all;
> Who cried "La belle Dame sans mercy
>   Hath thee in thrall!"   (37–40)

The kings and princes choose a strange mode of defining the knight's predicament. For reasons never explained in the poem, they change languages in midstream, with the movement from archaic French in line 39 to archaic English in line 40: the code switching after the enjambment allows the distant and unfamiliar to come threateningly close.

Yet this cross-linguistic moment is not as neat as it seems. The kings and princes start out not so much with archaic French as with a weird

Franglais: although Keats's orthography preserves the final -e's in "belle" and "Dame," his tetrameter eliminates the distinctively French [ə] sounds. To retain them would be to extend the line into a pentameter, as if the lady could be fully French only if she deserted the ballad for another genre (possibly epic?). Without them, her name veers away from French and toward the English "beldame," used generally for an older woman and more specifically for a witch.[38] The lady's potential acoustic shift from French to English is a disenchantment: the French "belle dame" masks what Kenneth Burke calls a "concealed offense," the lady's English "beldame" ugliness (51–60). Yet Keats does not actually write "beldame" (a word he uses in *The Eve of St. Agnes*): the orthography remains French, even as the pronunciation stutters between the two languages. A similar uncertainty lurks around "sans" and "mercy," both of which have French and English realizations; in the case of the second, the phonological difference is also a semantic one.[39] The poem flickers between visual and aural versions to create a non-interface, which ends quickly in the next line when the "kings and princes" speak English, not Keatsian Franglais.

Their first words, which look like the beginning of a description of the lady that might continue in Franglais, turn out to be a proper name. This linguistic shift is bad news for the knight because it means that the lady's quality of being "sans mercy" is not an attribute subject to later modification, but one so inherent that it has become her unpronounceable name. Even as the languages switch across the lines, a lingering partial rhyme "mercy / Hath thee" suggests that the lady's French name has the English words somewhat "in thrall."

Such resistance to pronounced English further explains why Romantic poems seemed so hard for their first readers. They undermined contemporary assumptions about the way that voice and print were supposed to work together. Foucault, quoting Beckett, focuses "What is an Author?" on the question, "What does it matter who is speaking?" (101), but (as Foucault would recognize), Romantic authors were not clear what it would mean to speak, since the very sound of words was under such debate. Although previous Romantic critics have emphasized the period's phonocentrism, they have underestimated how Romantic poets often seem eager not to assume voice but to move to a peculiar unheard voice available only in print.[40]

If we move from the undecidablity of English words to a more overt thematic level, we find that Romantic poetry does not like elocution. Book II of Cowper's *Task* provided the classic condemnation of the elocution teacher:

> He teaches those to read, whom schools dismiss'd,
> And colleges, untaught; sells accent, tone,
> And emphasis in score, and gives to prayer
> The *adagio* and *andante* it demands. (2.358–61)

Cowper's distaste for vulgar, mercenary elocution resonates throughout Romantic poetry. At best, oral recitation appears as a phase to be supplanted by silent meditation and composition. In *The Prelude*, Wordsworth remembers oral recitation with John Fleming as the naïve repetition of "favourite verses with one voice / . . . as happy as the birds / That round us chaunted" (5.564–66). When he describes his more mature project in the Prospectus to *The Recluse*, this social setting has given way to the paradoxical desire to "chant" his "spousal verse" in "lonely peace" (57–58). In Coleridge's "To William Wordsworth," Wordsworth's recitation leads Coleridge not to an oral response but to a silent prayer; in Keats's "On First Looking Into Chapman's Homer," hearing Chapman "speak out loud and bold" (8) leads not, as we might expect, to praise of elocution, but to images of silent vision. In "The Child Reading the Bible," Hemans praises a young boy not when he reads his Bible expressively, but when his head is "bow'd / In silence o'er the Book of Light" (26–27).[41]

A particularly strong condemnation of the elocutionary voice appears in Shelley's *Prometheus Unbound*. Prometheus, having forgotten his own curse, wants to overcome his failure of memory. Rather than asking for a written copy of his words, he conjures up a performance by the simulacrum of his nemesis, Jupiter. The Phantasm of Jupiter becomes a proto-technological medium of vocal reproduction, underscoring the proximity of elocution to possession. Prometheus's voice returns to him, but only in an alienated form: sound reproduction thrusts Prometheus into the realm of shadows, repeating the concern I noted earlier about the male voice's phantasmagoric detachability. According to the elocutionists, the oral performance of a text should increase an audience's sympathy with its message. Yet rather than feeling sympathy, as the elocutionists claimed, Prometheus feels only disgust at hearing his words: "It doth repent me: words are quick and vain; / Grief for awhile is blind, and so was mine"

(1.303–04). In Shelley, the technologization of voice through the medium of the Phantasm occurs simultaneously with Prometheus's recognition that it is obsolete: the play supersedes the voice of the Phantasm's delivery with other media of communication.

The Romantic mistrust of vocal performance spreads to a larger problem with deixis, a fear of locating too specifically the sources of voice, as if doing so would make them too subject to elocutionary evaluation. One enduring sign of the problematic of the Romantic voice is the basic but unsolved quandary over just how to name the enunciator of a Romantic poem—a voice? an author? a writer? a speaker? a narrator? a persona? The location of voice in poems like Pope's "Epistle to Dr. Arbuthnot" or Gray's "Ode on a Distant Prospect of Eton College" is far more specific than in poems like "Tintern Abbey" or "To Autumn," if these latter poems even have voice. William, for example, sees and hears Dorothy in "Tintern Abbey"'s dramatic present, but what exactly is her relation to what is happening? Does she actually hear him, or is she stuck only reading his "lines" and "exhortations" after the fact? If not, just what exactly is Wordsworth doing in the poem? The poem is characteristic of much Romantic poetry in its peculiar dismantling of the grounds of a speech act.[42]

Given the reluctance of the Romantics to specify the provenance of enunciation, they might have seemed to be eager to turn to the expository English of the Scottish academics as an alternative. The explosion of the Romantic paratext is a partial indication that they did just that, as if to make up in prose for a radical uncertainty about recitability. The first-generation Romantics seemed particularly eager to adapt poetry to the requirements of prose in their use of blank verse; even Blake notes that *Jerusalem* has prosaic parts (Plate 3, "To the Public"). Yet as Romantic blank verse loudly sets itself against elocutionary English, it retains certain markers of potential voice; as Wolfson notes, the voicing of blank verse was a "revealing crux" of the period (*Formal Charges* 27).[43] Romantic poets absorb this white space into their blank verse through a particular elocutionary device, the pause. Paradoxically, the privation of sound in Romantic blank verse prevents it from becoming too much like prose. The emphasis provided by the capital letter at the beginning of the line and the brief pause of blank space at the end gives the blank verse line an autonomy from the syntax of pure English through which the agency of the Romantic author could emerge.

Wordsworth's "Nutting" provides a complex example of the blank verse pause:

> Even then, when from the bower I turn'd away,
> Exulting, rich beyond the wealth of kings—
> I felt a sense of pain when I beheld
> The silent trees and the intruding sky.— (48–51)

Of the two dashes, the first dash has some manuscript authority; the second seems to have been added by the printer and kept by Wordsworth, and precedes the blank space marking the transition between verse paragraphs.[44] The line before the second pause ("The silent trees and the intruding sky") fits uncomfortably into an iambic pentameter, as Wordsworth recognized when he later revised it as "The silent trees, and saw the intruding sky." As first published, it feels more like a collapse into prose, as if poetry has given out. Yet, immediately after "intruding sky," we get a double pause—first, the dash; then, a blank space before the poem's final lines. If we consider enjambment as well, there is a further pause after "beheld," of the kind that Christopher Ricks describes as "delicately fertile of surmises" (*Force of Poetry* 110). The arrival of "the silent trees" at the beginning of the next line elevates them from their syntactic status as the object of a verb to a poetic status as the occupiers of the beginning of a line: they become more important in poetry than they would be in prose. The typography insists that, counter to the ideals of expository prose, meaning does not reside solely in semantics. However prosaic Wordsworth's English has become, he still retains a trace of the typographic voice found in the elocutionists' experimental layouts and Robinson's Della Cruscan verse, whose poetic diction otherwise could not be more different from Wordsworth's. Yet where Robinson located the unheard voice in manipulations of typeface, Wordsworth locates it in visual markers of the pause, at the level of the dash, enjambment, and blank line.

Wordsworth's grammar and diction in the passage are straightforward: the passage exemplifies the clearness and brevity praised by the Scottish academics. Yet in Wordsworth, as in much other Romantic blank verse, proximity to the ideals of good prose produces not certain comprehensibility, but haunting obscurity. The local lexical coherence of the passage contrasts with the difficulty of understanding it within the larger context of the poem as a whole. The problem, as has often been noted in Wordsworth, is the unconventional relationship between cause and effect. Wordsworth writes as if it should be obvious why seeing "silent trees" and an "intruding sky" should cause pain, but does not explain his reaction. Romantic poets often reserve their prosaicism for such moments that assert causal relations without explaining them, as in Blake's "The Virgin started from her seat, & with a shriek / Fled back unhinderd till she came into the vales of Har" ("Thel" Plate 6, 21–22) or Shelley's concluding lines in *Mont Blanc*: "And what were thou, and earth, and stars, and sea, / If to the human mind's imaginings / Silence and solitude were vacancy?" (142–44). As Keach notes about Shelley's passage, "vacancy" carries much of the potential prosaicism because it "seems both to yield to and to resist the rhyming power of the compositional will" (*Shelley's Style* 200). It is as if the best way for a Romantic poet to reach the sublime were to write very good prose, in poetry.

In terms of the larger scope of British literary history, Romantic poetry's most creative challenge to eighteenth-century English was a new mode. It drew on a principle of sound in poetry that competed with the inflections prized by the elocutionists. Peter Manning argues that once Romantic poetry was "freed from the exigency of communication," it found that "sound patterns" could become "ever more intricate and various" ("'The Birthday of Typography'" 77). I would extend Manning's remark by suggesting that sound patterns become "more intricate and various" in two ways. The first, which I call "patterned Romanticism," was typically found in pentameter verse like Keats's "To Autumn," and involved the creation of a dense web of minute acoustic repetitions and variations within a pentameter. The second, which I call "percussive Romanticism," appears in tetrameter meters or meters involving anapestic patterns. It involves a pounding regularity of meter that largely obviated the need for the complicated rules for pause, emphasis, cadence, and climax that typified elocutionary English: getting the right words in the right place and time carried the poem. Internal assonance and consonance, while present, are less audible than the regularly recurring, thumping beat. There are various sources for this mode, such as Thomas Percy's *Reliques*, Coleridge's *Christabel*, and especially Thomas Moore's *Irish Melodies*, with their huge influence on second-generation Romantics.

According to William Mitford's 1804 discussion of prosody, sophisticated hearers can tolerate irregular versification:

When verse is proposed for recitation without music, it behoves the poet to be diligent and ingenious in the use of the scanty resources for variety, which the tones of common discourse afford . . . Ruder ears, indeed, as we have already observed, are apt to be disappointed by the failure of the strong acute in its expected place: but the more practised organ, not wanting the continual return of the more forcible time-beating, is relieved and gratified by its occasional and not unfrequent remission. (*Inquiry* 95–96)

For Mitford, poetic meter seduces with dangerous pleasures. If regularity forces itself too vigorously on the ear, it becomes "forcible time-beating." A sophisticated listener needs relief and prefers the "not unfrequent remission" of the barrage of regularity. "Ruder ears," however, as Mitford recognizes, succumb to the assault; their rudeness is incapable of the finer pleasures of "remission" and instead needs to be beaten into enjoyment.

Percussive Romanticism upsets Mitford's categories by privileging the "forcible time-beating" that he disparages, as in Byron:

> The black bands came over
>   The Alps and their snow;
> With Bourbon, the rover,
>   They passed the broad Po.
> We have beaten all foemen,
>   We have captured a King,
> We have turned back on no men,
>   And so let us sing!   (*Deformed Transformed* 1.2.123–30)

In this soldiers' song, meter overrides the supposedly "natural" inflections prized by elocutionary English, so that, for example, "no men" is hastened along by the need to rhyme with "foemen" (giving a fleeting aural glimpse of "omen"). What John Hollander has termed the "metrical contract" created an early association between percussive Romanticism and historical, often military subjects ("Blake and the Metrical Contract"). The pulse of the meter becomes a metaphor for the subordination of the individual to a larger, collective entity, as in the case of Byron's soldiers. So strong is the pulse that these works both invite and eschew voice: the meter can be "heard" even in silent reading, to the extent that, in longer poems, one can find oneself reading the meter rather than the words. Comprehension happens almost automatically because the meter hurtles the audience through the poem.

In an important article, "How the Romantics Recited Poetry," David Perkins surveys the evidence about the vocal performances of Wordsworth, Coleridge, Keats, Shelley, and Hunt, and concludes,

[The] style of recitation was in transition during the Romantic age. A poem might be half chanted in a sustained rhythm, or it might be delivered with many and long pauses and a highly varying inflection . . . Whether it was closer to chanting or to singing, Romantic recitation was far more musical than we now conceive. Tempo, volume, and tone of voice altered to express changing emotions, and the whole effect was more emotional and less inhibited than it usually is at present. (665)

Perkins describes the "transition" as moving from "the more regular, sustained rhythm of Augustan recitation" to a more modern "accentually based delivery" (660). Although he does not argue that the Romantics resisted this transition, his evidence suggests that they did because all the contemporary hearers of these poets used "chanting" to describe their reading; as Perkins notes, such chanting is a style that "the elocutionists unanimously condemned" (661). I would add to Perkins's argument that the Romantic poets developed percussive Romanticism to encourage the persistence of a "chanting" style in the face of the elocutionists' attempt to cast it as an outmoded form of delivery.

John Stuart Mill famously claimed, "Poetry and eloquence are both alike the expression or utterance forth of feeling. But if we may be excused the seeming affectation of the antithesis, we should say that eloquence is *heard*, poetry is *over*heard" ("What is Poetry?" 12). His distinction dismissed the best-known and best-loved poetry of the nineteenth century. Percussive Romanticism dominated the nineteenth-century popular recitation anthologies. For Victorian readers, the high Romantic ode was negligible next to such works as Byron's "The Destruction of Sennacherib," Southey's "Bishop Hatto," Hood's "The Dream of Eugene Aram," and, most famously of all, Hemans's "Casabianca."[45] This mode later achieved its high points in Longfellow's romances, Tennyson's "Charge of the Light Brigade," and the ballads of Kipling. Its haunted parody was in its adaptation to the nightmarish ecstasies of Poe's "The Raven," Browning's "A Toccata of Galuppi's," and much of Swinburne. As such, percussive Romanticism became an unexpected success, eventually achieving the link between poetry and the national imaginary that so many Romantic poets believed was impossible.

Academic Romantic scholarship has never liked this mode and has much preferred what I have called "patterned Romanticism," which is hospitable to the much-discussed Romantic subject. Percussive Romanticism, in contrast, looks too much like doggerel. Yet in its historical context percussive Romanticism emerged as a successful attempt to beat elocution at its own game. Elocution in the eighteenth century avoided poems whose metrical scheme was too "forcible," to use Mitford's term. It aimed for the subtle variety of vocal inflections that might be brought to bear on print: blank verse or prose were favored texts to demonstrate this variety. Yet as elocution progressed in the nineteenth century, the most popular poems for oral recitation were those of percussive Romanticism. Poems that originally countered the prescriptions for elocution paradoxically came to become the most beloved chestnuts of oral recitation.

Percussive Romanticism let poetry challenge the novel in its claim to comprehensibility. If no one understood "Tintern Abbey" or *Prometheus Unbound,* everyone was presumably able to understand "Casabianca," insofar as it became required recitation for generations of schoolchildren. If they did not understand it, they could at least pronounce it, and pronouncing would suffice. Part of the point of percussive Romanticism was to change what it meant to understand a poem. Whether or not the many young reciters of Hemans's poem had the background to grasp the poem's topical references, the poem's "forcible time-beating" meant that a successful reading might involve nothing more than getting the right phonemes in the right place at the right time. Percussive Romanticism insisted on the metrical beat's power to produce a version of comprehension that went beyond the semantic surface of the text.

By the end of the Romantic period, the interfaces of elocution and expository prose had reshaped the relation between poetry and novel. The novel soared in accessibility precisely because it did not need to be pronounced: instead, it became the site at which readers could take on the position of the omniscient narrator judging the voices of others. The novelistic adaptation of elocution and expository prose allowed the voice of the novelist to be the voice of truth. Poetry rebelled against both the elocutionary voice and the assumed truth value of expository prose.

In the previous chapter, I argued that the purification of English led Romantic poetry to position itself between the poles of the individual style of genius and the transpersonal language of poeticity. To link these developments to those discussed in this chapter, experiments with unvoicing elocution or subtle voicings of prosaic poetry characterized the texture of genius, the unreproduceable distinctiveness of style. Percussive Romanticism, in contrast, belonged to "poeticity," a transpersonal mode of writing that came to stand for the distinctive mode of poetry. Works of percussive Romanticism are more alike than they are different: one thundering poem sounds much like the next. They have little room either for individual subjectivity or for the quirks of individual style. Instead, they foregrounded nation or empire, as if pounding metrical regularity could become an apt aural metaphor for political unity.

Through these responses to eighteenth-century interfaces, the novel and the poem as literary modes developed generalizing tendencies in relation to English that transcended style as traditionally conceived in literary criticism. Instead, they each acquired modes of authority that made up for the loss of linguistic power resulting from English's purification. If the English experts directed language, novelists could, within the fictional contact, gain a voice of truth that could never be subject to the qualifications and in-fighting of the English experts' work. Poets developed a highly popular, specialized mode of English that bypassed elocutionary niceties and that came to embody patriotic, nationalistic sentiments, whether or not its English usage was absolutely standard. To become an author meant fitting one's English into these rapidly conventionalized sociolects: mastering them became necessary groundwork for competence in a genre. As such, they functioned neither as *langue* nor as *parole* but as enabling constraints on language use, the rules from which literary English could emerge.

§ 5 Sentencing Romanticism

If, as I noted in the previous chapter, the novel's omniscient narrator embodied the ideals of expository prose, why did the novel not gain more authority as an exemplar of usage? Moreover, what was the relation of expository prose to the actual prose of the Romantic period? Understanding the effects of expository prose depends on investigating its fundamental unit, the sentence. Although the sentence, rather than the word or the letter, forms the basis of printed prose, traditional grammars tend not to treat it as a distinctive aspect of prose, as opposed to other modes of communication. Instead, in a much-repeated definition, the sentence possesses a special ability to express a "complete thought." It takes little effort to dismantle this definition, since what counts as "complete" or as a "thought" is never defined. Yet the promise of epistemological completeness has traditionally elevated the sentence into an icon of linguistic totality.

The sentence does indeed have a special magic, but it has more to do with its form than with its completeness. The printed sentence has a beginning, middle, and end that are not *the* beginning, middle, or end: it is a micro-totality compatible with larger macro-totalities (the paragraph, the essay, the novel). As such, it is a primary defense against the potential chaos of reading and writing. Sentences impose form at the microlevel, interrupting the stream of information with reminders that a unit is about to start or has finished. They at least look linear on the page, whether or not readers process them serially.

As Walter Kintsch has noted, this signaling has high cognitive stakes.

Although readers integrate new information continuously, their experience of the sentence's end stands out:

> The integration that takes place at the sentence end has a special status. . . . Except for very short sentences, working memory at this point is usually loaded to capacity and must be cleared to make room for the next sentence. . . . Except for one or two central propositions that are retained in the focus of attention because of their presumed relevance to further processing, all that has been constructed up to this point in working memory is now lost from consciousness/primary memory. (*Comprehension* 102)

For Kintsch, a competition occurs at the end of every sentence. While reading a sentence, the brain processes propositions continuously, but at the end, the limitations of working memory mean that the brain can retain only a few of them, while the rest are forced into the void. One might fear that in a long work this process would fragment the reading experience, creating "a sequence of disjoint structures, each corresponding to a sentence" (*Comprehension* 102). Yet Kintsch assures us that this fragmentation will not occur because bridging material remains in short-term memory, and the reader may also remember material from earlier in the work and from general semantic and episodic memory. This retrieved material lets the reader create an integrated macrostructure from sentences, rather than unconnected bits of information.

Yet the specter nevertheless lurks in Kintsch's account that integration into a larger structure may not happen as easily as it is supposed to do. The snag arises from a conflict between two kinds of totality: the local totality represented by the individual sentence, and the global totality represented by the reader's macrostructural representation of a work. The critical point is this: creating the second structure requires eradicating the first. In Kintsch's account, readers always conquer the sentence by integrating only the most relevant idea units into their memory. Yet the possibility remains that a given sentence might be stubborn. It could refuse or at least resist integration by being too self-sufficient or by being too representative. A sentence might be so tightly bounded, such a unity unto itself, that it blocks the reader's ability to break it into meaningful fragments and thereby stops easy assimilation into a larger memory representation. As Shelley noted in his *Defence of Poetry*, "A single sentence may be considered as a whole though it be found in the midst of a series of unassimilated portions" (515). A sentence may stick out from the surrounding texture and, even if only momentarily, break the flow of reading. In contrast, a sentence may sum up a given piece of writing so well that it cancels out the reader's ongoing mental representation by substituting for it. The painstaking, gradual integration described by Kintsch can be wiped away through the power of one sentence to encapsulate the whole work, as in the genres of the thesis sentence, the moral, the apothegm, or the slogan. The sentence has the potential both to say nothing, because it is only a moment in the reading process, and to say everything, because it may substitute for the entire work.

Print and the purification of English unleashed these tensions in the sentence, which had been less visible in its former incarnation as the rhetorical period. The history of the sentence has traditionally been written in terms of English syntax, in which the sentence is understood in contemporary linguistic terms and modern syntactic categories are projected backwards into Anglo-Saxon, and middle and early modern English.[1] These investigations say more about the history of particular syntactic formations than about the sentence as an idea. As Ian Robinson has noted, linguistic historians have given the sentence a longer history than it deserves because English translations use "sentence" for words that in Latin or Greek writings do not correspond to what academic linguistic theory calls a sentence; they consequently obscure the peculiar modernity of the printed sentence (*Establishment of Modern English Prose*, "Appendix 1: The History of the Sentence").

To understand the sentence's history, it is helpful to think of it as an unstable meeting point for several linguistic forms:

1. The logical sentence: the linguistic expression of a "complete thought."
2. The period: a device from classical rhetoric consisting of a grouping of ideas felt by the speaker to comprise a larger unit.
3. The grammatical sentence: the syntactic domain of a finite verb.
4. The manuscript sentence: a written unit bounded by more or less conventional visual signals.
5. The typographic sentence: a printed unit that conventionally begins with a capital letter and ends with terminal punctuation.
6. The sententia: a rhetorical figure stating a maxim or authoritative pronouncement.

Not only is this list not complete, each item in it is a definitional minefield. Yet definitions that are too precise would not help with a history characterized by looseness and overlaps in meaning. Nor have I touched on the meaning of "sentence" most common in Romantic literature, the sentence as a literal or metaphorical punishment. Despite tantalizing parallels between changing understandings of the English sentence and the late eighteenth-century revision of the English penal code, I will bracket the legal sense of "sentence" in this chapter in order to follow through on the logic described in chapter 1, whereby the history of English is allowed not to be a second-order reflection of some other, supposedly more important history.

Most uses of "sentence" in the eighteenth century conflate some of the senses that I have listed above. This blurriness arose because English writers inherited two classical traditions relevant to understanding the sentence, corresponding to the first two items on my list: the logical tradition (sentence as complete thought) and the rhetorical one (sentence as a speech unit). Of the two, the rhetorical tradition had been hotly debated during the seventeenth century in a long, well-documented battle.[2]

These debates heightened attention to problems in English that could not be solved by looking to classical models. At a surface level, stylistic prescriptions about orating in Latin and Greek needed drastic overhauling to be helpful for printed English: as many writers argued, English syntax made the Ciceronian periodic style awkward. Admittedly, the need to revise long-held assumptions is not necessarily visible in overt pronouncements of the English experts. Eighteenth-century grammar books present a monotonous repetition of the logical definition of the sentence:

> A *Sentence* comprehends at least a *Name* and a *Verb*; by which some sentiment, or Thought of the Mind, is expressed. (Fisher, *New Grammar* 116)

> What is a Sentence? A Sentence is any Thought of the Mind, expressed by two or more Words joined together in proper Order. (Buchanan, *British Grammar* 165)

> A SENTENCE is an assemblage of words, expressed in proper form, and ranged in proper order, and concurring to make a complete sense. (Lowth, *Short Introduction* 67–68)[3]

> A sentence or period in language ought to express one entire thought or mental proposition; and different thoughts ought to be separated in the expression by placing them in different sentences or periods. (Kames, *Elements of Criticism* 2:263)

SENTENCE, in grammar, a period or set of words, comprehending some perfect sense or sentiment of the mind. ("Sentence," *Encyclopædia Britannica* 3:578)

A sentence is any number of words so arranged as to express distinctly any opinion or sentiment which we wish to communicate to the hearer. The words so combined are said to make a *complete sense*, because the end of speech is then answered. (Hazlitt, *New and Improved Grammar* 2:73)

The sameness of these definitions should not mask the drift from rhetorical completeness to a linkage between epistemological and syntactic totalities. The best account of this change is Jean-Pierre Seguin's *L'invention de la phrase au XVIIIe siècle*. Seguin, who confines his discussion to French, argues that in the eighteenth century, the sentence underwent a series of shifts: from oral to written; from a lexical unity to a syntactic entity; from a constructed arrangement to a structural model; from a set phrase to the semantic expression of a subjectivity; from an incidental object to myth; and from the core of oratory to the defining trait of prose.[4] There is an interesting tension in Seguin's categories: the sentence simultaneously becomes more linguistically abstract (it becomes written and a syntactic entity) and more socially weighty (it expresses subjectivity and becomes a myth). Insofar as Seguin's list applies to English as well as French, and I believe it does, the source for both the shifts and tensions he describes was Locke's transformative description of language in his *Essay on Human Understanding* (1690).

Although the classical period expressed a complete sense, definitions of this completeness remained vague. Everything from pithy apothegms to elaborate perorations could count as complete because perceived completeness existed at the level of the rhetorical unit. Locke's empiricism shrank completeness from rhetoric to words: *"Words, in their primary or immediate Signification, stand for nothing but the* Ideas *in the Mind of him that uses them"* (2:4). For Locke, thoughts are ideas, and ideas are expressed in words. Words, not sentences, equal complete thoughts. The completeness of the sentence was a higher-level mode of completeness that arose from linkages between distinct ideas.

Locke theorized those linkages in a strange, isolated, but influential chapter, "Of Particles." In it, he notes that all words in a language are not the same. Although most words express ideas, language also includes words "that are made use of, to signify the *Connection* that the Mind gives to *Ideas, or Propositions, one with another*" (2:71); Locke calls such words "particles." He believes that traditional grammar has neglected particles and that they need attention because they are "of such constant and indispensable use in Language, and do much to contribute to Mens (*sic*) well expressing themselves" (2:72). Locke skirts the problem that the mere presence of connecting particles does not in itself guarantee coherence. Instead, he writes as if particles carried the burden of the whole sentence: the mind "has found a way to intimate to others by these particles, some whereof constantly, and others in certain Constructions, have the Sense of a whole Sentence contained in them" (2:73).

Although Locke's chapter on particles is quite brief and, by his own admission, only a sketch, it had major implications: it renovated the sentence as a micromedium. If the idea was located no longer in the rhetorical unit but in individual words, then what counted as the sentence's complete sense had to be rethought. Sentence completeness now depended on using particles to integrate separate idea-words into a convincing unit. Under the pressure of Locke's philosophy, coherence in discourse shrank from a skillful arrangement of rhetorical commonplaces to the epistemological unity of the sentence, in which idea-words and particles would mirror the mind's operations. This shift demanded a greatly heightened attention to local matters of grammar and (as an extension of Locke's concerns) punctuation, since these would bind together idea-words. Although in the seventeenth century, "the basic linguistic unit was the letter, sound, syllable, or word," in the early eighteenth century, "it is the syntactical function," because Locke had made this function central to thinking (Cohen, *Sensible Words* 51).

This attention to syntax had an epistemological edge. Although words might stand for ideas, only by combining them could the mind reveal itself. At a fundamental level, without syntax, thinking did not happen: the sentence, as the site for combining ideas into a larger unit, became the prime medium of all subjectivity. The epistemological power of post-Lockean syntax explains the peculiar tension in Seguin's account of the sentence, whereby the sentence simultaneously becomes more abstract (as a syntactic unit) and more subjective (as the semantic expression of interiority).

To some early eighteenth-century writers, Locke's philosophy bolstered the claims of English over those of Greek and Latin. For them, the mind worked the way English did. Although the role of the building blocks of language in shaping cognitive perception (the Whorfian hypothesis) remains a debated topic in current psycholinguistics, in the early eighteenth century English writers assumed that there was no debate: English was right and other languages were wrong.[5] As Richard Blackmore claimed,

> An *English* Writer is unpardonable, if the Order of his Words is not plain and obvious, for which perhaps no Language in the World affords such great Advantages; no other admits and preserves that regular Succession of the Words as our own. In the *Greek, Latin, Italian, German,* and *Spanish* Tongues, especially in the two first, the unnatural Transposition of the Terms extreamly obscures the Sentiments of the Writer; their Periods are inverted from the Order in which the Mind form'd its Conceptions; and if the Words are the Images of our Thoughts, this is to represent them in a very irregular and distorted manner; as if a Man were drawn with his Head between his Feet, or his Heels in the Air. ("Essay on the Nature and Constitution of Epick Poetry" 108–09)

Blackmore makes fun of classical and European languages by linking syntax to cognition: "But the English express their Thoughts in the same Train and Method in which the Mind conceives them." For Blackmore, a universal pattern of mental understanding exists and English, unlike Latin or Greek, follows it. If English users have sense enough not to let rhetorical flourishes like "unnatural Transposition" of words get in the way, English should be a perfect medium between minds.

Later grammarians rushed to codify English syntax and punctuation to make the benefits described by Blackmore available to all. Good English would guarantee good thinking. In this effort, actual definitions may have mattered less than examples. Ann Fisher's *New Grammar* (1750) presented a landmark innovation, though one modeled on traditional Latin grammars: the bad sentence for the pupil to fix. Previous English grammars had had parsing exercises in which students named each part of speech in a sentence.[6] Fisher's textbook did more by providing actual English sentences to be corrected:

A Man's Manners commonly shapes his Fortune.

O Lord, thou is our Father; thou has made Summer and Winter.

Learning and Knowledge is Ornaments in Youth. (130)

Fisher's innovation caught on. Later authors like James Buchanan, James Gough, Peter Walkden Fogg, and John Knowles incorporated bad sentences into their textbooks, so that the English sentence in need of improvement became a cornerstone of eighteenth-century pedagogy, and one that remains a fixture today in the grade-school classroom (Görlach, "A New Text Type").

As time went on, these exercises became more ambitious. Lindley Murray's *English Grammar* (1795) included not only instructions for grammatical correctness but also an influential appendix about good style. Although his grammar book itself did not have student exercises, Murray wrote separate *Exercises* "adapted to Murray's English grammar designed for the benefit of private learners, as well as for the use of schools." It included examples of sentences that had problems with style, not just grammar. For example, one rule was "*to dispose of the capital word, or words, in that place of the sentence, where they will make the fullest impression*" (*EG* 205). To help learn this rule, the students face sentences like the following; the corrections, which I have put immediately after the sentences, appear in a separate "key" for the teacher:

> Whether a choice altogether unexceptionable, has, in any country, been made, seems doubtful.
> [Whether, *in any country*, a choice altogether unexceptionable has been made, seems doubtful.]
>
> And Philip the Fourth was obliged, at last, to conclude a peace, on terms repugnant to his inclination, to that of his people, to the interest of Spain, and to that of all Europe, in the Pyrenean treaty.
> [And, *at last, in the Pyrenean treaty*, Philip the Fourth was obliged to conclude a peace, on terms repugnant to his inclination, to that of his people, to the interest of Spain, and to that of all Europe.]
>
> Were instruction an essential circumstance in epic poetry, I doubt whether a single instance could be given of this species of composition, in any language.
> [Were instruction an essential circumstance in epic poetry I doubt whether, *in any language*, a single instance could be given of this species of composition.] (*Exercises, Adapted to Murray's English Grammar* 1:149; 2:117–18)

Readers may be surprised by Murray's corrections because the corrected sentences are not obviously better than the uncorrected ones; at least, one might argue that the best word order depends on a sentence's role in a larger context. But Murray, like previous grammarians, worships the isolated sentence and assumes that the good student will recognize the ideal word order. His book acquires a mysterious authority by promulgating rules that seem to admit variation and debate, even though they are learned through exercises whose answers are either right or wrong.

Murray's model was Lectures 20, 21, and 22 of Hugh Blair's *Lectures on Rhetoric and Belles Lettres*. In these, Blair comments on three essays from *The Spectator* typographic sentence by typographic sentence, with unprecedented detail and precision. In a footnote, Blair explains that actual classroom experience led him to this exercise. Teaching in a "part of the kingdom . . . where the ordinary spoken language often differs much from what is used by good English authors," he gave essays from *The Spectator* so that students could "analize and examine . . . the structure of Mr. Addison's sentences" (1:430). The results provided the content of these three famous chapters.

Blair's comments on the sentences are so detailed that they overwhelm Addison. For example, in *The Spectator* 412, Addison writes, "There may, indeed, be something so terrible or offensive, that the horror, or loathsomeness of an object, may overbear the pleasure which results from its novelty, greatness, or beauty; but still there will be such a mixture of delight in the very disgust it gives us, as any of these three qualifications are most conspicuous and prevailing." Blair quotes Addison's sentence and then clobbers it:

> This sentence must be acknowledged to be an unfortunate one. The sense is obscure and embarrassed, and the expression loose and irregular. The beginning of it is perplexed by the wrong position of the words *something* and *object*. The natural arrangement would have been, *There may, indeed, be something in an object so terrible or offensive, that the horror or loathsomeness of it may overbear.*—These two epithets, *horror* or *loathsomeness*, are awkwardly joined together. *Loathsomeness,* is, indeed, a quality which may be ascribed to an object; but *horror* is not; it is a feeling excited in the mind. The Language would have been much more correct, had our Author said, *There may, indeed, be something in an object so terrible or offensive, that the horror or disgust which it excites may overbear.*—The first two epithets, *terrible* or *offensive*, would then have expressed the qualities of an object; the latter, *horror* or *disgust*, the corresponding sentiments which these qualities produce in us. (1:431–32)[7]

What may strike readers now as a pedantic exercise was for eighteenth-century readers a virtuosic debugging of English, an invaluable series of adjustments to enable the code to work as it should. This partial quotation gives some idea of the detail and minuteness of Blair's scrutiny. He jumps between criticism of style (the wrong position of "something" and

"object," made especially confusing because Blair does not actually rec-
ommend altering the position of "something") and of content (the need
to introduce a distinction between objective "loathsomeness" and subjective "horror"). Addison is subjected to a full-scale onslaught, in which
every possible fault is exposed.

Addison's larger argument vanishes under Blair's scrutiny. Blair rarely,
if ever, adduces as a criterion of judgment the link between one sentence
and the next: his spotlight shines on each sentence in turn, and no memory of one sentence carries to the next. Like bad sentences in schoolbook
grammars, the isolated sentence is the unquestioned unit of analysis.
Blair's stylistic choices in his own sentences reveal as much as his actual
criticisms of Addison; his sentence structure competes with Addison's.
Most obviously, while Addison writes long sentences still indebted to classical periodicity, Blair writes short, tight sentences praised by the Scottish
academics. By isolating Addison's sentences and commenting on them in
such a clipped style, Blair suggests that Addison's sentences are not yet
ready for modern print.

From Fisher to Blair to Murray, attention to bad sentences did more
than foreground the isolated, typographic sentence. It linked English textbooks to one of the most popular literary genres of the day, the maxim
collection. Maxims had a long history going back to the Book of Proverbs; their presence is felt throughout English literature from Chaucer's
Tale of Melibee to Shakespeare's Polonius. They remained extraordinarily
popular in the eighteenth century. Robert Dodsley's *The Oeconomy of
Human Life* (1750), for example, was one of the eighteenth-century's best-
sellers and was one of the first English books stereotyped.[8] It consists of
short, quasi-biblical paragraphs, of one or two typographical sentences,
that look much like the strings of sentences in grammar books:

> A fool is provoked with insolent speeches, but a wise man laugheth them
> to scorn.
>
> Harbour not revenge in thy breast; it will torment thy heart, and discolour
> its best inclinations.
>
> Be always more ready to forgive than to return an injury: he that watches
> for an opportunity of revenge, lieth in wait against himself, and draweth
> down mischief on his own head. (37)

When Ann Fisher first introduced bad sentences in her textbook, the sentences she used were all *sententiae* like Dodsley's. By the time of Hugh Blair

and Lindley Murray's exercises, however, some sentences were *sententiae*; others, not. In Blair, all Addison's sentences were equal, whether or not they look like traditional *sententiae*. In Murray, a respectable Addisonian maxim like "Let us endeavour to establish to ourselves an interest in him, who holds the reins of the whole creation in his hands" appears on the same page with the following quotation from Swift: "It is likewise urged, that there are, by computation, in this kingdom, above ten thousand parsons, whose revenues, added to those of the bishops, would suffice to maintain, &c." (*sic*) (*Exercises* 149). Whereas the Addisonian sentence is a *sententia*, heavy with moral value, the Swift, out of context, looks like neutral expository prose (it's actually from the satiric "An Argument Against Abolishing Christianity" [1708]). If early grammar books linked moral and grammatical instruction by using *sententiae* for grammatical practice, by the time of Murray, the *sententia* no longer dominated.

Nevertheless, in Blair and Murray, a stylistically good English sentence inherits the gravity of a traditional *sententia*. This gravity consists in its maxim-like autonomy. Blair stresses that "during the course of the sentence, the scene should be changed as little as possible"; that "things which have . . . little connection" should not be in the same sentence (1:217); and that the sentence should "always" come "to a full and perfect close" (1:223); Murray follows him closely. Their strictures construct the sentence's perfect self-sufficiency, trimmed of unnecessary words and arranged to have an unambiguous start, middle, and stop.

This ideal of the sentence induced a crisis from which English prose has yet to recover. Although the self-enclosed, autonomous sentence fit perfectly with the Scottish ideal of expository prose, with its emphasis on clarity and brevity, there was a lurking problem. Such sentences did not necessarily add up to perfect clarity at the macrostructural level. The gap in Locke whereby particles alone created a relation between microstructure and macrostructure becomes a gaping chasm in Blair and Murray. They assumed that their advice about individual sentences would lead to larger structures that possessed the same virtues of clearness, unity, and strength: a metonymic relation should pertain between the sentence as a unit and the larger discourse. But it was just as likely that the relation between the sentence and the larger unit would be competitive rather than metonymic, especially given their stylistic prescriptions. Their theorization of the sentence encouraged choppy prose by giving no guidance about sequencing ideas beyond the sentence.

Blair and Murray were relatively untroubled by this potential conflict because the sentences they liked fit well in their favorite prose genre, Christian religious writing. In Blair's hugely popular sermons, the well-turned, atomized sentence dominates.[9] Blair attains a macrostructure through lists:

> He who is of a cowardly mind is, and must be, a slave to the world. He fashions his whole conduct according to its hopes and fears. He smiles, and fawns, and betrays, from abject considerations of personal safely. He is incapable of either conceiving, or executing, any great design. He can neither stand the clamour of the multitude, nor the frowns of the mighty. The winds of popular favor, or the threats of power, are sufficient to shake his most determined purpose. (*Sermons* 3:133)

While all Blair's sentences relate to a common topic, as in the older collections of maxims, no causal relation links one sentence to the next. The paragraph's cohesion depends on pronouns: the repetition of "he" at the start of each sentence, and in one case of "its." But within the list, there is no particular reason that one sentence needs to follow the next: the order could be shuffled with minimal change. Without the pronouns, the sentences would stand alone as perfect *sententiae*: a pile-up of isolated pronouncements about the coward.

Such sentences, however well suited to sermons, were less suitable to genres based on narrative, technical description, or argumentation that needed stronger causal enchainment between clauses. These genres were either emerging in the late eighteenth century or were reshaping themselves in light of print's demands. As a result, the sentence had a somewhat different relation to authorial agency than did pure English. Whereas the rules of pure English quickly came to be a central constraint on both the writing and reception of printed English, the well-formed sentence did not impose itself quite so universally. Literary authors may have lost their ability to define the future of English usage, but the battle over the future of the sentence was more open. One sign of this is the emergence of the sentence as an overt topic in literary writing, especially in the novel. In Samuel Johnson's *Rasselas* (1759), for example, typographic sentences often coincide both with the traditional sententia and with the well-formed stylistic sentence as theorized by linguists. Indeed, the novel's weighty, balanced typographical sentences are even more atomized than those of Addison or Blair. As Boswell noted, "The fund of thinking which the work contains is such, that almost every sentence of it may furnish a subject of long meditation" (*Life* 242). He treats *Rasselas* as if the overall work deserves less attention than its isolated sentences, each of which merited close, detailed thought.

Yet the content of *Rasselas* undercuts its form. The closure that Johnson's sentences achieve in isolation contrasts with the novel's open-endedness, with its "conclusion in which nothing is concluded." Throughout *Rasselas*, Johnson questions "the emptiness of rhetorical sound, and the inefficacy of polished periods and studied sentences" (104). In particular, he accuses "studied sentences," meaning both *sententiae* and well-formed sentences, of lacking a genuine "complete sense." This quotation occurs when a philosopher confronts the inadequacy of human advice to ease devastating grief: tragedy renders all sentences, of any sort, incomplete.

Rasselas unmasks the vaunted completeness of the sentence as a pseudo-completeness that exists only at a syntactic or lexical level. The unsolved Lockean problem inherited and ignored by eighteenth-century English experts was the relation between microstructure and macrostructure. Johnson re-poses the question by changing the definition of macrostructure so that it pertains not to the macrostructure of a discourse, but of all human experience. The continuity between linguistic and mental experience that the Lockean sentence promised is undercut by his demonstration of the sentence's inadequacy to encompass the full range of emotion.

Different as *Tristram Shandy* (1759–67) is from *Rasselas*, Sterne resembles Johnson in his sense of the incompatibility of the microstructure of the sentence and the macrostructure of human experience:

> I think, replied my uncle *Toby*, taking his pipe from his mouth, and striking the head of it two or three times upon the nail of his left thumb, as he began his sentence,——I think, says he:——But to enter rightly into my uncle *Toby's* sentiments upon this matter, you must be made to enter first a little into his character, the out-lines of which I shall just give you, and then the dialogue between him and my father will go on as well again. (56)

Sterne, like Johnson, brings perspectives never considered by the linguists to bear on the notion of the sentence's completeness. According to Sterne, finishing Uncle Toby's sentence would be pointless because the reader would not know enough about Uncle Toby to understand it. The typographically complete sentence on the page would not translate into a semantically complete one in the reader's mind.

Elsewhere, Sterne teasingly suggests that a censored sentence may actually present a more complete sense than a complete one. Uncle Toby claims, when explaining why his sister does not want a male doctor, "My sister, I dare say, added he, does not care to let a man come so near her ****." Tristram then adds, "I will not say whether my uncle *Toby* had compleated the sentence or not;—'tis for his advantage to suppose he had,—as, I think, he could have added no ONE WORD which would have improved it" (we also learn that Tristram's father has snapped his pipe right at the moment of the asterisks, as another cause for the break) (89).[10] Sterne presents a typographically complete sentence that has been rendered semantically incomplete through the deletion of the final word. Yet his narrator plays with the reader by assuming that what originally looks like a bit of censorship (the asterisks substitute for a bawdy word) may actually stand in for an ellipsis or dash (Uncle Toby said nothing and left his meaning implicit). Sterne continues with a detailed account of Uncle Toby's sentence and its different possible endings, concluding with a parody of Locke when he urges his countrymen to remember on what "small particles your eloquence and your fame depend" (89). Sterne zeroes in on the weak spot in defining the sentence as a complete thought by demonstrating that, paradoxically, the only logically complete sentence is a syntactically incomplete one.

Subsequent writers of the late eighteenth-century novel display more confidence than Johnson and Sterne in the sentence's ability to represent human experience. For them, the micro/macrostructure problem resides at a level more internal to the text. In particular, the more well-formed the sentence is, the less well the sentence fits into a developing narrative because each sentence seems potentially autonomous. Writers struggle to reconcile the demands of a forward-moving narration with the demands of the well-formed sentence valorized by the English experts. The result can look to later readers like a bizarre mesh of suspenseful plot and cumbersome style, as in this passage from Ann Radcliffe's *The Italian* (1797):

> Vivaldi listened with submitting patience to this mention of morals and decorum from a person, who, with the most perfect self-applause, was violating some of the plainest obligations of humanity and justice; who had conspired to tear an orphan from her home, and who designed to deprive her for life of liberty, with all the blessings it inherits. But, when she proceeded to speak of Ellena with the caustic of severe reprobation, and to hint at the punishment, which her public rejection of the vows had incurred, the patience of

Vivaldi submitted no longer; indignation and contempt rose high against the Superior, and he exhibited a portrait of herself in the strong colours of truth. But the mind, which compassion could not persuade, reason could not appal; selfishness had hardened it alike to the influence of each; her pride only was affected, and she retaliated the mortification she suffered by menace and denunciation. (120)

At times, Radcliffe's sentences turn into momentary *sententiae*. It would take only a little tinkering for a clause like "But the mind, which compassion could not persuade, reason could not appal" to find a niche in collections of maxims like Dodsley's or in a sermon by Blair. Elsewhere, however, her novel links causally connected events in sentences that are quite unlike maxims. Moreover, each sentence hardly contains a single "complete thought": Radcliffe (or her compositor) unites several clauses into a single typographical sentence. Nevertheless, Radcliffe's prose keeps the traits of the well-formed sentence: each "capital word" counts; each sentence uses elaborate parallelisms; and end-stopping brings each typographical sentence to a resounding halt.

This closural aspect sits uneasily beside *The Italian*'s forward narrative thrust: for a reader wanting to find out what happens next, it takes a mini-eternity to wade through these sentences. Signs that even Radcliffe's first readers found her style awkward are evident less in the reviews of the novels themselves (which often praise the elegance of her style) than in the reviews of her travel writing. Scenic description favored the well-formed sentence more than narrative did because descriptions could list individual features. Reviewers thought that her travel writings were simpler and less encumbered than her novels: "She is very properly contented with a less laboured and artificial diction than is found in many parts of her novels," and she uses "generally plain and simple" language in her descriptions.[11] Their comments point to a perpetual and unresolved tension in Radcliffe's work between the macrostructure, which depends on forward motion, suspense, anxiety, and breathless mystery, and the stasis of the microstructure, which depends on the well-formed sentence's insularity.

As I described in the previous chapter, the Romantic novel in general brilliantly adapted the principles of expository prose to the device of the omniscient narrator. Yet the well-formed sentence was a sticking-point: good sentences made bad novels. For the novel to acquire real authority, it would have to transcend the link between sentence and *sententia* to relocate authority at the level not of the sentence but of the narrative persona. Believability would reside not in the gem-like isolated sentence but in the gist impression of a wise observer on the action and the ability of characters to come close to or to reject that wisdom. Austen and Scott treat the English experts' sentence as if it were a serious impediment to novelistic authority and develop an alternative praxis of the sentence, better suited to what they view as the aims of the novel.

Given that the well-formed sentence was especially well suited to clerical discourse, Austen and Scott parody it in their clerics. In *Pride and Prejudice*, Mr. Collins mixes well-formed sentences with misfires:

> Be assured, my dear Sir, that Mrs. Collins and myself sincerely sympathise with you, and all your respectable family, in your present distress, which must be of the bitterest kind, because proceeding from a cause which no time can remove. No arguments shall be wanting on my part, that can alleviate so severe a misfortune; or that may comfort you, under a circumstance that must be of all others most afflicting to a parent's mind . . . And it is the more to be lamented, because there is reason to suppose, as my dear Charlotte informs me, that this licentiousness of behaviour in your daughter, has proceeded from a faulty degree of indulgence, though at the same time, for the consolation of yourself and Mrs. Bennet, I am inclined to think that her own disposition must be naturally bad, or she could not be guilty of such an enormity, at so early an age. (327)

As is typical of Austen's depictions of the clergy, Austen (daughter of a clergyman) avoids giving Mr. Collins bits and pieces of moral maxims standard in earlier representations of foolish or self-satisfied clergymen, although he notes that he would be eager to provide such "arguments." Yet he does not need *sententiae* to make a fool of himself because he has sentences. Mr. Collins's first and second sentences are carefully structured on the best linguistic models, complete with climactic closes ("a cause which no time can remove"; "most afflicting to a parent's mind") and parallel structures ("that can alleviate . . . that may comfort"). Yet his well-formed sentences are trumped by his ill-formed ones. To subject this letter to a Blairite analysis, one might note that the last sentence quoted breaks all Murray's rules for the sentence's unity: (1) "*We should not be hurried by sudden transitions . . . from subject to subject*" (*EG* 196): Mr. Collins swerves drastically from blaming the Bennets to blaming

Lydia; (2) *"Never . . . crowd into one sentence, things which have so little connection, that they could bear to be divided into two or three sentences"* (*EG* 197): Mr. Collins overloads his sentence with clauses; (3) *"Keep clear of all unnecessary parentheses"* (*EG* 200): Mr. Collins masters the obnoxious parenthetical phrase ("as my dear Charlotte informs me," "for the consolation of yourself and Mrs. Bennet").

Mr. Collins's repulsiveness in his letter does not exist only at the level of the sentence: it permeates all aspects of his rhetoric. Austen's point is that the well-formed sentence belongs to a self-enclosed mind, incapable of sympathetic connections with others and eager to inflict as much pain as is compatible with a thin veneer of politeness. Whereas Blair judged the Addisonian sentence as a completely autonomous unit, Austen judges the sentence as the product of a pre-existing moral agent. What counts is the sentence's ability to reveal that agent, not to enshrine a free-standing morsel of truth.

Mr. Darcy's letter to Elizabeth, in contrast, features a quite different practice of the sentence, along with an odd form of punctuation (though one found in previous novels):

> —I will only say farther, that from what passed that evening, my opinion of all parties was confirmed, and every inducement heightened, which could have led me before, to preserve my friend from what I esteemed a most unhappy connection.—He left Netherfield for London, on the day following, as you, I am certain, remember, with the design of soon returning.—The part which I acted, is now to be explained.—His sisters' uneasiness had been equally excited with my own; our coincidence of feeling was soon discovered; and, alike sensible that no time was to be lost in detaching their brother, we shortly resolved on joining him directly in London.— (220–21)

The dashes in Mr. Darcy's letter transform the typographical sentence by physically making each sentence continuous with the next one. While we may recognize that punctuation in this text, or any work of the period, cannot be attributed exclusively to the biographical author, I am less concerned with the biographical Austen than with the historical text of *Pride and Prejudice*. The dashes insist that each sentence is not self-sufficient but belongs to a larger macrostructure. Most of Mr. Darcy's justification consists not of organized arguments like those of Mr. Collins but of narrative. Rather than being self-contained, each sentence leads to the next in a chronologically ordered, causal sequence of events. The dashes fill the typographical space as visible images of semantic connections between sentences, which cannot be separated into maxim-like nuggets of wisdom. The letter's totality exists not in the typographical sentence but in the described event.

While Darcy's sentences conform to pure English, they care less about the well-formed sentence. In a work like *Tristram Shandy*, dashes signal disconnection and the failure of the typographic sentence to embody a genuinely complete thought. In *Pride and Prejudice*, dashes also indicate that the complete thought does not obtain at the level of the sentence, but rather than breaking off, as in Sterne, they connect successive sentences into a larger whole. The dashes work against the danger lurking in Kintsch's account of reading, whereby sentences refuse integration into a larger whole. The dashes at the end of one sentence flag readers not to abandon the information in the sentence as they move on to the next, but to track a larger flow of events. Just as Mr. Collins's sentences pointed to the state of his moral consciousness, so Darcy's dashes insist that his point of view depends on presenting a totality in the form of a complete history, of which Elizabeth is unaware.

Earlier in the novel, variation in writing style has characterized the difference between Bingley and Mr. Darcy. After teasing Mr. Darcy for studying "too much for words of four syllables" in his letter writing, Bingley turns to himself: "My ideas flow so rapidly that I have not time to express them—by which means my letters sometimes convey no idea at all to my correspondents" (52). Unable to tolerate being teased, Mr. Darcy unmasks Bingley's modesty about his letters as self-indulgence: "You consider them as proceeding from a rapidity of thought and carelessness of execution, which if not estimable, you think at least highly interesting" (53). Yet later in the book, when we read letters, Mr. Darcy's style turns out to be closer to Bingley's, while Mr. Collins's style is closer to the one that Mr. Darcy is initially supposed to write. Mr. Collins writes the stilted sentences that draw attention to their own constructedness, while Mr. Darcy's dashes indicate, if not sloppiness in composition, an eagerness to privilege substance over style.

Austen's English underscores the importance of this counter-practice of the sentence in her treatment of the sentence as motif. *Pride and Prejudice* is unusual among works of the romantic period in that it never uses "sentence" in its legal or juridical sense. Instead, its characters have internalized Blair's lesson that the sentence is the key to discourse. In their eyes, human communication has a particular unit, the sentence, as its corner-stone. Yet sentences that they analyze do not work in quite the way that eighteenth-century grammarians might lead us to suspect, as when Eliza-beth reads Mr. Darcy's letter: "She read, with an eagerness which hardly left her power of comprehension, and from impatience of knowing what the next sentence might bring, was incapable of attending to the sense of the one before her eyes" (226). Elizabeth's eagerness to know what will come next arises both from the content of Mr. Darcy's letter and from the typographical presentation of his sentences, which physically run together so as to make "what the next sentence might bring" appear closely linked to "the sense of the one before her eyes." She has no interest in perfect closure because for her, as for Mr. Darcy, completeness of the communi-cation lies not in sentences but in the overall event.

Elsewhere, when Austen draws attention to sentences, she does so to emphasize not the individual sentence but the cumulative power of a se-ries. Sentences are bits of information that create and then intensify an impression:

Elizabeth noticed every sentence conveying the idea of uneasiness. (210)

Every sentence that he uttered was increasing her embarrassment. (278)

She . . . gloried in . . . every sentence of her uncle, which marked his intel-ligence, his taste, or his good manners. (282)

Her joy burst forth, and every following sentence added to its exuberance. (337)

Every sentence of kindness was a fresh source of happiness. (384)

The sentence's informational content, its expression of a "complete thought," takes a back seat to the ability of sentences to flow together to intensify a mood, either positive or negative. Locke's concern with particles to link idea-words becomes less important to Austen than the sentence's cumulative power to represent emotion. Emotion's truth is not guaranteed unless it is represented through a sequence of sentences, whose moment-to-moment meaning is less important than the totality that it enables. In *Pride and Prejudice*, however fragmented sentences may be on the page, sentences matter to the characters for their ability to create and then sus-tain a new kind of complete sense, a totality at the level of feeling.

Walter Scott takes the novelistic battle against the grammarians' sen-tences a step further by developing a new principle of sentence construction: speed. I focus on a novel obsessed with sentences and speed, *The Monastery* (1820). Forms of the word "haste" appear almost eighty times in it, averaging more than four occurrences per chapter. Whereas sentences in *Pride and Prejudice* arose in the context of conversation and of letters, sentences in *The Monastery* are more directly tied to literacy. Bad Catholic reading leads to bad sentences, which are bad not because they are ungrammatical or badly formed but because they take too long. Good Protestant reading leads to good sentences, although this association is complicated by gender. On the surface, this split seems like a familiar association between Protestantism and plain speaking that had become a stereotype of the English (not necessarily Scottish) character.[12] Yet in the context of the anti-novelistic rise of the well-formed sentence, this familiar opposition acquired unexpected overtones. In rejecting the bad literacy of the Catholic characters, Scott also rejects a model of textuality associated with the well-formed sentence and its atomized perfection; against it, he poses the new novelistic sentence, marked above all by its tight causal cohesion with its surroundings.

Although Scott's priests resemble Mr. Collins in their self-important sentences, the premier bad sentencer in *The Monastery* is the Catholic Sir Piercie Shafton, often called "the Euphuist," who has read too much Tudor prose for his own good:

> "Pretty and quaint, fairest lady," answered the Euphuist. "Ah, that I had with me my Anatomy of Wit—that all-to-be-unparalleled volume—that quintessence of human wit—that treasury of quaint invention—that exquisitely-pleasant-to-read, and inevitably-necessary-to-be-remembered manual, of all that is worthy to be known—which indoctrines the rude in civility, the dull in intellectuality, the heavy in jocosity, the blunt in gentility, the vulgar in nobility, and all of them in that unutterable perfection of human utterance, that eloquence which no other eloquence is sufficient to praise, that art which, when we call it by its own name of Euphuism, we bestow on it its richest panegyric." (136)

Shafton's Euphuism (not an especially good imitation of Elizabethan prose) combines extravagant vocabulary, elaborately patterned language, and, most of all, very long sentences, whose gist is wildly out of proportion to their word count. Throughout the novel, his speech violates Grice's maxim of quantity, as when he sings "without mercy or remorse about five hundred verses" of "the poesy of the un-to-be imitated Astrophel."[13] A running gag consists of characters finding themselves bewildered by Shafton's discourse or trying desperately to cut short his endless sentences.

Scott sets these bad sentences against the good ones of virtuous Protestant characters, Alice of Avenel, her daughter Mary, and the novel's hero, Halbert Glendenning. The book that inspires them to their sentence-making is the Avenel family's Bible in English, treated by the Catholic monks as dangerous property. Alice of Avenel preserves it from the wreck of her fortunes; in humble retirement, she reads "small detached passages" (51) to her daughter and servants. That a mother should read the Bible to her family is unremarkable: more striking is Scott's specificity that Alice reads only short bits, as if reading too much might be intrinsically dangerous. Part of Alice's virtue inheres in knowing how to transform the Bible into traditional *sententiae*. Long narratives acquire an aura of impropriety, but detached passages prove her ability to glean true value.

Although Alice dies before she can fully instruct her daughter and her Bible is twice confiscated by priests, a supernatural White Lady protects the Avenel family by ensuring that their Bible always returns to them. Alice's daughter Mary, directed to the Bible's presence, at last reads it and discovers that it is much more than simple text. Her mother has inserted "slips of paper" into it, of two kinds: ones pointing out "the errors and human inventions with which the Church of Rome had defaced the simple edifice of Christianity," complete with the support of "necessary proofs and references" (280); and others presenting "the simple effusions of a devout mind communing with itself" (281). Scott includes among these "effusions" a mini-anthology of "those affecting texts to which the heart has recourse in affliction" (281), which consists of short sentences: "She read the affecting promise, 'I will never leave thee nor forsake thee,' and the consoling exhortation, 'Call upon me in the day of trouble, and I will deliver thee'" (281). Although not properly an "effusion," this anthology of *sententiae* attracts Mary "above all the other lessons" (281). Mary becomes a quick study and converts to Protestantism in one morning solely on the basis of reading this Bible.

The familiar Protestant emphasis on the unmediated availability of the Gospel becomes in Scott's hands a valorization of speed reading, which needs the safe mediation of a mother's editing. Considering that Catholicism was stereotypically associated with glossing and Protestantism with the naked truth of scripture, the scene is a striking inversion. The unmarked Bible is a risky document that needs to be whittled down to safe

Protestant sentences. In Scott's hands, the readable Bible becomes a docu-ment like Dodsley's *Oeconomy of Human Life*, a string of commonplaces that are comforting precisely because they are commonplace.

Exposure to these sentences transforms Mary's speech: after reading them, she never speaks again. Extracting herself from a bad Catholic cul-ture of long-windedness has as its price complete silence. The novel jux-taposes her silence with the speech of her beloved Halbert Glendenning, whom the Avenel Bible also transforms. Early in the story, he is a rough, violent youth with no head for learning, whose speech is filled with Scot-ticisms and short sentences strung together by dashes. Jealous of the per-ceived intimacy between Mary and his brother Edward, he seeks out the supernatural White Lady. She had promised to teach him the Bible, and he comes to redeem her promise, hoping thereby to ingratiate himself with Mary. Explaining that the book contains the "mystery of mysteries" (115), the White Lady helps him to recover it from a magical cave.

Given this spectacular lead up, we expect Halbert to read the Avenel Bible and become a changed man as a result. He does indeed change: "It was evident to all, that . . . young Halbert was an altered man; that he acted with the steadiness, promptitude, and determination which be-longed to riper years" (138). Yet, oddly enough, he never actually reads the Bible; he just hides it in his room. Nevertheless, the effect on his sentences is dramatic. He gains the speech that Mary loses to become the model Protestant speaker. Unlike the Catholic characters, he avoids long, elaborately patterned sententiousness. Unlike the lower-class Scottish characters, he suddenly loses his Scotticisms, except in the case of some proverbs that he explicitly identifies as Scottish. Instead, he produces per-fectly grammatical English that is an ideal medium between formality and informality, written and oral, politeness and directness. Above all, his sentences are as short as possible while being compatible with his status as a gentleman, and much of his time is spent emphasizing his desire to avoid delay: "Your noble proffer doth but hasten the execution of a reso-lution which I have long since formed" (179); "You should have abidden in England had you desired to waste time in words, for here we spend it in blows" (200); "There is no time to expound anything" (206); "I must answer in brief, that I cannot profit by them" (222); "I will hasten as fast as you will" (320); "Halbert Glendinning briefly told the story" (336).

Scott thus creates a peculiar gendered division of labor: Mary becomes a good Protestant by speed-reading the Bible and not talking; Halbert, simply by touching the Bible and by speaking in short, direct sentences. This division allows Scott to avoid the perceived dangers of Catholic long-windedness and of bad Protestant enthusiasm, the possibility that reading the Bible too closely will produce not model brevity but streams of speech larded with Biblical diction. He represents this danger in the character of Henry Warden, an enthusiast so extreme as to have been exiled by Elizabeth from England. As such, he is the Protestant equivalent of the Catholic Father Eustace: both are essentially good men deluded by doctrinal extremes and both, when pressed, defend their religious positions at length. When Scott's narrator asks rhetorically, "What can ensure the good temper and moderation of polemics?" (303), the implied answer is "nothing."

We might expect that Scott's narrator would model himself after Halbert and write in similarly terse sentences. Instead, Scott writes as if he recognizes a potential trade-off between brevity and cohesion: sentences that are too short may actually slow down a work by eliding connections between one sentence and the next. Scott's narrator values not brevity but cohesiveness, the easy connection between one sentence and the next through clear markers of relational and causal cohesion.[14] Unlike Mary's mother, who looked for excerptable chunks of biblical wisdom, Scott writes in a style that exchanges excerptability for cohesive wholeness. It guarantees that no individual sentences stick out as memorable. As Walter Bagehot noted perceptively, "Nobody rises from his works without a most vivid idea of what is related, and no one is able to quote a single phrase in which it has been narrated" (q. in Hayden, ed., *Scott: The Critical Heritage* 420); for Virginia Woolf, Scott was a great novelist, and "great novelists who are going to fill seventy volumes write after all in pages, not in sentences" ("The Antiquary" 63). None of Scott's narrative sentences has any pretense at being free-standing; each makes sense only in the larger context of the narrative. Unlike the English experts' sentences, with their well-chosen openings and resounding conclusions, Scott's sentences end with no firm closure. Instead, the requirements of the macrostructure overwhelm the well-formedness of the sentence as microstructure.

Scott's narrative style may strike later readers as flat, but the swift unsententiousness of his sentences was a powerful novelty in early nineteenth-century narrative. He maintained the Enlightenment goal of creating English as a disappearing medium, but the actual interface that eighteenth-century linguists had developed for such a medium, the well-formed sentence, turned out to be ill-suited for such work in the novel: its constructedness drew attention to it. Instead, Scott's cohesive style renovated the sentence by relocating clarity away from the typographic sentence to the narrative, just as Jane Austen privileged Mr. Darcy's writing over Mr. Collins's.

Scott's first readers associated his novelistic style above all with speed. Scott's novels seemed to be written by him and read by an eager public with almost indecent haste. Francis Jeffrey, writing about *Waverley*, noted, "Here is a thing obviously very hastily . . . written." Other reviewers note that his novels "have followed each other very rapidly"; speak of "the unpardonable haste and carelessness with which his latter productions have been sent forth from the press"; and claim that "it is almost impossible to keep pace with the pen of this prolific Writer." Hazlitt condemned "the innumerable and incessant instances of bad and slovenly English in them, more, we believe, than in any other works now printed. We should think the writer could not possibly read the manuscript after he has once written it, or overlook the press" (q. in Hayden, ed., *Scott: The Critical Heritage* 79, 104, 165, 188, 289). In the case of *The Monastery*, critics worried that Scott had actually been too hasty: "the march of genius may be too rapid" ("Review of *The Monastery*"). For these critics, the impression of haste came not only from the speed of Scott's output but also from the rush of his writing, the sense that he cared nothing for the niceties of the well-formed sentence.

Given Scott's enormous popularity throughout the nineteenth century, it might seem that his speedy style effectively killed off the well-formed sentence as a model. In Scott's new style, what mattered was not the rhetorical form of the sentence but a style that disappeared into the representation of vivid characters and events. As Leslie Stephen noted in 1871, Scott was remarkable for "that easy flow of narrative never heightening into epigram . . . No man ever depended more on the perfectly spontaneous flow of his narratives" (q. in Hayden, ed., *Scott: The Critical Heritage* 446). The whole point of his flow was that nothing about the language was to be remembered, only the situation. The effect was not to banish the well-formed sentence *per se* (what Stephens described as heightening "into epigram"), but to suggest that novels could dispense with them.

Yet, in the long run, Scott's renovation of the sentence had a cost. For all Scott's popularity, there remained a lingering suspicion of how much authority any work could have that flouted so completely the norms of the well-formed sentence. In particular, the well-formed sentence was particularly suited, as I have noted, to conventional moral maxims, and much nineteenth-century criticism of Scott worried about the depth of his morality. The point was not whether his works were moral, but whether they engaged moral issues at a deep enough level. This moral debate had a stylistic edge: the cohesiveness of Scott's sentences discourages the kind of moral epigrams that such critics desired. Much of the history of the Victorian novel can be seen as an attempt to develop a style that would allow novelists to regain the moral ground that Scott had lost, less through the content of his plots than through the swiftness of his sentences.[15]

Moreover, the speediness of Scott's writing guaranteed that, while he would be universally admired, he would never become a model for good sentence-making of the kind advocated by the linguists. For all his success, he was no Addison. Since Blair and Murray dominated prescriptions for English throughout the nineteenth century, any writing that flouted them was academically marginalized. As the quotation from Hazlitt reveals, Scott's novels could be praised as many things, but not as good English. Those wanting to learn how to employ the well-formed sentence would have to look elsewhere, such as to the eighteenth-century novels like *Rasselas* or Goldsmith's *Vicar of Wakefield* (1766) that remained "cheap and plentiful" in the nineteenth century (*RN* 472–73). Scott had made the novel respectable by incorporating history and what seemed to be useful information, but his problematic style pointed to the need for a writer who could combine the virtues of swift and interesting historical information with a style that modeled the virtues praised by Blair and Murray.

Whereas novelists like Austen and Scott treat the well-formed sentence as an impediment to narrative authority and develop alternatives to it, it might seem that the sentence as theorized by linguists would be irrelevant to poetry. Poetry should have had little need to care about sentences because it had other markers for organizing micro- and macrostructure: the line and the stanza or verse paragraph. For the most part, Romantic poets write as if they had never heard about the stylistic recommendations for sentences of eighteenth-century linguists, nor does it seem as if the sentence was a particularly useful site of evaluation for their contemporaries: Georgian critics look at syntax, diction, or metrics when they review poetry, but rarely sentence style. The consensus seemed to be that other forms of demarcation in poetry, such as the line, the stanza, or the verse paragraph, mattered more. The word "sentence" in Romantic poetry usually refers to sentence in its juridical sense, either literally or metaphorically, rather than to its linguistic one.

This absence is no surprise: the well-formed sentence as developed in the eighteenth century belonged to prose, not poetry. Grammars like James Buchanan's *The British Grammar* asked students to translate poetry into prose by providing the sentence's "natural Order" and by "supplying the Ellipsis." For example, the compact couplet "He who will true Examples learn to give, / First let him learn to die, and then to live" became "He who will learn to give true Examples, let him first learn to die, and then let him learn to live" (218).[16] Buchanan pays no attention to the possible loss in meaning created by taking words out of iambic pentameter and by eliminating rhyme: the couplet is simply on a par with other prose examples that Buchanan provides. Pope had famously asked critics to look in poetry for "what oft was *Thought*, but ne'er so well *Exprest*" (*Essay on Criticism* [1711] 298), but the grammarians suggested that nothing in poetry could be as well expressed as in prose. For the English experts, poetry is a messy code, filled with irregular word order and unnatural ellipsis, which a good student can improve by rewriting as solid prose.

It would seem, then, that Romantic poetry could be safely skipped in an account of the history of the sentence. Yet doing so would focus only on the surface form of the sentence and miss the more important issue it raises, the relation between micro- and macrostructure. If the sentence itself is not critical to Romantic poetry, the issues that the sentence was meant to engage are central. Moreover, they had a particular historical context often overlooked in studies of Romanticism: the rise of the excerpt. Given the emphasis that critics from M. H. Abrams to Clifford Siskin have put on organic development as a master trope for Romantic literature, the importance of excerptability in the period has been understated or ignored. The familiar Romantic thematics of development occurred in the face of a larger cultural demand for the instantaneous, synchronic bit that could be easily consumed.[17] The excerpt, like the atomized sentence, assumes that a microstructure is perfectly self-contained and can be extracted from a larger whole with little loss; indeed, the larger whole can best be appreciated fully through skilled extraction.

The marketability of extracts from longer works skyrocketed in the eighteenth century: the rise of the periodical press in particular encouraged excerpting in reviews and in collections of free-standing excerpts.

These excerpts typically consisted of episodes from prose works and short poems or selected passages from volumes of poetry. Vicesimus Knox's widely-selling *Elegant Extracts* was an exemplary text, mentioned by Wordsworth, Coleridge, Byron, and Austen: at least 23,000 copies were sold between 1796 and 1824 (*RN* 540). By 1820, one reviewer could refer to the "numberless tomes, of all sizes and prices, which, under the titles of 'Specimens,' 'Beauties,' 'Selections,' 'Elegant Extracts,' &c have rendered" much of British poetry familiar ("Aikin's British Poets" 501). While collections like Knox's were made up of older poetry that had gone out of copyright, the habit of "extraction" from new works had many outlets: book reviews, commonplace books, books designed for school use, epigraphs in novels and expository prose, and collections of "beauties." Following the increasing visibility of the poem as commodity discussed in chapter 2, these sites treated poetry as an early form of clip art, often reproduced without reference to author or title of the original work.

The excerpt seemed especially pertinent to longer works like the novel. In such cases, the excerpter judged which bits and pieces of the longer text worked best as free-standing units. Extracting from a volume of poetry seemed to require less skill because one simply chose shorter poems. Moreover, poetry had formats useful to excerpters: the verse paragraph and the stanza. In general, actual collections of extracts tended less to chop up longer poems than to reprint shorter lyrics. For example, the extensive *Elegant Extracts in Poetry, Selected for the Use of Young Persons* contains for the most part complete poems, although it does break Cowper's *Task* down into excerpts such as "The Want of Discipline in the English Universities" and "Happy the Freedom of the Man whom Grace makes free" (2:508–9); it also presents many of Shakespeare's plays in excerpts. St. Clair has noted, however, the prevalence of shorter excerpts from poems in commonplace books of the period (*RN* 224–29).[18]

Even more than pure English, extraction challenged poets of the Romantic period by guaranteeing that their reception would depend not on their work as a whole but on its excerptability. Conventions of pure English could be contested; excerpting could not. The problem at the heart of the sentence, the relation between micro- and macrostructure, dominates poetry of the Romantic period, even if the sentence itself is not the site of conflict. Excerpting threw into question just where to locate an author: was the author of an extract the same as the author of the work as a whole? Could there be good extracts from bad poems, and bad extracts from good poems? How accountable should authors be for pre-excerpting their works, so as to make them available for easy reproduction?

In *Don Juan*, Byron throws in a scorching commentary on excerpting when describing Juan's military exploits:

> And as he rushed along, it came to pass he
>   Fell in with what was late the second column,
> Under the orders of the General Lascy,
>   But now reduced, as is a bulky volume
> Into an elegant extract (much less massy)
>   Of heroism, and took his place with solemn
> Air 'midst the rest, who kept their valiant faces
> And levelled weapons still against the glacis.   (8.34)

Byron compares decimating an army to creating an "elegant extract" from a "bulky volume," which becomes "much less massy," and, by a near-pun, less "messy" as well. The simile links bloodshed to literature's commodification as elegant extracts. Byron holds them both responsible for norms of efficiency that eliminate excess, either of pages or of lives. *Don Juan*, in contrast, is "massy" and inefficient, loudly foregounding its pleasure in digressiveness, inconsequentiality, and linguistic play.

Yet, paradoxically, the digressive roominess of *Don Juan* is what made it so elegantly extractable: most readers who encountered the poem did so as an excerpt, and such excerpting began almost as soon as it was published.[19] Byron's ironic swipe at the culture of excerpting did little to counter its ability to engulf *Don Juan*. The result was double-edged. *Don Juan*'s excerptability assured its wide dissemination but blunted its satirical edge, especially in relation to sexual mores. Byron's wide-ranging survey of hypocrisy and folly could be chopped down to a witty stanza or two, turning a powerful epic to fluffy light verse, a problem that shadows *Don Juan*'s reception to this day. *Don Juan* posed and continues to pose at the level of the stanza the familiar eighteenth-century problem of the sentence, the microstructure's ability to block or even cancel out the macrostructure. Though within the context of a stanza, Byron's language often deviates from the strictures of the English experts, his stanza remains closer to the well-formed sentence than he might want to admit.

In contrast to Byron, Wordsworth most strongly resisted the accommodation to marketability that excerpting allowed. His 1815 *Poems*, introduced with a loud attack on contemporary audiences, attempts to guarantee the integrity of a volume by presenting poems "arranged according to subject, genre, chronology, or even the mental faculty most prominent in their inception" (Fraistat, *The Poem and the Book* 35) and then specific orderings within each group to mirror the course of a human life. To remove a poem from this context would be to lose a substantial part of its meaning.

Yet even before the 1815 volume, Wordsworth's poems counter excerpting through their long sweeps of narrative and gradually accumulating details. In his stanzaic verse, as in many of the *Lyrical Ballads*, conventions of narrative or of dialogue hold the stanzas together through causal cohesion: a continuing action unfolds among characters, much as in Darcy's letter in *Pride and Prejudice*. This resistance to excerpting brings Wordsworth's prosaicism into a complicated relationship with the eighteenth-century well-formed sentence. In his 1800 "Preface" to *Lyrical Ballads*, Wordsworth famously argued that "some of the most interesting parts of the best poems will be found to be strictly the language of prose when prose is well written" (*Lyrical Ballads and Other Poems* 748). He aims to disprove grammarians like Buchanan by showing that poetry can be just as "well written" as prose.

Yet despite Wordsworth's valorization of prose "when it is well written," what he wrote bore little resemblance to the English experts' recommendations:

> Upon the Forest-side in Grasmere Vale
> There dwelt a Shepherd, Michael was his name,
> An old man, stout of heart, and strong of limb.
> His bodily frame had been from youth to age
> Of an unusual strength: his mind was keen,
> Intense and frugal, apt for all affairs,
> And in his Shepherd's calling he was prompt
> And watchful more than ordinary men.   (40–8)

The surface differences between the Addisonian prose prized by the English experts and Wordsworth's poetic prosaicism are apparent: Addison's vocabulary is heavily Latinate, Wordsworth's is not; Addison favors parallel structure, Wordsworth does not; Addison retains Latin periodicity by saving the climax for the end, Wordsworth does not.

Beneath these stylistic differences are deeper shifts in technologies of communication. As I have noted, English experts insisted that a good writer should "*dispose of the capital word, or words, in that place of the sentence, where they will make the fullest impression*," usually near the beginning or end (*EG* 205). A Buchanan-like revision of Wordsworth's sentence might read as follows: "An old shepherd named Michael, who had a stout heart and strong limbs, dwelt upon the forest-side of Grasmere Vale." Rather than writing such a sentence, Wordsworth breaks down information into discrete units that he lists: "There dwelt a Shepherd, Michael was his name, / An old man, stout of heart, and strong of limb." Wordsworth's sentences are, from the point of view of the English experts, inefficient, chiefly because of their overemphasis on anaphoric coherence: "a Shepherd," "Michael," "his," "an old man," "his bodily frame," "his mind," "his Shepherd's calling."

The Wordsworthian sentence as collage recalls Sterne by challenging the well-formed sentence's ability to depict a "complete thought." Wordsworth's grammar works against the possibility of such completeness by overloading the sentences with information. They conclude less with a sharp rhetorical flourish than with a sense of quiet letdown, as if they had exhausted themselves by keeping so much material in a single syntactic unit. For all Wordsworth's desire to insist on the closeness of poetry to prose, his most prosaic blank verse follows quite different rules for the sentence than those promulgated by the English experts of his day. It promotes incompletion over completeness, accumulation over linearity, parenthesis over unity, and anticlimax over closure.

Such sentences make all Wordsworth's poems feel like fragments in spite of themselves, even the ones that are complete. Their fragmentariness, counterintuitively, works against their excerptability. The good excerpt, like the well-formed sentence, is entirely self-sufficient, or at least can appear so when reproduced out of context. The fragment, in contrast, presents a perpetual reminder of its dependence on material outside of its bounds: the macrostructure of which it is part can never be adequately grasped. Wordsworth's poetry refuses to present the complete sense upon which the mystique of the sentence depended.

Percy Shelley went even further. Although he was perfectly capable of writing well-formed sentences, his stanzaic poetry attempts something quite different. What William Keach notes about "To a Skylark" is true of much of Shelley's poetry more generally: "Grammatical arrangement and especially rhythmic patterning . . . urge the reader past the separation imposed by punctuation and stanzaic division" (*Shelley's Style* 161).[20] Whereas

Wordsworth writes in larger, cumulative units like the verse paragraph, Shelley produces stanzas that resist the Byronic parallel between the stanza and the sentence, as in this moment from *The Witch of Atlas* (1824):

> A haven beneath whose translucent floor
>   The tremulous stars sparkled unfathomably,
> And around which, the solid vapours hoar,
>   Based on the level waters, to the sky
> Lifted their dreadful crags; and like a shore
>   Of wintry mountains, inaccessibly
> Hemmed in with rifts and precipices grey
> And hanging crags, many a cove and bay.   (433–40)

Most obviously, the stanza is not a syntactic sentence, though it appears as a typographical one. Syntactically, it is a huge noun phrase amplifying the description of the "haven" that the Witch builds in the previous stanza. Unlike the syntactically self-contained stanzas in *Don Juan*, this stanza does not imitate the propositional sentence: it is not a "complete sense" in the understanding of that phrase by the English experts. Instead, it depends entirely on cohesive renaming of an earlier phrase.

But the stanza's lack of a "complete sense" goes beyond syntax because it eschews the lingering connection between sentence and *sententia*. As I have suggested, the well-formed sentence's complete sense originated in close association with moral maxims like Dodsley's. Shelley avoids the sentence both as maxim and as form. In this stanza, his syntax looks like a particularly tough assignment for schoolboys tutored in Buchanan's textbook. "Inaccessibly hemmed in" initially appears to be a past participle modifying the subject "wintry mountains," leading to the expectation of a main verb in the last line. But no such verb appears, leaving "many a cove and bay" as a peculiarly inconclusive stop. Actually, "hemmed in" turns out to be one of two verbs governed by the subject "solid vapours hoar," which "lifted their dreadful crags" and "hemmed in . . . many a cove and bay," as if the vapours were "a shore / Of wintry mountains." The syntax pulls in two directions: initially, it appears that the stanza is a pile-up of isolated images. Actually, when thoroughly parsed, the images are more closely related syntactically than may first appear, but the initial impression of a sequential list of only tentatively related images is hard to erase.

The overall effect is as far from the well-formed sentence as could be imagined, so that the stanza remains stubbornly unexcerptable: it contains none of the characteristics of a good excerpt since it does not contain a memorable bit of wisdom, a well-formed bit of description, or a beautifully isolated piece of language. At the same time, it coheres only loosely with the stanzas surrounding it, since it provides a fantastic extension of a place named in the previous stanza, but serves no causal role in the poem's narrative, slight as that is. Shelley's stanza is neither autonomous, like Byron's, nor cohesive, like Scott's sentences, but a strange hybrid that conforms to the expectations of neither a micro- nor a macrostructure. Instead, it collapses the ideology of the excerpt from within by adopting a stanza form that seems to invite excerpting and then refusing to link form to content in expected ways. The result is a breakdown in the familiar distinction between micro- and macrostructure, since it is not clear that a stanza such as the one that I have quoted fits comfortably into either category. *The Witch of Atlas*, like much of Shelley's poetry, avoids a clearly identifiable climactic line or stanza that could serve as a convenient metonymy of the whole.

Of all Romantic poems, the one most self-conscious about the excerpt's allure is Keats's "Ode on a Grecian Urn" (1820). Most evidently, the urn itself is an elegant extract, a piece of art that, placed on display, has lost the historical context that gave it meaning. Keats reveals the museum as a visual version of the excerpt collection, one that removes works from their first surroundings to give them a new status as icons of consumption. Yet, unlike *Childe Harold's Pilgrimage*, the urn resists easy consumption, at least in Keats's eyes, because it is a bad excerpt. A good excerpt has a meaning despite the loss of context; the urn does not.

When Keats describes what he sees on the urn, he becomes another version of an elegant extractor, offering us glimpses of a larger whole that do not necessarily cohere. The fourth stanza makes this lack particularly vivid:

Who are these coming to the sacrifice?
   To what green altar, O mysterious priest,
Lead'st thou that heifer lowing at the skies,
   And all her silken flanks with garlands drest?
What little town by river or sea shore,
   Or mountain-built with peaceful citadel,
      Is emptied of this folk, this pious morn?
And, little town, thy streets for evermore
   Will silent be; and not a soul to tell
      Why thou art desolate, can e'er return.   (31–40)

If this stanza disappeared from the poem, the ode would lose nothing in the way of lexical cohesion. Indeed, it would arguably gain in coherence: most of the images in stanza five, such as the "brede / Of marble men and maidens overwrought, / With forest branches and the trodden weed" (41–43), refer more obviously to images from stanzas two and three than to the rites described in stanza four.

Despite many interpretations treating Keats's fourth stanza as a bridge from the third to the fifth one, it may be more helpful to focus on its lack of fit, its dramatization of the vexed relation between part and whole. Separate from the poem, the stanza lacks the self-sufficiency of a *sententia* because the reader would not know that the scene described was on a Grecian urn. Yet the stanza sits uncomfortably in its context, as if it were the beginning of a new direction in the ode that never develops. It works neither as a self-sufficient microstructure nor as a seamless part of a larger macrostructure. Just as the urn alone does not lend itself to easy comprehensibility, so the urn's extracts do not quite work the way extracts should. Instead, the stanza remains in a strange limbo, a leaky parenthesis or an inelegant extract. It looks like it belongs to the poem because it follows the same stanza structure. But it tests how far its subject matter can stray from its surroundings and still remain part of the same poem.

The urn itself gives voice to imperfect excerptability in its final sentence: "'Beauty is truth, truth beauty,'—that is all / Ye know on earth, and all ye need to know" (49–50, in the punctuation of the 1820 volume). Whether or not the urn speaks the entire two lines or just part of them matters less than the similarity of these lines to the traditional genre of the *sententia*. This is the nugget of wisdom that resembles a secular version of the pieties found in works like Dodsley's *Oeconomy of Human Life*. Yet, like the fourth stanza, this concluding *sententia* is only imperfectly excerptable. In itself, it is a vacuous sendoff. Only through the poem's larger context do the "beauty" and "truth" described acquire concreteness and meaning as a charmed fiction, against which the speaker subtly protests through the poem.

Behind what Keats perceives to be the urn's confident *sententia* lies a Johnsonian suspicion of the adequacy of "polished periods" to the miseries of human experience. The macrostructure of the poem meditates on the loss that excerptability entails, even as it recognizes such excerptability as the inevitable starting point for interpretation. The poem becomes a test case for a reader's relation to excerpting, as the final lines function as a concession to the reader who insists that a poem, like a sentence, must conclude with the most important words at the end. Yet the concession is only a pseudo-concession, an acknowledgement of the wish-fulfillment surrounding the conventions of closure.

Despite resistance shown by Romantic poems to excerptability, poets were far less successful than novelists in avoiding the effect of excerpting on their later reception. If poets did not write in excerpts, excerpting was forced on them. Wordsworth's *Prelude*, Blake's epics, Shelley's *Prometheus Unbound*: all became known primarily through extracts. The model of poeticity that I discussed in chapter 2 found its most convenient outlet in such short clips of poetry, blocks of language that conformed to a recognizable model of poetry. Francis Turner Palgrave's mid-Victorian *Golden Treasury* (still in print) may be the most familiar monument of this vision of the Romantic period, but it influences widely-used classroom anthologies even today. Only after poets had succeeded as items in an anthology did they achieve enough prestige for later readers to tackle their longer works; only then could they be perceived as geniuses whose personalities ran throughout their *oeuvre*. For geniuses, excerpting was a crime: only in their totality could they be truly appreciated.

Yet the history that I have traced raises an interesting challenge: does reading every line of a work necessarily give a better picture of it than reading an excerpt? The deeply ingrained academic assumption that the authentic experience of a work, or at least the only one deserving scholarly attention, must take account of the whole was not necessarily held either by Romantic readers or writers. Some works may be better in excerpt than in their entirety, and a good excerpter may help readers get to the heart of a work better than they would on their own. Yet current literary criticism rarely considers excerpting equivalent to the production of knowledge about a work: knowledge production depends on writing essays. It would be easy to present a radically different picture of the Romantic period by choosing less-familiar excerpts from familiar authors, yet the inertia whereby certain texts and certain excerpts reappear in anthology after anthology masks the continuing interpretive centrality of excerpting. The challenge of the well-formed sentence resurfaces in the relation of the individual poem to the authorial career.

My discussion of the sentence has avoided nonfictional prose, the mode in which the sentence might seem to be most central. Nonfictional prose of the Romantic period generally reads as if Addison, Blair, and

Murray had never existed and there was no consensus at all about what a sentence should be. Even as textbooks popularized certain familiar prescriptions, their consensus had little obvious effect on mature prose writers of the period. This lack arose from the fierce politicization of prose during and after the French Revolution and the Napoleonic wars. The neutral style that Blair promoted buckled before the perceived urgencies of what Olivia Smith describes as the split between vulgar and refined language.[21] While this division is too simple to cover the wide range of prose styles that developed during the Romantic period, Smith is right that, at least in the short term, the eighteenth-century dream of a common style gave way to everything from the demotic bluntness of radicals like Tom Paine and William Cobbett to the lofty sophistication of the *Edinburgh Review*, from the fiery rhetoric of Burke to the loopy escapades of *Blackwood's*. In terms of experimentalism, it is as if the relative positions of late eighteenth-century poetry and periodical prose switched at the beginning of the nineteenth century: poetry's English becomes less experimental, while prose becomes much more so. As many critics have argued, political positions became stylistic positions: Burke versus Paine, the *Quarterly Review* vs. the *Edinburgh Review*, Coleridge versus Bentham, and so forth.[22]

By the 1820s, however, a different stylistic polarity had emerged that no longer fit the older political divisions. Instead, it resembled the split that I described earlier for poetry: the contrast between a seemingly generalized style that came to exemplify a respectable version of the mode, and an eccentric style that stood for genius. Given the close association between sentence style and the Scottish intelligentsia, it is not surprising that these styles came from the work of two men with Scottish roots: Thomas Babington Macaulay (whose father, Zachary Macaulay, was born in Scotland) and Thomas Carlyle. Both were protégés of Francis Jeffrey and both launched their careers through Jeffrey's vehicle, the *Edinburgh Review*. They also hated each other, although in public they maintained a thin layer of civility. In their early years as reviewers, they competed for the same topics: Macaulay wrote the essay on Byron that Carlyle had hoped to write for the *Edinburgh Review*; both wrote essays on history and on Boswell's *Life of Johnson* (Macaulay for the *Edinburgh*, Carlyle for *Fraser's*).[23] Yet the similarities between them only heighten the drastic difference in their styles between the all-purpose familiar style (Macaulay) and the prophetic mode of genius (Carlyle).

Of the two writers, Carlyle has received more attention; I give more space to Macaulay because he has largely dropped out of critical discussion. As a Victorian author born during the Romantic period whose frame of reference is the age of Johnson, his best essays describe eighteenth-century figures: Johnson, Addison, Burney, Hastings, Clive, Pitt, and others. This peculiar historical positioning has made him a bad fit for the academic canon of Victorian writers, but it allowed him in the nineteenth century to acquire remarkable authority. His work and its reception provide the critical link for transmitting eighteenth-century ideals of the sentence to the twenty-first century and beyond.

It is hard to underestimate just how influential Macaulay's familiar style became in the English-speaking world. American editions of his essays were so popular that eventually Macaulay bowed to pressure from the publishers of the *Edinburgh Review* to collect his essays, which were published by Longman ("Preface" vii–viii). According to Henry Curwen, the essays were "the most remunerative collection of essays ever published in this or any other country" (*History of Booksellers* 105). Macaulay's nephew George Trevelyan, author of his official *Life and Letters*, noted that the "astonishing success" of the essays was "something of far higher consequence than a mere literary or commercial triumph"; the essays had "awakened in hundreds of thousands of minds the taste for letters and the yearning for knowledge" (2:114). At times, nineteenth-century critics wrote as if Macaulay's essays had educated the entire English-speaking world; Edmund Gosse, for example, noted that "countless readers found in the pages of Macaulay's 'Essays' their earliest stimulus to independent thought, and the humane study of letters" (*Short History* 332).[24] In America, which operated with less attention to copyright, his essays were widely available even sooner. According to Harold J. Laski, "Everyone knows that even in the log cabins of the American frontier, the traveller would find, apart from the Bible and Shakespeare, a well-thumbed copy of Macaulay's *Essays*" (*Faith, Reason, and Civilization* 114).

My purpose is not to recover Macaulay by giving new readings of his essays but to describe his status as the icon of English prose and the history of the sentence. I concentrate on his breakthrough "Essay on Milton" (1825), the essay that first brought him widespread attention and the essay closest in time to Romanticism and the eighteenth-century English experts. Nominally a review of the newly discovered *De Doctrina Christiana*, it was a pioneering example of the review as mini-monograph; it quickly moved away from the work supposedly under discussion to the philosophy of aesthetics and to the historiography of the British Civil War. Macaulay splits the essay into two halves, one on Milton's poetry, the other on his politics.[25] In so doing, he makes a simple but salient point: aesthetics and politics are different. After years of reviews, tracts, prefaces, and footnotes that insisted on the inseparability of art and politics, Macaulay made art freestanding, and develops his understanding of Milton's poetry not in terms of his politics but through an extended comparison with Dante. He then abandons the poetry altogether and defends Milton and the regicides against their detractors.[26]

The essay quickly brought Macaulay to the attention of London's Whig intelligentsia, but the most interesting response to the essay came not to its content, but to its form; Jeffrey wrote, "The more I think, the less I can conceive where you picked up that style" (q. in Trevelyan, *Life and Letters* 1:117). In a way, the surprise is that Jeffrey was surprised at all, for any schoolchild of the day would have recognized where Macaulay "picked up his style": the prescriptions for the well-formed sentence that Blair and Murray had disseminated. Jeffrey's surprise indicates how few writers earlier in the century actually wrote as if those prescriptions were meant for them (Hazlitt is a major exception, and one with considerable influence on Macaulay's early writings).[27]

Comparing Jeffrey's prose and Macaulay's makes visible Macaulay's art of the sentence; these excerpts come from essays written only eight years apart, both first published in the *Edinburgh Review*:

> When we have said that his observations are generally right, we have said, in substance, that they are not generally original; for the beauties of Shakespeare are not of so dim or equivocal a nature as to be visible only to learned eyes—and undoubtedly his finest passages are those which please all classes of readers, and are admired for the same qualities by judges from every school of criticism. Even with regard to those passages, however, a skilful commentator will find something worth hearing to tell. Many persons are very sensible of the effect of fine poetry on their feelings, who do not well know how to refer these feelings to their causes; and it is always a delightful thing to be made to see clearly the sources from which our delight has proceeded—and to trace back the mingled stream that has flowed upon our hearts, to the remoter fountains from which it has been gathered; and when this is done with warmth as well as precision, and embodied in an eloquent description of the beauty which is explained, it forms one of the most attractive, and not

the least instructive, of literary exercises. (Jeffrey, "[Review of *Characters of Shakespeare's Plays* by William Hazlitt]" 472–73)

> But though we think the conduct of the regicides blameable, that of Milton appears to us in a very different light. The deed was done. It could not be undone. The evil was incurred; and the object was to render it as small as possible. We censure the chiefs of the army for not yielding to the popular opinion; but we cannot censure Milton for wishing to change that opinion. The very feeling which would have restrained us from committing the act, would have led us, after it had been committed, to defend it against the ravings of servility and superstition. For the sake of public liberty, we wish that the thing had not been done, while the people disapproved of it. But, for the sake of public liberty, we should also have wished the people to approve of it when it was done. (Macaulay, "Review of *Joannis Miltoni, Angli, De Doctrina Christiana*" 334)

Macaulay responds to Murray's injunction that "long, involved, and intricate sentences, are great blemishes in composition" (*EG* 198), while Jeffrey still writes with vestiges of Latin periodicity. Although Macaulay admired Jeffrey and dedicated his collected essays to his memory, he was aware of his stylistic differences from Jeffrey. When Jeffrey revised one of Macaulay's essays for the *Edinburgh Review* by inserting some passages of his own, Macaulay noted that the passages did not fit in because Jeffrey was "fond of omitting his *thats* and *whiches*, a thing which I never do" (Trevelyan, *Life and Letters* 1:222). Macaulay, unlike Jeffrey, obediently follows Murray's prescriptions; for Murray, "in all writings of a serious and dignified kind," the "practice of omitting the relative . . . ought to be avoided" (*EG* 203). He also boasted of how carefully he wrote; describing his essay on Bacon to Macvey Napier, he noted that "there is not a sentence in the latter half of the article which has not been repeatedly recast" (q. in Napier, ed., *Selections* 181).[28]

Macaulay's handling of the well-formed sentence differed from the atomization of Blair's sermons and the run-on style of Scott's novels. His solution generally was to narrate histories about which his assumed audiences had considerable background knowledge. Unlike in Scott, few would read a historical essay by Macaulay with breathless anticipation to find out what happened next. Instead, writing on more familiar topics, like the Civil War, Macaulay foregrounded not the presentation of events themselves but his running commentary on them. The forward thrust of narrative takes a second place to the epigrammatic, well-formed sentences in which Macaulay voices his opinions of major players and events he describes. Macaulay could focus the complete thought of the sentence at the level of commentary because he moved quickly through the narration of events that preoccupied Scott. He joins solid history to the precise bite of the well-formed sentence.

As a result, Macaulay could be a model of prose style in a way that Scott never was. For all Scott's popularity, his stylistic sloppiness kept him out of the schoolroom. Macaulay, in contrast, could straddle the popular and the academic: he presented the golden model of a popular intellectual style. Just as Hemans's style could stand for poetry itself in the 1820s, so Macaulay's sentences could stand for a perfect exemplar of good prose. His work created the mirage that all knowledge could be made accessible with enough attention to style; the tension described by Guillory between "clarity" and "technicity" would be won triumphantly by Macaulayan clarity.

Just as the eccentric genius of *Don Juan* shadowed Hemans's achievement, the tight, beautifully constructed Macaulayan sentence met its dark twin in the work of Thomas Carlyle, whose "Signs of the Times" appeared in the *Edinburgh Review* only four years after Macaulay's "Essay on Milton." Carlyle's prose leaves every rule of the prescriptivists in the dust:

> These and the like facts are so familiar, the truths which they preach so obvious, and have in all past times been so universally believed and acted on, that we should almost feel ashamed for repeating them; were it not that, on every hand, the memory of them seems to have passed away, or at best died into a faint tradition, of no value as a practical principle. To judge by the loud clamour of our Constitution-builders, Statists, Economists, directors, creators, reformers of Public Societies; in a word, all manner of Mechanists, from the Cartwright up to the Code-maker; and by the nearly total silence of all Preachers and Teachers who should give a voice to Poetry, Religion and Morality, we might fancy either that man's Dynamical nature was, to all spiritual intents, extinct—or else so perfected, that nothing more was to be made of it by the old means; and henceforth only in his Mechanical contrivances did any hope exist for him. ("Signs of the Times" 452)

Even before the advent of the Germanisms that crowd *Sartor Resartus*, Carlyle has developed his distinctive approach to the sentence. For him, each sentence looks like the start of an unpredictable adventure, characterized by long lists of unexpected words, jarring transitions, and sweeping generalizations. Rather than presenting a complete thought, Carlyle's sentences present too many thoughts, jumbling over each other in chaotic profusion. Yet, as with Byron's style, simply listing linguistic features does not do justice to Carlyle. The linguistic wildness accompanies a particular mental picture of the writer as sage, a voice crying in the wilderness. Whereas Macaulay writes as the impersonal voice of commonsense Whiggery, Carlyle appears as the outcast prophet. Even though he tells us no autobiographical details about himself, the sense of his style is inseparable from the impression of a man behind the style, and the response to the style is as much to the perceived persona of the writer as to specific linguistic cues.

As Geoffrey Hartman notes, Carlyle "challenged the principle of decorum on which cultural commentary had proceeded: that . . . it should be an extension of the familiar essay or the letter to the *Spectator* or *Gentleman's Magazine*" (*Criticism in the Wilderness* 137). Macaulay followed this principle of decorum; Carlyle did not. To model oneself on Macaulay was to conform to a widely-admired norm for English prose. To model oneself on Carlyle made you only a secondhand Carlyle; Matthew Arnold told Frederic Harrison to "flee Carlylese as the very devil" (q. in Harrison, "On Style in English Prose" 941). Between them, they charted out possible futures for the well-formed sentence as theorized by the eighteenth-century English experts: its transformation into a model of middlebrow seriousness, or its destruction before the seemingly relentless onslaught of genius.

Yet, in the long run, the differences between Macaulay and Carlyle may have been less important than what they shared: both wrote for the *Edinburgh Review* and, as such, were committed to the image of a literate sphere for educated readers. Their versions of English, however different, all assumed a general reader who would be interested in what they had to say. As such, they masked the fact that, even in the early nineteenth century, disciplinary and professional specialization were countering this general reader with a more specialized one, for whom sentence structure mattered less than technical vocabulary and field knowledge. In business and professional prose, niceties of sentence structure would matter far less than other aspects of communication. Yet the popularity of Macaulay and eventually Carlyle kept the threat of specialized prose largely hidden through most of the nineteenth century: it still seemed possible for the prose of a writer like Macaulay to be imagined as a universal model, one that provided a style adequate to all occasions and all places.

The mythology of the sentence as a representation of a complete thought continues to haunt writing in English. It is easy to point out the inadequacies of these definitions of the sentence but less easy to demarcate internal divisions within print without resorting to some notion of completeness. My point in this chapter is that ideas of completeness during the Romantic period quickly acquired generic associations and, with them, varying levels of centrality within categories of authorship. The rise of the sentence enforced new distinctions in writing that have become invisible through their familiarity, even though they still constrain communication in media that rely on print.

§ 6 Afterlives
Philology, Elocution, Composition

By the 1820s, literature had met the challenges of pure English. The novel absorbed elocution and expository prose but gave up claims to linguistic exemplarity by abandoning the well-formed sentence. The division between the genius and the generic meant that poetry and nonfictional prose had developed modes of departing from and conforming to the norms of pure English. Possibilities for the production and reception of the author as a category in relation to English had been defined. This flexibility positioned Romantic English well to have a varied and useful afterlife in the classroom, a history that I will trace in this chapter.

Although English continued to develop and change after the Romantic period, the school, which had always helped to define good English, became even more important during the nineteenth century. Romantic literature's effect on the English language depends on the school. As a result, the novel fades from the effects of Romantic English because, while it entered the school curriculum sooner than literary critics sometimes claim, it did not disseminate knowledge about usage. In three case studies, I describe the fate of the English of Romantic poetry and prose. The studies are histories of the rise of vernacular literary study and also histories of loss. They examine ways of reading that flourished in the nineteenth and early twentieth centuries and withered after the reorganization of literary study in the 1940s. I offer them not only as stories about the past but also as provocations for the present, to reflect on the costs of roads left behind.

Although school anthologies with Romantic poets (especially Scott and Byron) appeared even during the Regency, copyright restrictions and the peculiar publication histories of several of the major Romantics meant that most Romantic poetry was not widely available in Britain until long after the poets died. As soon as republication was legal (and sometimes even before), poems appeared in dictionaries, elocution manuals, grade-school readers, guides to usage, literary anthologies, collections of model quotations, school examinations, and other sites for spreading good English.[1] Although the rise of the English experts meant that literary writers no longer primarily defined English, the challenge faced by nineteenth-century educators was figuring out how to use literature in the schools.

For the lower levels, Lindley Murray's *Exercises* made literature the basis of sentences for correction, as described in the previous chapter. For more advanced students, an anthology like *Elegant Extracts in Poetry* (1816) reveals some uncertainty about just what to do with it. The "Preface" asserts that poetry provides entertainment and moral instruction. Yet the writer's confidence decreases when confronting the specifics of practice, since entertainment and instruction could conceivably happen outside the school. The "Preface" defensively claims to find it "unnecessary" and even "impertinent to point out the mode of using the collection to the best advantage," but then recommends that it be used "in recitation, transcription, the exercise of the memory, or in imitation," noting that it can be used "just as the Latin and Greek authors are read at the *grammar-schools*" ("Preface" to *Elegant Extracts* vii). Although the author refers to grammar-school pedagogy as an obvious precedent, it was in considerable flux when this anthology appeared, and its usefulness as a model would be far less obvious than the author implies. The suggestions offered range among quite different options: recitation (skills of public vocal performance), transcription (handwriting and penmanship), the exercise of memory (cognitive skills), and imitation (the cultivation of stylistic discernment).[2]

Nevertheless, this vagueness did not pose a problem until much later in the century, possibly because the number of schoolchildren who would have used an anthology like *Elegant Extracts in Poetry* was small. Later anthologists, coming after the reforms in Victorian education, had to do a better job defining not just why poetry was good, but why it should be studied. A leader in this effort was John Wesley Hales, Fellow at Cambridge, then teacher at the King's College in London and later Professor at the Bedford College for Woman. In 1867, Hales published an important essay, "The Teaching of English," arguing for the importance of instruction in the English language in schools. Even more significantly, in 1872, he published an anthology, *Longer English Poems, With Notes, Philological and Explanatory, and an Introduction on the Teaching of English, Chiefly for Use in Schools.* For roughly fifty years, Hales's anthology was the most significant vehicle for learning English poetry in high schools and colleges, although, to my knowledge, it has never received scholarly attention.[3]

Hales introduces his volume with a manifesto for change in the teaching of English: "It is certain that a great revolution is now taking place in the educational world" (xi). According to Hales, just as, in the Renaissance, "Greek and 'the New Philosophy' at last found a place in our schools and universities, so now Modern Languages and Natural Science appear to be establishing themselves" (xii). Hales aims to show to "those who may still regard English as a subject somewhat barren of such material as the teacher requires, how abundant and rich it is in fact" (xv). To prove that English was classroom worthy, he provides a twenty-page lesson plan, and, although his anthology starts with Spenser, he chooses a Romantic poem as his example: Walter Scott's "Rosabelle" from *The Lay of the Last Minstrel.* He imagines teaching possibilities for this poem in great detail, including attention to elocution, structure, overall unity, historical background, genre, prosody, and biography. Above all, he gives minute attention to grammar and semantics: "What part of the verb is *listen*, is *mourns*, is *cross* in st. 4, is *chide* in st. 6, *buried* in st. 12, &c." (xxviii). For those using this anthology, detailed study of the English language is inseparable from the analysis of English poetry in general and Romantic poems in particular.

Hales does more than introduce the book; his anthology stood out for the detail and completeness of the *"Notes, Philological and Explanatory"* advertised in the title. Placed at the back, these take the form of philological and historical glosses and study questions set off in brackets. Answers to the questions are not given, and are not always especially obvious. Rather than heightening Hales's authority as editor, they encourage potential dialogue and debate among reader, work, and teacher, although whether or not such discussions actually happened would have depended on particular classroom settings.

Each section of notes begins with a biography of the author, but when Hales moves to the glosses themselves, the author disappears in favor of English: *parole* gives way to *langue.* We move from claims that Coleridge "was a living Hamlet, full of the most splendid thoughts and the noblest purposes, but a most incompetent doer" (378) to "With what part of the sentence is *like God's own head* connected?", "What is meant by the *furrow* following free?", and "What part of speech is *all* here?" (in reference to "All in a hot and copper sky") (382).[4] According to Foucault, the "author" in modern literary criticism becomes "the principle of a certain unity in writing," whereby "contradictions are resolved, where incomparable elements are at last tied together or organized around a fundamental or originating contradiction" ("What is an Author?" 111). But Hales's questions free the student from worrying about a unifying authorial purpose. His questions can be answered without reference to biography, organic unity, or even overall intention.

For Hales, only through painstaking attention to syntax and semantics can good reading occur. Critics have usually understood such glossing as an attempt to force classical philology onto English literature. Yet classical philology provided Victorians like Hales with a poor model for the study of English literature because many of its building blocks were useless.[5] Traditional philology glossed unfamiliar words or constructions in Latin or Greek; the language of ·Romantic poetry was for the most part familiar to students and did not need such glossing. Traditional philology compared and evaluated varying readings from surviving manuscripts; Hales and others like him had access to no manuscripts of the Romantics. Traditional philology debated the findings of ancient critics like Servius; Romantic poetry had no comparable tradition of textual commentary.

Far from grafting the teaching of English onto familiar classical models, philologists like Hales, eager to argue for English's legitimacy, were forced into an unfamiliar disciplinary space that required ingenuity and experimentation about questions that might be asked. When Hales annotates works from before the Romantic period, his questions typically focus on defining or parsing individual words:

> Was paynted all with variable flowers (Spenser, "Prothalamion," l. 13)
>
> [What is meant by *paynted* here?] (206)
>
> I hear the far off curfeu sound (Milton, "Il Penseroso," l. 74)
>
> [What part of speech is *sound* here?] (248)
>
> Fought all his battles o'er again (Dryden, "Alexander's Feast," l. 53)
>
> [Is *fought* a "strong" pret. or a "weak"?] (283)

At such moments, Hales encourages a localized attention to individual word choice and grammatical placement within the line. Although his procedure comes from the study of Greek and Latin, his questions insist that interpreting English poetry requires not taste, culture, discrimination, sensibility, national pride, knowledge of authorial intention, recognition of theme, or understanding of cultural milieu, but a command of a metalanguage about English. According to John Guillory's treatment of the canon, "all canonical works can be regarded as exemplifying a language essentially different from the language spoken by 'real men,' namely, 'literary language'" (*Cultural Capital* 133); this distinction is defined by the operations of the school. In Guillory's account, the school creates an absolute split between ordinary English and literary English. Yet Hales's philology challenges this split. Literary English appears not as the absolute opposite of ordinary English but as a metonymy of it: students are not asked to learn a new language so much as to draw upon, extend, and increase what they should already know about English.

When Hales's anthology reaches Romantic poetry, the pressure to provide definitions fades as the language of the poetry becomes more contemporary with that of his students, although he does include certain poems like *The Rime of the Ancient Mariner* to display his philological prowess. While his questions continue to ask for definitions and parsing, their quality shifts subtly but notably. Rather than asking about unfamiliar words, he asks about familiar words used in unfamiliar contexts: for the line, "And all the boards did shrink" (Coleridge, *Rime of the Ancient Mariner* 120), he asks, "What is the force of *and* here?" (381); for the line, "Another race hath been, and other palms are won" (Wordsworth, "Ode: Intimations of Immortality" 199), he asks, "What is meant by *race* here?" (396). His increased use of the second person acknowledges the greater importance of the reader in determining appropriate meanings: for the lines "of a mood / Which 'gainst the world in war had stood" (Byron, *The Prisoner of Chillon* 94–5), he asks, "What is the force of *had stood* here? How would you explain this usage?" (402); for the lines, "She closed the door, she panted, all akin / To spirits of the air, and visions wide" (Keats, *The Eve of St. Agnes* 201–02), he asks, "What do you think is meant by *visions wide*?" (410).

His glosses even praise usages that a grammarian might view as errors but that he justifies, as in his reading of lines from Byron's *The Prisoner of Chillon* on Bonnivard's reaction to his younger brother's death: "So tearless, yet so tender–kind, / And grieved for those he left behind" (188–189). Hales notes, "There is much delicacy in this plural. By such a fanciful multiplying of the survivors the elder brother prevents self-intrusion; himself and his loneliness are, as it were, kept out of sight and forgotten" (402–03). Hales picks up on the strangeness of Byron's pronoun "those," since the only person "left behind" by the younger brother's death is Bonnivard himself. Rather than seeing this usage as an error or as an instance of Byron's sloppiness, he sees it as a mark of "delicacy" in masking the painful solitude that Bonnivard's brother's death creates for him and him alone. Where most nineteenth-century critics emphasized the egomania of Byron's heroes, Hales, through close philological attention, finds an important counter-moment of self-effacement. Maybe his most telling gloss occurs when he confronts two lines from *Adonais*: "And keep thy heart light, lest it make thee sink / When hope has kindled hope, and lured thee to the brink" (422–23). He writes what a contemporary editor would never admit: "I cannot explain these two lines" (422). Giving up any persona of mastery, he does not blame his failure on Shelley in the way that T. S. Eliot would in the twentieth century, but poses his failure as a challenge to the reader: maybe we can explain what he could not.[6] The closer that Hales's glosses come to questions about philology, the less authoritative their presentation gets. Hales asks questions without providing answers and even confesses when he does not have an answer.

Hales's notes expand the exemplary function of poetry in relation to English. To study earlier poetry is to learn definitions (many archaic) and to reinforce knowledge of English grammar. To learn Romantic poetry also requires knowledge of definitions and grammar, but then asks the reader to put that knowledge to use in the context of what I have called stylization: recognizing how an author has manipulated English grammar and syntax for local effect. Hales's experimental philology asks students to look carefully at poetry, but does not require them to subordinate their knowledge to larger governing unities. Indeed, his method raises a challenge similar to the one that I described in the previous chapter in relation to the culture of the extract: does the requirement to make sense of the work as a whole detract from the ability to understand its parts?[7] Even more, why should a global interpretation be privileged over a local gloss?

His glosses have another function as well: to emphasize the heterogeneous, shifting nature of English. Rather than appearing as a mystical code embodying the genius of the nation, English in *Longer English Poems* combines old and new meanings, dialect with respectable English, classicism with vernacularity. In an essay of 1867, Hales loudly defended dialects: "Let us then carefully remember what is meant by calling the provincial languages of England English dialects—that, in calling them so, we acknowledge them to be of as good blood and birth as that language to which we now arrogate the name of English" ("English Dialects" 558). Studying English poetry, for Hales, let students remain in contact with English dialects even as they went to elite schools and universities. Philological understanding was potentially a form of political understanding because it encouraged an inclusive picture of the nation.

The question remains of how Hales's textbook was actually used. It certainly proved exportable. From the evidence that I have found, Hales's work, like that of Blair and Campbell, found an even more enthusiastic audience in the United States than in Britain itself.[8] Cornell University's register for 1877–78 notes, for example, that Hales's *Longer English Poems* was required for both semesters of the third year (*Cornell University Register* 63); J. M. Hart notes similarly in 1886 that Hales's anthology occupies an entire year in the English major at the University of Cincinnati ("Rhetoric—Style—Meter" 103).

It also found a friendly reception in the colonies. When examining students at the Higher Training College in Cairo in 1926, Robert Graves learned that much of their instruction came from Hales's anthology. Graves believed that this instruction created a "moralistic, character-forming view of English literature" among Egyptian students (*Good-Bye to All That* 307). Yet the account of actual students in a colonial setting suggests that the effects of Hales's anthology were not necessarily so predictable. Students writing about their college days in Lahore between 1909 and 1911 reveal that their teacher followed Hales, but also challenged him:

> When teaching Hales' "Longer English Poems," Dr. Iqbal was at his best. It was a great pleasure to listen to a poet of Iqbal's eminence explaining the elegance and charm of a poem, and elucidating the meaning which the poet wished to convey. It was our rare good luck that we had such a teacher.

Another student remembered that Iqbal "would usually teach only one stanza in a period . . . He would quote corresponding Urdu, Persian, or even Arabic verses, to bring home the thought contained in the poem. . . . The Allama created so much interest that the students felt as if they themselves were the authors of the poem" (q. in Masud-Ul-Hasan, *Life of Iqbal* 1:88–89). The slow pace of Iqbal's class suggests the seriousness

of his philological approach. Like Hales, he finds the local moment to be
more telling than a larger thematic interpretation.

The teacher whom these students describe, Muhammad Iqbal, is a central figure in the founding of modern Pakistan, one whose poetry, philosophy, and politics continue to be widely studied and praised.[9] He is
acknowledged as Pakistan's national poet and a critical figure in developing
an ideology calling for a separate Muslim state, although he died before the
establishment of Pakistan.[10] Many intellectual and political influences went
into Iqbal's work, and I would not want to overstate the significance of his
time using Hales's anthology. Yet his students' descriptions of his pedagogy are notable in two respects. First, using Hales provided another venue
for Iqbal's characteristic movement back and forth between European and
Islamic sources; just as his philosophical writings use comparisons and
contrasts with European philosophy to explain major Islamic texts, so his
pedagogy might be understood as an example of what Dipesh Chakrabarty
calls "provincializing Europe," using texts from the Islamic tradition to understand *Longer English Poems.* Whereas Hales's notes refer to other English
poems, as well as to texts from Greek and Latin, as appropriate sources,
Iqbal embeds Halesian philology in a different linguistic context.

Second, the many languages that Iqbal used suggest that Hales's anthology allowed him to demonstrate a key aspect of his understanding of
Islam, its multilingualism. In "The Muslim Community," a lecture from
1911, he noted, "It is not the unity of language or country . . . that consti-
tutes the basic principle of our nationality" (*Speeches, Writings, and Statements* 104). In his own writing, Iqbal was a multilingual author, writing
major works in Urdu, Persian, and English. Teaching English poetry became an occasion not to reinforce the hegemony of the English language,
but to extend Halesian philology in ways that underscored the linguistic
richness of the Islamic past. Far from being a moribund exercise in pedantry, Iqbal used a philological pedagogy to transform English literature
in ways that his students found mesmerizing.

Yet the approach that provided the springboard for Iqbal's inspired
pedagogy in colonial India was loudly condemned by New Critics in
America, as this quotation from *The Well Wrought Urn* reveals:

> In order to understand Shakespeare, we simply have to understand what
> Shakespeare's words mean. And the implications of this latter point are im-
> mense; for they go far beyond the mere matter of restoring a few obsolete

meanings. Tied in with language may be a way of apprehending reality, a philosophy, a whole world-view. (Brooks 236)

In light of such an attack, Hales's quirky, experimental glosses of Romantic poems faded before the close reading of organic unities; his privileged category of English gave way to the interpretation, the critic, and the difficult otherworldliness of literature; *Understanding Poetry* took over for *Longer English Poems*. Many of the activities required by Hales were ceded to other disciplines, such as communication and linguistics. Most of all, the philological awareness that was primary for Hales and Iqbal gave way before the all-conquering power of the expressive totality of organic form, the "whole world-view" that Brooks claims is the real object of analysis.[11]

Losing Hales's methodology has created a vexed situation in literary studies, whereby close attention to textual detail continues to be valued, especially in the undergraduate classroom, but the linguistic metalanguage that would enable such attention is not. Students are rightly baffled, especially those without the skills to intuit from a teacher's examples exactly how a close reading should proceed. Neither older categories like taste and discrimination nor newer ones like critical thinking or theoretical awareness can compensate for the inability to recognize syntactic, phonological, metrical, and semantic aspects of English as a surface code. The result mystifies the classroom's relation to literature in English by assuming that the language of the literary work that is read and taught is the same as the language spoken and written by its students, which is supposedly also the same as the disciplined English of the professor. Avoiding philology keeps alive the assumptions behind this supposedly obvious continuity among Englishes; it creates the illusion of linguistic common ground where none exists.

The dream of pure English survives even among teachers who may reject many of the specific recommendations of the eighteenth-century English experts. Not foregrounding English as a code enables it to become an unquestioned given and bypasses the educational agency of the literature classroom. This avoidance neither prepares students to be careful readers of literature nor provides them with the analytic skills to understand the changing role of English in a global culture. Hales's anthology stands as a challenge to reimagine the tools of philology in light of contemporary educational, aesthetic, cultural, and political goals.

My second case study concerns the afterlife of elocution. In 1929,

J. Clifford Turner made sound recordings for His Master's Voice of eight poems (HMV B3151 and 3152), which represented an unprecedented re-mapping of British literary history through the oral performance of short Romantic lyrics.[12] Four poems on the recordings are by canonical Romantic poets (Blake, Wordsworth, Shelley, and Keats); the others represent either a Romantic afterlife (Tennyson's "Now Sleeps the Crimson Petal" and Browning's "Prospice") or earlier poems that can be assimilated to the Romantic model of generic poeticity (Shakespeare's Sonnet 30 and an excerpt from Milton's *Samson Agonistes*). At first glance, this repertoire seems unexceptionable: the poems and authors are familiar, and they are short enough for a 78 rpm recording. Yet this familiarity should not mask the document's novelty: so far as I have found, nothing like it had ever been sold before. Clifford Turner's work represents the first widely available sound anthology not only of Romantic poems, but of any British poetry at all, which had previously had a small place in sound recordings. I want to examine who Clifford Turner was, why Romantic poetry played such a large role in his recording, and what it says about the cultural history of Romanticism and voice.

In Turner's recordings, two complex histories come together: the history of the performance of Romantic poetry, and the history of recorded sound. During the Romantic period, discomfort with voice did not prevent the Romantic poets from reading their own poetry aloud, sometimes with dramatic effects, as in Coleridge's recitations of *Christabel*.[13] Yet the actual sale and circulation of works by Romantic poets (Scott, Byron, and Hemans excepted) were so small that such readings reached only a fraction of the population. A larger listening audience for Romanticism had to wait until much later in the century when cheaper editions and anthologies of shorter poems or excerpts became available.

In the case of Hales, I focused on his use in the schools, but the reading of Romantic poetry was also part of the more general Victorian pastime of reading aloud.[14] The period from the late nineteenth century to roughly World War II was a golden age for the widespread accessibility and popularity of poetry as a vehicle for oral recitation.[15] Only in rare cases, however, was the poetry contemporary; it tended to be poetry from much earlier in the nineteenth century, like that of Tennyson or Longfellow. Oral recitation encouraged anthologies designed less for classroom study, like Hales's, than for reading aloud, although there was certainly overlap between books used at home and in the classroom.

What may be most striking about such anthologies is the relatively small role played in them by introspective lyric poetry. Victorian elocution largely avoided the poems that form the backbone of Hales's *Longer English Poems*. Instead, it favored what I have termed in chapter 4 percussive Romanticism, in which a pounding regularity of meter does the work of voice. William Ernest Henley's *Lyra Heroica: A Book of Verse for Boys*, for example, has no Shelley and little Keats ("On First Looking Into Chapman's Homer" is retitled "To the Adventurous"), though it includes much Byron and the usual Hemans ("Casabianca" and "The Pilgrim Fathers"). A successful, or at least adequate, reading of these poems can be achieved by sticking, with little compromise, to a regular metrical scheme, in ways quite unlike the complexities of Romantic lyrics. Such poems were part of a canon of texts that circulated widely through anthologies in English-speaking countries in the late nineteenth and early twentieth centuries.

Yet once this culture of oral recitations reached its peak, the gramophone changed it. Although I have earlier described the eighteenth-century conflict between the proto-scientific expository prose of the Scottish academics and the humanist culture of elocution, one of the ironies of nineteenth-century sciences is that elocution spurred several scientific inventions, including the telephone and the gramophone, through its mechanization of the voice and concern with voice reproduction.[16] The gramophone dispensed with the complex language of face and gesture central to oral recitation: the multi-dimensional aspects of communication theorized during the eighteenth and nineteenth centuries disappeared. Instead, the machine replaced the body as the medium of transmission.

According to Kittler, the gramophone demanded a new relation between auditor and text because it empties "out words by bypassing their imaginary aspect (as signifieds) for their real aspects (the physiology of the voice)" (*Discourse Networks* 246). But vocal physiology had been a subject of concern long before the appearance of gramophones, through the work of elocutionists like Bell. What was new about the gramophone was that it made the voice infinitely reproducible. Edison inaugurated his gramophone company with a quotation from Wordsworth: "Shall I call thee bird, or but a wandering voice?" (q. in Camlot, "Early Talking Books" 154). Yet his quotation missed the point: the gramophone prevented a voice from wandering because, on the machine, it would always sound the same. Cut off from the bodily culture of gesture, the voice became pure articulation. Not surprisingly, by far the most common use of early spoken word recording was to teach correct English diction, as in Shaw's *Pygmalion* (1914). Pronunciation of English could become authoritative only once the gramophone froze it forever, cut off from the vicissitudes of the body.

In terms of its relation to imaginative literature, early sound recording continued the late-Victorian culture of oral recitation in mixing high culture (poetry and Shakespearean speeches) and low (comic monologues). Yet, as Camlot has documented, it also acknowledged the presence of the new medium; early sound recording compensated for the loss of gesture and of co-presence in space and time of performer and audience by overemphasizing the role of sound ("Early Talking Books"). For example, comic monologues on early recordings typically featured nonstandard Englishes (as in the highly popular monologues in the person of Cohen the Jew, or Fred Terry's drunk scene from *The Scarlet Pimpernel*) or mimics who imitated famous actors, as in Bransby Williams's 1914 monologue copying George Alexander, Forbes Robertson, and others.[17] As for high culture, in addition to scenes from Shakespeare, two classics of percussive Romanticism received a disproportionate share of recordings because they were sound spectaculars: Poe's "The Bells" (1849) and Tennyson's "Charge of the Light Brigade" (1854). In both, the phonological quality of the poems trumps their semantic content in ways that made them perfect for the contextless void of the gramophone sound. The regularity of the meter may also have helped the medium's low fidelity: meter could be heard even if the words were not.

In this context, Clifford Turner's recordings of Romantic poetry were a striking innovation. In recording Romantic lyrics, Clifford Turner reacted against Victorian elocution and the self-reflexivity of early recorded sound. Given his background, this reaction was not surprising. He came not from the class of amateur readers and music hall actors, but from a group of London-based professionals who transformed the sound of the English public voice.[18] At the center of this new vocal culture was London's Central School of Speech and Drama, founded in 1906 by Elsie Fogerty. Although the school later became famous as a training-ground for actors, Fogerty understood herself chiefly as a voice teacher eager to demolish elocution: "We must throw away the horrible false tradition of 'recitation,' which stood self-condemned in that it never succeeded in interpreting anything but the worst, the most vulgar and meaningless of verse" (*The Speaking of English Verse* x). In place of this "false tradition," she developed her own high modernist aesthetics, encouraging students to extinguish their personalities to become pure media for poetic voice: "Dear: it's all *in* the words; we are only instruments to *convey* the meaning. Just let the poet speak" (q. in Cole, *Fogie* 51). Fogerty made sure that real poets knew about the results of her work: she asked many leading poets of the day, including Yeats, Laurence Binyon, and Gordon Bottomley, to adjudicate her school's annual Diction Examinations (*Fogie* 51). Later, she played a key role in the modernist revival of the poetic drama, since she trained the speakers who performed the first choruses in Eliot's *The Rock* and *Murder in the Cathedral* and also taught Laurence Olivier and John Gielgud how to speak Shakespeare (*Fogie* 36, 155, 164–69).

More significantly for my purposes, she was also Clifford Turner's teacher: she regarded him as a star pupil. He came to her attention at the famous Oxford Recitations, established by John Masefield in 1923; these annual competitions during the 1920s, judged by prestigious poets and critics, raised national awareness of and skill in oral recitation of poetry.[19] Masefield and the judges moved from the heterogeneous mixture of the Victorian recitation anthologies to a more recognizably elite canon: Chaucer, Shakespeare, Donne, Milton, Gray, and the major Romantics. Of these, the poets closest to Masefield's heart were the Romantics, whom he viewed as the spring of all subsequent poetry.[20] For Masefield, the Oxford Recitations reproached both the older elocutionary tradition of percussive Romanticism and Eliot's high modernist aesthetics by taking what he saw as the best of the English verse to a wide audience.[21]

Although Masefield intended to promote amateur speakers, speakers with professional training soon dominated the Oxford Recitations, especially those from Fogerty's school. Clifford Turner was one of the earliest and best proponents of this new style. He had met Elsie Fogerty as a competitor, and she offered him a scholarship to the Central School; in 1926, he won the Men's Medal in the competition (Cole, *Fogie* 107). He and other winners from Fogerty's school credentialized her new mode of public speaking, one that rejected Victorian methods for a modern style of voice characterized by precise diction, absence of musical accompaniment, a reduced gestural vocabulary, a privileging of voice against meter, and a restrained range of volume and inflection.

Those not able to attend the recitations longed to have access to the new style of English speaking that they featured. In 1926, the prestigious

Anglo-Saxonist W. J. Sedgefield wrote to the *Times Literary Supplement* that any poetry lover "doubtless has his own way of reading verse, but he may not be persuaded that it is the best possible way." For poetry lovers to learn the "best possible way," Oxford Recitation winners should make recordings, since they were "acknowledged by poets or by good judges of poetry to be really competent" ("Records of Recitations" 218). A writer to *The Gramophone* who signed himself "B. P. L. C." agreed with Sedgefield and hoped that "lovers of English poetry" would "attend to the matter themselves" by creating such recordings, with or without recording companies ("Recording of English" 66).

Luckily for readers like Sedgefield, Clifford Turner's recordings for the Education Department of His Master's Voice in 1929 gave them what they wanted: an Oxford Recitation winner reciting poetry.[22] Although I have found no evidence that Masefield dictated Clifford Turner's choice of poems, the repertoire fits exactly into the image of English poetry promoted by Masefield at the Oxford Recitations, with the Romantic lyric as the blueprint. In my discussion of Romanticism's response to elocution, I contrasted two ways in which sound became prominent, patterned and percussive Romanticism. Clifford Turner's recordings replaced the second with the first, and thereby rejected the older elocutionary style for a new one designed for electronic reproduction.[23] His readings exchange the sharp fluctuations in pitch, volume, and timbre characterizing earlier sound recordings for a quieter, restrained intoning. His voice combines clarity of pronunciation with a deliberate, sustained articulation that is not quite chanting but steers away from conversational speech. While Clifford Turner's readings are hardly devoid of emotion, the overall effect is one of presenting the poems rather than inhabiting them, as if, in accordance with Elsie Fogerty's instructions, the speaker strove to be a medium for the poet's words.

Clifford Turner's speaking style suited new technological developments in the recorded sound of the 1920s, especially electronic recording. Electronic recording increased fidelity and freed the performer from bellowing into a horn. Whereas older recordings played to the presence of technology by drawing attention to sound, Clifford Turner's did the opposite by refusing to acknowledge any technological mediation whatsoever. His recordings created an idealized image of a voice polished into an all-purpose clarity of diction and articulation, an ideal that hid its careful suitability for the particular medium of electronic sound reproduction.

The Romantic lyric was the perfect vehicle for this pioneering use of the medium. The Romantic lyric used by Clifford Turner represents the voice of a subject who is never explicitly aware of the formal mechanisms enabling that voice. While many Romantic poems present subjects who are intensely aware that they are part of a poem, as in Wordsworth's *Prelude*, lyrics that came to be most identified with the Romantic period in the early twentieth century aim to present an unmediated interiority, even as their language arises in relation to complex verse techniques. As such, this divorce between content and form mapped perfectly onto the technological project of Clifford Turner's recording. In these poems, an individual expressive voice emerges from a complex set of technological materials that the voice itself never acknowledges.

By the mid-1930s, the boom in the oral recitation of poetry represented by the Oxford Recitations and Clifford Turner's recordings had diminished, though it had a long, interesting afterlife in schoolrooms, poetry festivals, and the BBC's Third Programme.[24] This diminishment coincided with the rise of the talking cinema and of television. Although neither form proved friendly to spoken poetry, both required the voice that Clifford Turner had cultivated for his recordings of Romantic lyric, one that could move seamlessly from the auditorium to the intimate medium of the microphone. As such, his articulation acquired enormous cultural power, largely through his position as voice teacher at Fogerty's Central School of Speech and Drama and also at the Royal Academy of Dramatic Arts (RADA). As a teacher, Clifford Turner trained the voices of major actors of the twentieth century, including Peter O'Toole, Albert Finney, Theodore Bikel, and Alan Bates; his 1950 *Voice and Speech in Theatre* is still in print and is recognized as a classic.[25] From Clifford Turner came the notorious RADA voice, a particular style of enunciation common to these actors that, through the medium of film, has come to have enormous influence on perceptions of Britishness, the relation of language to nation, the representation of subjectivity, images of empire, and markers of class.[26]

His pupils' memoirs indicate the importance of Romantic poetry, especially Keats, to his vocal training. Martin Jarvis, for example, remembers struggling through Keats's "Ode to a Nightingale." The assignment was particularly daunting because Keats was Clifford Turner's "favourite poet"; according to Jarvis, the best he received was a "nice try" (*Acting Strangely* 28–29).[27] Jarvis underscores that Keats functioned as a kind of Everest for Clifford Turner's students: rather than being asked to produce believable non-standard English or to recite a piece from Shakespeare or Shaw, the ultimate exercise for the production of voice was Keats.

To be able to recite the ode successfully meant that the student had developed a cultured voice that could be applied to any medium: film, radio, sound recording, or live theater. No matter what role a student might play or what medium he or she might employ, the RADA voice retained its distinctive presence, an unchanging base of technique on which individualizing accents, gestures, costumes, and other markers of performance could be draped. Through Clifford Turner's work, the Romantic lyric provided the critical medium for the formation of this voice because of its resistance to the elocutionary foregrounding of sound. A good performance of Romantic lyrics had to acknowledge but hide their formal mediation in the same way that the skilled performer had to acknowledge but hide the technological mediation of sound reproduction. In the twentieth century, the unheard melodies of Romanticism enabled an older technology of the human voice to be reinvented for an era of mechanical reproduction.

The afterlife of Romantic pronunciation has a second, parallel history in the American academy. In narratives that English professors have written about their discipline's history, oral recitation's large role has mostly vanished. This forgetting has occurred because oral recitation left English departments early in the century and relocated in speech departments, which have since become communication departments. What was once a thriving educational and scholarly enterprise exists now only in a few vestigial forms, such as high school speech contests.

Teaching oral recitation assumed that it alone enabled "*the development of adequate mental and emotional responsiveness to the meaning of literature,*" to quote Wayland Maxfield Parrish, author of a key textbook in the field, *Reading Aloud* (18). Particularly interesting is Parrish's sense of the value of oral reading for the English teacher, "for upon her interpretations will depend largely the taste for poetry of her pupils. Her example, in voice, in pronunciation, in melody, in feeling, in appreciation, will make or mar their taste for fine speech and fine literature" (23). Parrish connects the university to secondary education and links oral interpretation to female professionalism: historically, speech departments were among the first to employ and hire female faculty members and graduate students.

Equally relevant are the institutional underpinnings of Parrish's book: the oral interpretation of literature flourished in non-elite institutions (Parrish taught at the University of Pittsburgh), which admitted women long before the Ivy League.

For Parrish, the oral recitation of literature requires good pronunciation. Poetry in particular depends upon it; discussing Wordsworth's "It is a beauteous evening," he notes that "no matter how deep and rich the voice of the reader," the beauty of the opening lines "would be lost if they were read . . . thus, as by one with foreign dialect":

Eet ees a beaut-yus efenink, kem andt frree;
Thee howly time ees quiet ass a non
Breat-less wit' ad-o-rra-tion.   (175)

Whereas Wordsworth's prosaicism rebelled against Della Cruscan excess, the prosaicism that for Wordsworth resisted translation into audibility had become by the twentieth century the gold standard for good English. Wordsworth's poem lacks foregrounded aural features (assonance, iconic prosodic effects, rhyme) that would lead the ear to focus solely on them, yet retains enough markers of poetry (iambic pentameter) to prevent it from being heard merely as prose. For those listening to the recital, attention hones in on the purity of English diction, in a way that, for Parrish, cruelly exposes any imperfection.

Parrish's message for anyone with a "foreign" accent was plain: English poetry was not for them. Doing so masked the fact that what a "native" accent was for this poem is by no means clear. Parrish was teaching in Pittsburgh, where few of his students would have had a British accent; even if they had, the relation between twentieth-century British Received Pronunciation and the various pronunciations available when Wordsworth wrote was not straightforward. Parrish assumes that American English is not foreign to the pronunciation of British poetry, but that other Englishes are. Whereas Clifford Turner used the Romantic lyric to help credentialize professional actors, Parrish uses it as part of a more general stratifying system, separating those with good English from those without it.

New Criticism in the 1940s killed off the academic respectability of such oral recitation.[28] I. A. Richards declared that hearing a poem and reading it were the same: "Any line of verse or prose slowly read, will, for most people, sound mutely in the imagination somewhat as it would if read aloud" (*Principles* 91). René Wellek and Austin Warren's *Theory of Literature* maintained that oral recitation would wreck serious literary study:

> We must . . . distinguish between performance and pattern of sound. The reading aloud of a literary work of art is a performance, a realization of a pattern which adds something individual and personal and, on the other hand, may distort or even entirely ignore the pattern. Hence a real science of rhythmics and metrics cannot be based only on the study of individual recitals. (*Theory of Literature* 158)

Susanne Langer's immensely influential *Feeling and Form* noted, "The treatment of poetry as physical sound comparable to music rests, I believe, on an utter misconception of what a writer creates, and what is the role of sound in that creation" (277). This distaste for recitation lingers even in Paul de Man, who begins his lecture on "Time and History in Wordsworth" with notes on what it means to read a poem; oral recitation is the first mode he rejects (5).

In place of oral recitation, the New Critics reappropriated "voice," a unique, intangible entity conferring authenticity and pre-existing unity on a particular text or career; the concept has since become virtually omnipresent in literary, cultural, and composition studies.[29] A writer at last finds his or her voice; a critic should recognize subtle differences between different textual voices; those on the margins need to be given voice. In some cases, analysis of voice may attend to a work's sounds, but usually only at the level of phonemes safely inside the work. The array of inflections and gestural markers that eighteenth-century elocutionists also understood to be in the text, such as emphases, pauses, climaxes, and so forth, fell out of twentieth-century discussions of voice because they were too threateningly dependent on the individual reciter. Voice in literary criticism comes from writing, not speech.

The fall of oral recitation and the rise of textual voice accompanied changes in the social and institutional missions of criticism. Getting rid of oral recitation made a clean break with the tensions around the relation between British and American English that Parrish skirted in his discussion. In silence, it would be harder to notice the peculiar configuration of English studies as a multinational enterprise that pretended it was not one. New Criticism shifted the vanguard in professional literary study to elite universities and colleges, away from coeducational to all male institutions, from close connection with secondary education to a marked separation, and from a social setting for the literary experience to an elite academic one. The faintly queer aura that lingered over elocutionary practice, with its unsettling theatricality and numerous "single ladies" and "pretty gentlemen," faded before the New Critical investment in heterosexual imagery and plots.[30] Most importantly of all, New Criticism disseminated and reproduced itself through particular modes of expository prose: the textbook, the scholarly monograph, and the literary critical essay. All had existed before New Criticism, but the New Critics introduced different standards for producing and evaluating them. More than anything else, oral recitation died off from its inability to modernize the discipline through the reproducible form of printed prose. As Paul Edwards notes, "Interpretation's fading from American universities in the postwar era relates in part to its difficulty in developing a research agenda resulting in scholarly publication" (*Unstoried* 9–10). Next to reams of New Critical scholarship, oral interpretation looked thin.

Further aiding this distance from oral interpretation was the rise of a peculiar mode of credentialization, the disciplinary voice.[31] This voice belongs to what Ellen Messer-Davidow calls "the professional order," consisting of "the character and conduct of practitioners" by which disciplines imprint themselves on the bodies of their subjects (*Disciplining Feminism* 45).The disciplinary voice translates into aural terms all the strictures of expository prose, resulting in a firm antitheatricality, a narrow range of volume, pitch, and inflection, minimization of facial and bodily gestures, and, more recently, the emergence of overheads and Powerpoint slides to present an aural redundancy to a printed text. It uses a host of lecturing practices to signal resistance to aurality: microphone awkwardness, minimal distinction between critical prose and literary quotation, routinization of questions and answers. As such, it distinguishes itself from competing vocal modes, including those of the theater, the pulpit, the poetry slam, and the literary chat.

Perceptions of smartness are carefully coordinated with mastery of the professional voice, as displayed in the classroom, the departmental meeting, and the academic conference, with significant repercussions for pedagogy, workplace climate, and extra-academic relations. While many professors value oral recitation in the classrooms, it remains strictly in the classroom, not in higher-stakes venues, such as the hiring interview or the professional conference. As Roland Barthes notes, some speakers embody this voice straightforwardly or, by "correcting, adding, wavering," can signify discomfort with this authority and so be perceived as "human, too human—*liberal*," as when they add asides, or fill talks with arch puns and turns of phrase ("Writers, Intellectuals, Teachers" 192). What remains is a persistent discomfort with the physical performance of voice, even as "voice" and "performance" become omnipresent as objects of investigation.

Rejecting oral recitation mattered not only for literary criticism as a whole, but also for Romanticism in particular. Although the founding works on Romanticism in the United States, such as M. H. Abrams's *The Mirror and the Lamp* (1953) and Earl Wasserman's *The Finer Tone* (1953), rebelled against New Critical tenets, a major project in them was assimilating Romantic poetry to expository prose. Initially, this prose is largely that of Romantic criticism, as when Wasserman writes, "The mode of *Alastor* is best understood in the light of Shelley's earlier experiment with the skeptical and paradoxical manner of proceeding in his *Refutation of Deism*" (*Shelley* 12). Later, contextualizing historical documents and theoretical texts supplemented the role initially performed by such works as Shelley's tracts, Coleridge's philosophy, or Keats's letters, but, in all cases, Romantic poetry nested safely within expository prose. Even more, the longer, more prosaic a Romantic work was, the more academically respectable it became, as in the elevation of Blake's epics, Wordsworth's *Prelude*, Keats's *Fall of Hyperion*, or, more recently, the Romantic novel.

The result is a strange bifurcation in literary study whereby the restless exploration of new approaches and texts coexists with the ossification of the disciplinary voice. While the semantics of academic speech have altered, styles of presentation, forms of address, and general prosodic features have changed little; insofar as they have, they have further privileged the dominance of expository prose, as in the emergence of Powerpoint presentations. Why should anyone listen to a lecture that will later be published, virtually unchanged?

English professors remain an important source of information for students about what counts as good English, since we are often presumed to be native speakers, though not necessarily British ones. Moreover, spoken and heard English remains a chief medium for disseminating knowledge about literature, yet the profession of literary criticism has virtually no conceptual frameworks for understanding or evaluating it as medium, only as topic. As a result, we are poorly prepared to understand changes to literary study that will occur as a result of changes in spoken English, from the globalization of English, the increasing multilingualism of the classroom, and the rise of computerized modes of voice reproduction that claim to be both more correct and more emotionally apposite than actual speakers.

Calls for an increased role for oral recitation in the classroom are sometimes couched in a vocabulary of immediacy, as if a good reading were equivalent to a transparent experience of a work of literature. No one in the Romantic period would have believed this: the rise of elocution had made clear how complicated the stakes were in any act of reading aloud. The voice of the teacher is different from the voice of the student, both in terms of the physical quality of enunciation and in terms of the social valorization of voice. To realize a literary work orally results in quite different kinds of performances. Moreover, the voices of students in a classroom are likely to represent a wide range of possible relations to English, in terms of various fluencies, modes of articulation, accents, and pronunciation preferences, as well as differences arising from age, geography, gender, and socioeconomic status.

My point is not to prevent professors from encouraging students to read aloud or to rob anyone of the pleasure of listening to and performing oral reading and listening. But reading aloud instantiates a particular use of the author stemming from the Romantic period. In reciting a poem by Wordsworth or Keats, it is easy to use the metonymy that one is "reciting Wordsworth" or "reciting Keats," as if the author and the poem were one. What this metonymy masks is that recitation also involves speaking English. The fiction of the author makes it seem that all speakers share in the author's mystical unity, since they are all reciting him or her. It presents a different version of the problem created by the loss of philology, whereby English becomes the unexamined common ground that elides historical difference. Reading aloud is not merely interpretation by other means: it is also a site for the battle over control of voice. As such, it offers a powerful site for analyzing the role of the university and of English literature in producing more and less valued voicings of English.

For my third case study, I turn to the later history of the sentence and the pivotal work of John Wesley Hales. In his landmark essay on English teaching, Hales singled out the sentence as the cornerstone of what the young needed to know. He argued that the student

> should be shown that language is logical,—that it is not capricious and arbitrary in its arrangements, but reflects the operations of the mind. In fact, he should be made thoroughly familiar with the *sentence*—with the sentence in

all its varieties, simple and compound; should acquaint himself thoroughly
with the relation to each other of the various parts of it, with the modifica-
tions of the general sense that each one produces, with the significance of the
order in which they come, and the results that would ensue from any transposition or inversion of them,—in short, with the subtle, delicate, vigorous
expressiveness of the sentence. ("Teaching of English" 306)

Hales's pedagogical goals for the sentence begin conventionally by recognizing rhetorical differences between simple and compound sentences.
Yet as his list goes on, it abandons the conceptual framework of the eighteenth-century English experts and becomes increasingly complex. His
goals for studying the sentence move away from the atomized sentence
to its role in a larger discourse. Students need to learn how each sentence
modifies "the general sense," how they are ordered, and how the sense
would change if the order were changed. Rather than theorizing the paragraph or the thesis sentence, Hales uses the sentence to grapple with the
Lockean question of the relation between small units of discourse and
larger units of thought.

Sadly for later teaching, Hales never wrote a textbook comparable to
Longer English Poems to disseminate such an approach to prose. His vision
went largely unrealized, at least in terms of the textbook presentation of
sentences. One reason was that English literature already had a writer
who could supposedly serve as a model for sentence study: Macaulay.
Tributes to his clarity and to his sentences had become a commonplace of
nineteenth-century criticism: "The wonderful clearness, point and vigor
of his style, send his thoughts right into every brain" (Whipple, "Macaulay," 1:13); "As to its clearness, one may read a sentence of Macaulay twice,
to judge of its full force, never to comprehend its meaning" (Milman,
"Memoir" xxiv); "One can trace in his writing a constant effort to make
himself intelligible to the meanest capacity" (Minto, *Manual* 104); "He
never wrote an obscure sentence in his life" (Morley, "Macaulay" 388);
"His *Essays* and his *History* exhibit the most popular style which any English author has ever possessed" (Saintsbury, *Specimens* 364).

Interestingly, this fixation on Macaulay's clarity accompanied certain
reservations: it seemed to many to be purchased at the cost of shallowness, and the contrast was often drawn between Macaulay's perfect style
and shallow thought and Carlyle's chaotic writing but supposedly deeper
message.[32] Such comparisons may have reacted against Macaulay's evident
popularity: anyone who sold so many copies had to have flaws. Yet it also

suggested ambivalence about Macaulay as a prose model. It made him a bit too textbookish, a good writer for younger learners, but one who might be surpassed by those aspiring to more advanced thought.

What made the relation between Macaulay and Carlyle of more than merely historical interest is that the relation between them became ingrained in American pedagogy and continues to affect the teaching of writing. In the late nineteenth century, American colleges and universities created entrance exams, and in 1893, "the Association of Colleges and Preparatory Schools of the Middle States and Maryland set the pattern for the development of uniform college entrance examinations. These examinations tested the reading of a fixed list of English masterpieces" (Smith, "Development of Departments of Speech" 452). Year after year one of Macaulay's essays was a mandatory piece for study, in ways that altered high school curricula across the nation.[33]

American English professors agreed that, whatever their reservations about Macaulay, he was obviously the right choice for the young.[34] As Edwin L. Miller noted, "A thorough study of one of Macaulay's essays will do more to make him [the student] despise looseness of language and of logic than all the precepts in the rhetorics . . . He is the greatest of all awakeners of an enthusiasm for clear, exact, polished, manly utterance" ("Literary Study" 289). A thorough study of the Macaulayan sentence would filter who could and could not be considered worthy of college.

Macaulay's presence affected more than students: a generation of English professors in American universities like Stanford, Princeton, Cornell, and Yale gained their most prestigious publications by editing Macaulay's essays for high school use. When just what counted as research for an English professor was unclear, Macaulay came to the rescue. Editing Macaulay allowed professors a neat balancing act, whereby they could seem specialized and popular at the same time. While they displayed their specialization in their detailed introductions and editorial apparatus, these editions were designed for students, so their professorial erudition could seem to be designed not for narrow specialists but for a mass elite of high school students planning to go to college.

Macaulay's magical style enabled this balancing act; as a Yale professor noted,

> Every sentence is crisp, clear, and strong. The boy or girl who studies Macaulay's style is taking a composition tonic. It is the best remedy that can be sought for the diffuseness and inaccuracy of thought, loose and ineffective

sentence structure, and feeble use of words, that beset the average untrained writer. Clearness and force in thinking, speaking, and writing are the qualities best worth cultivating. "The first rule of all writing," said Macaulay, "that rule to which every other is subordinate, is that the words used by the writer shall be such as most fully and precisely convey his meaning to the great body of his readers." It is a rule which we may well make our motto. The teacher who makes the best use of Macaulay will not fail to direct continual attention to his style. (Smith, *Macaulay's Essays* xvi)

Repeatedly, American textbooks of the "Essay on Milton" foreground the need to study Macaulay's sentences:

Point out and discuss the characteristics of six sentences which may be taken as typical examples of Macaulay's sentence structure.

Give six examples of sentences which may be taken as models of excellence in construction. Explain, so far as possible, their specific points of excellence.

Mark ten examples of the loose sentence. Append a discussion of its nature and character as compared with other types. What cautions should be observed in regard to its use?

Ten examples of the periodic sentence. Discuss its use as in the preceding exercise. Show that the frequent employment of the period counteracts tendencies towards diffuseness and verbosity in sentence structure.

Ten examples of the balanced sentence, noting carefully its parallelisms— parallel phrases and clauses.

Compare it with other types for elegance, rhythm, harmony, antithetical effect. In what connection can it be used to best advantage? Arguments, descriptions, comparisons of objects, etc.

(Pearson, ed., *Macaulay's Essay on Milton* 33–34)

One might expect to find business prose consecrated for study, since guides to writing such prose were prevalent throughout the nineteenth century. Writing good business prose was a marketable skill, and prescriptions for business English followed all the rules of the Scottish academics.[35] But Macaulay's familiar prose seemed to offer a superior alternative to business prose because his essays combined the presentation of information (masses of historical data) with what was supposed to be an effective, interesting style for the general reader, as manifested by the magic of his sentences. The eighteenth-century purification of English aimed to create a common language that could unite Britain; the nineteenth-century elevation of Macaulay aimed to create a common style that could unite all readers and writers of English, regardless of national boundaires.

If American professors had reservations about Macaulay's shallowness, they appeased them by making Carlyle also a college entrance requirement, especially his "Essay on Burns." American high schools institutionalized the familiar division between a general model of familiar prose (Macaulay) and the unique work of genius (Carlyle). The textbooks of Carlyle emphasize that Carlyle, whatever his virtues, was no stylistic model: "Even at his best, Carlyle is a dangerous model to place before students who are not able to discriminate clearly . . . For this reason, the rhetorical study of this essay should be distinctively subordinate and incidental" (Farrand, ed. *Carlyle's "Essay on Burns"* xlviii).[36] "Any attempt to bring the essay as a whole, or by paragraphs, or even sentence by sentence, within the rules of modern composition is unavailing" (Aiton, ed. *"Burns" by Thomas Carlyle* 34). While textbooks of Macaulay's essays typically have writing exercises based on Macaulay's sentences, textbooks of Carlyle's do not.

One particular editor of Macaulay and Carlyle had great influence on the English sentence. In his edition of Macaulay's and Carlyle's essays on Boswell's *Life of Johnson*, he, like almost all Macaulay's admirers, praised Macaulay's sentences: "Macaulay is admirably clear. His professed aim was to write no sentence that did not disclose its meaning on first reading." He also admires Macaulay's "infrequency of metaphor and the almost total absence of digression," as well as his "short sentences," "*repeated structure*," and "strong sense of contrast."[37] It is only a small step from this praise to later, more famous advice: "Vigorous writing is concise. A sentence should contain no unnecessary words, a paragraph no unnecessary sentences, for the same reason that a drawing should have no unnecessary lines and a machine no unnecessary parts. This requires not that the writer make all his sentences short, or that he avoid all detail and treat his subjects only in outline, but that every word tell."[38] These sentences come from William Strunk, Jr.'s *The Elements of Style*. Originally written for his Cornell students, it became a phenomenon after E. B. White revised and expanded it in the late 1950s. As the most widely recognized work of prescriptive English ever written, it remains frequently recommended. It is also a standing embarrassment for composition studies, which has worked to distance itself from Strunk's quirky prescriptivism.[39]

The sentence's path from Blair and Murray through Macaulay to Strunk and White represents a line of succession whereby the eighteenth-century well-formed sentence has been passed down, almost unchanged, to the twenty-first century. At first, it may seem as if Macaulay is the odd man out in this succession because he was a popular historian, not a grammarian. But his presence is critical because he provided early academics like Strunk with an icon of familiar style, proof that good writing could cross boundaries of class and discipline to be available to all. Every time a piece of academic writing is condemned for "using jargon" or being "too specialized," norms created by the reception of Macaulay reassert themselves.

Macaulay's role in the teaching of English composition diminished dramatically after World War I, although one can find composition teachers recommending him well into the 1950s.[40] Yet Strunk's book and other works of prescriptive stylistics took over where Macaulay left off by enshrining the compositional principles that had been the basis of Macaulay's American success. At the same time, as I noted, a certain unease attended Macaulay's institutionalization. Although the Strunk and White tradition strove to hide this unease, it persisted nevertheless in a counter-tradition of sentence making found not in America's schools, but in its high modernist writers, especially in Gertrude Stein. Although Stein scholars have linked her experimental writing to many prominent intellectual trends, she herself wrote to Sherwood Anderson that she was "making a desperate effort to find out what is and isn't a sentence, having been brought up in a good old public school grammar and sentences are a fascinating subject to me. I struggled all last year with grammar, vocabulary is easier, and now I think before more grammar I must find out what is the essence of a sentence, sometimes I almost know but not yet quite" (*Sherwood Anderson/Gertrude Stein* 68).[41] In her 1931 *How to Write*, Stein returns to the fundamental challenges of the sentence that had never been resolved since its eighteenth-century theorization and that the enshrining of Macaulay had hidden rather than answered.

Stein's sentences take the abstract definitions of the English experts and subject them to minute scrutiny, pondering line by line what counts as a "complete thought," a grammatical sentence, a rhetorical sentence, a maxim, and a logical proposition:

> He looks like a young man grown old. That is a sentence that they could use.

> I was overcome with remorse. It was my fault that my wife did not have a cow. This sentence they cannot use. (*How to Write* 25)

Stein mixes model sentences with running commentary on them. Yet because the commentary also takes the form of sentences, the commentary comments on itself. The first sentence ("He looks like a young man grown old") counts as a "proper" sentence, one "they could use," because it fits all the requirements of a correct sentence. It also, however, alludes wittily to the dark mythology surrounding pure English, its close association between correctness and death. The syntax of the sentence is useable, but the meaning of the sentence implies that such usability has a cost: premature senescence.

The second set of sentences is more complex. It consists of three sentences: the first two are the examples, and the third the commentary, which also appears to comment on itself. If the first set of sentences examined a single sentence, Stein now moves to the effect of two associated sentences. It appears that when Stein writes "This sentence they cannot use," she refers to the second sentence, "It was my fault that my wife did not have a cow." Presumably, her condemnation refers to semantics: high-frequency collocation would lead to the expectation that the object of the sentence should be "baby," not "cow." "They cannot use" this sentence because, in terms of the context provided, it does not "make sense" in a way that "they" desire.

Yet the issue of usability reveals a sociolinguistic edge to sentences: it says more about the "they" than about sentences themselves. Stein insists on bringing large issues of politics, gender, and sexuality down to the micro-level of the sentence: to understand the sentence, she suggests, is to understand the operations of power and modernity. Readers literal-minded enough to reject this sentence as nonsense may also be closed to the hint of a nonce coding of "cow" as "orgasm." Stein revises an ancient metaphor connecting grammar to sexuality by underscoring the assumed patriarchal power of usable sentences. Even more, she may be condemning just what is meant by "use" when she reflects on sentences: what "they" can "use" may not be the best yardstick for judging the success or failure of a sentence.

In *How to Write*, Stein dissects sentences and paragraphs at multiple levels: what makes the start of a sentence ("Every sentence which has a beginning makes it be left more to them" [26]); what makes a sentence a fragment ("A part of a sentence may be a sentence without their meaning" [26]); what connects grammatical forms and thought ("Now what is the difference between a sentence and I mean" [31]); what emotional valences sentences produce ("Sentences make one sigh" [32]); and what gender has to do with sentences ("The difference in a sentence is that they will wish women" [31]). She introduces "Sentences and Paragraphs" with the epigraph, "A Sentence is not emotional a paragraph is" (23), as if it were a ringing affirmation or discovery, but the following exploration calls into question the confidence with which she asserts their difference.

Stein's *How to Write* turns out to be a better guide to English sentences than either Strunk and White or many textbooks in linguistics. Her work with the sentence has in turn inspired Ron Silliman in his theorization of the poetry of the L=A=N=G=U=A=G=E school. In his well-known essay on "The New Sentence," Silliman explicitly invokes Stein as his model. Like *How to Write*, the New Sentence joins the syntactic sentence to the absence of conventional discourse coherence, in ways that simultaneously invite and discourage what Silliman calls a "*secondary* syllogistic movement to create or convey an overall impression of unity" (92). The atomism of the New Sentence privileges grammar over author in ways that counter the mystique of voice that I discussed in relation to oral recitation. It also looks less like a rebellion against the well-formed sentence of Blair and Murray than a very literal-minded realization of it. A medium developed to ensure absolute clarity of information transfer between writer and reader has become an experimental site of writing designed to disrupt, question, and unsettle the possibilities of such transfer.

In contrast, traditional pedagogy in composition has never solved the problems posed by the well-formed sentence, especially its association with the familiar style developed by Macaulay and perpetuated by Strunk and White. Conventional prescriptivism stemming from Blair and Murray has given writing instructors a rich vocabulary for critiquing individual sentences at the level of grammar, punctuation, and style. At the larger discourse level, such as the paragraph or essay, many composition textbooks are organized around rhetorical structures, such as problem-response, comparison-contrast, definition, process, or cause-effect. The problem remains the gap between the two. Prescriptive works on the sentence rarely examine how to put together sentences to create a larger whole, except at the problematic level of the paragraph. In a widely used textbook, for example, advice for writing paragraphs first recapitulates advice for writing sentences ("Focus on a main point," "Develop the main point") and then recommends that paragraphs follow the same structures as complete essays ("Examples and Illustrations," "Narration," "Description," "Process") (Hacker, *Writer's Reference* 24–37). The paragraph appears not as a logical unit unto itself, but a confused hybrid: part sentence and part essay. Textbooks give little attention to building the paragraph from individual sentences or to scaffolding paragraphs into an overall argument.

Peter Elbow puts the difficulty well:

> Sentences are the basic building blocks of energy in words. That's why lots of writing teachers and stylists focus so intently on them. (In his widely read book on style, Joseph Williams works mostly with sentences.) But I ruin my writing experience and drive students crazy if I am too preoccupied with sentences alone. For we can read long passages of well-energized sentences and still experience a serious lack of organization. Whole texts need larger global pieces of energy. ("Music of Form" 627)

The overdevelopment of the sentence as the site of writing pedagogy has incurred the underdevelopment of an adequate metalanguage to describe how to move between micro- and macrostructures. What Elbow calls "global pieces of energy" depend on linking individual sentences to a larger unit of discourse, but traditional conceptions of the sentence block analysis of how to get from one to the other.

The fundamental difficulty is that creating such a linkage is impossible without adequate background knowledge of the topic on the writer's part. The fantasy of the familiar style is that such linkages can be taught purely at the level of rhetoric rather than at the level of content. Yet no amount of rhetorical training can compensate for lack of topic knowledge, although topic knowledge alone is necessary but not sufficient for good writing. Composition teachers have for years been unfairly blamed for not turning out students with adequate writing skills, as if writing skills could be abstracted from knowledge. On the contrary, composition instructors have struggled with an impossible task, teaching grammatical and rhetorical skills in advance of the knowledge levels that would allow them to be fully effective and that could motivate students to engage a topic deeply.[42] Although initiatives to move to writing within the disciplines have involved more professors in the teaching of writing, they have not solved the fundamental problem of the relation between specialized and general knowledge, only spread it more thinly. The result is the continued split that Elbow has diagnosed between the polarization of the sentence, analyzed at the level of grammar and style, and structure, analyzed at the level of rhetoric, with no metalanguage for describing the interrelation between them. Of course, graders of student writing address such issues at a practical level all the time, but, having learned effective links between micro- and macrostructure for one paper, students have difficulty transferring what they have learned to another paper in the same class, let alone in other classes.

The composition classroom thereby continues the tendency to treat English as the assumed common ground of relations between teachers, students, and texts that goes back to the enshrining of Macaulay in the American academy. What is needed is an alternative conception of the sentence, one suggested by Hales, not as a rhetorical unit but as a psychological one that plays a rôle in a reader's attempt to process information. A skilled reader may develop a macrostructural representation even of a fragmented text, given adequate motivation and background knowledge; readers with less skill, background, or motivation will not. A writing pedagogy that united a psychology of writing with a psychology of reading would supply a critical missing element in writing pedagogy identified by Elbow, the difficulty of teaching how to create large-scale coherence when rhetoric focuses on either the local or the global level.

In describing pedagogical effects of engagements with Romantic English, I am not recommending turning back the clock. English as a field of study will not suddenly acquire major institutional power if students can gloss the Anglo-Saxon roots of select words in poems, offering stirring recitals of "The Destruction of Sennacherib," or imitate select sentences in Macaulay's "Essay on Milton." The pedagogical methods described in this chapter were not golden keys to fine pedagogy: all could and probably did find quite mind-numbing realizations in particular classrooms. Yet they encouraged close attention to language without carrying with them some of the ideological burdens that close attention to language acquired with New Criticism and that have since become embedded in the practice of literary criticism: the production of the literary critical essay, the reduction of agency to the figure of the author, the privileging of totalities located either at the level of the work or of the cultural phenomenon.

Moreover, their loss has enabled the ossification of assumptions about the visibility of authorship and the invisibility of English that continue to function as problem points in the practice and teaching of literary criticism. These points are especially troublesome because the global status of

English has changed dramatically since the rise of New Criticism and its obliteration of older modes of pedagogy. English is no longer the site for a peculiar tension between Britain and the United States because it is now world-wide. Current criticism has responded to these changes in English primarily in terms of media studies: examinations of the effects of new modes of communication, such as email, blogs, vlogs, podcasts, and the internet. Yet to focus on the medium at the expense of the code is to mistake interactions for main effects. The globalization of English has given literature professors a remarkable opportunity to reinvent building blocks of literary criticism in light of a renovated understanding of philology.

Afterword

This book sprang from a fascination with prescriptive English. As an adolescent, I pored over books like Theodore Bernstein's *Watch Your Language*, memorized lists of stylistic recommendations, and studied the ins and outs of debated cruxes. Seeing movies, I had a soft spot for the fine-speaking villains who opposed the slangy hero, whose vital vernacularity was supposed to represent a breath of fresh air. The hero's casualness came with a high cost, like compulsory heterosexuality and conformity to nationalized codes of masculinity, which those who used pure English could ignore.

As a scholar, my interest is no longer in prescriptivism so much as in the effects of English as a code in relation to literary study. Yet I suspect that many English professors have had awkward experiences similar to mine: when we inform people we have just met that we are English professors, we sometimes hear, "Oh, now I'm going to have to watch my grammar" or "I was never really very good at spelling." More generally, we sometimes become for friends and family a court of final appeal for small points of grammar, pronunciation, or punctuation. The polite thing to do in such situations is to reassure those to whom we speak that we are not stern arbiters of usage. Yet this dodge masks what our relations to English may be. Although literary critics may not be prescriptive grammarians (and, indeed, many feel that prescriptive grammar is deluded), the fact remains that as educated professionals, we do use a privileged language variety. The ability to speak and write "good English" remains an often-unspoken qualification for becoming an English professor, and it marks our professional standing as a particular kind of intellectual laborer. There may be an edge of class contestation for those who worry that, in our presence, they will have to watch their language. These conversations are reminders, however unwelcome, that our relation to English does matter, and that we owe to it status and power.

These are increasingly vexed in relation to both the classroom's growing multilingualism and the globalization of English as the language of international finance, aided by the development of personal computers and the internet. Such tensions over language have always undergirded the study of English ever since Americans started teaching it, with a consequently uncertain relation to Britain. Yet now more than ever, assuming that English is common ground between professors, students, and the authors on the syllabus is problematic. I outlined in the previous chapter pedagogical problems that linger as a result of banishing philological investigation from literary criticism. My point is not that students all should take courses in the history of English, but that the fundamental aspects of what it means to study English in the twenty-first century have less to do with culture or literariness than with the status of English as a code. At the levels of writing, speaking, and reading, English professors and their students deserve closer attention to the historical status of English and the role of literary study in sustaining that status.

Before I began this book, I understood literary criticism as a rapidly changing field in which various approaches succeeded each other in quick succession. Studying philology has led me to a longer view, in which the persistence of certain enabling assumptions now makes the field look far more conservative to me. Questions about authorial agency that once were an important ground of discussion and debate have either dropped from sight or are relegated to books specifically about intention and authorship. In everyday practical criticism, authorship is largely taken for granted in ways that skirt some of the most interesting challenges presented by the opportunity to analyze literature in the first place. The history of literariness vanishes, to be replaced by a peculiar treatment of the literary canon as the obvious right place from which to launch a historical investigation of virtually any topic. While the concept of a new formalism is gaining increasing traction, it will not go significantly beyond the old formalism unless the concept of form itself is subject to the kind of scrutiny that philological analysis demands.

Given the historicist turn in Romanticism and in literary criticism more generally, blindness to the history of English appears a significant weak spot in much contemporary criticism. Any moment of practical criticism in which a critic engages closely with the language of a literary work needs a thorough awareness of the work's relation to English and the complicated array of possibilities that defined English usage during a period. This awareness should go beyond a vague sense of vulgar and refined usage to attend to the ramifications of syntactic choices, phonological arrangements, and lexical innovation. It also should avoid the assumption that authors' explicit pronouncements about language, intellectual backgrounds, or political positions are enough to explain their English. As I have emphasized throughout, English also has a history of its own that matters for the language of literary works.

An aspect of New Critical practice that remains an unquestioned foundation of much contemporary criticism is the association between the essay or book and the production of knowledge. An entire system of research and evaluation swirls around these forms, to the exclusion of all others. This system has erased a variety of older modes for creating knowledge about literature, such as the gloss, the recitation, the excerpt, and the imitation. For criticism to take philology seriously, it will need to investigate new genres and modes for registering interpretive insight. Admittedly, it is easier to call for such experiments than to realize them in practice: disciplinary habits die hard. Moreover, previous calls for experimental criticism have been disappointing insofar as their chief effect was to encourage autobiographical self-reflection. Nevertheless, the emergence of on-line scholarship opens up the opportunity for experiments with critical modes that is largely being ignored. Most on-line scholarship now remains content with reproducing older scholarly genres and, with them, a host of assumptions about the relations among author, work, and reader that can be usefully questioned.

Johnson's downbeat conclusion to his *Dictionary*'s "Preface" is a haunting reminder of the dangers of waxing too enthusiastic about the possibilities for change that any work of philology can create. No development has had a greater effect on contemporary English than computerization, in terms of adding words, revising mechanics, and creating new styles. The ability to produce printed English is now welded to the ability to work with software, yet the language governing the software is invisible and incomprehensible. Just as the English experts took over English from authors in the eighteenth century, so producers of code have taken over language from the school in the twenty-first century. No matter how deft

English professors become at developing websites and using online pedagogical tools, they will always work at a higher level of abstraction than that needed to understand and generate computer codes. English's globalization is paradoxically enabled by its demotion in the language chain to an aftereffect of far more arcane languages.

Yet the absence of English as a topic from literary criticism in English about English literature is too yawning a gap to remain unaddressed. Useful as the term "philology" has been as a descriptor, neither old-style philology nor contemporary linguistics is adequate to the task of examining the work of English in literary studies. My own disciplinary trajectory as a consequence of writing this book has been to turn to psychology as a means of investigating language production, reading comprehension, and writing strategies. My goal is not to advise all English professors to become psychologists but to encourage them to use the examination of English's history as a catalyst for breaking free of disciplinary assumptions that require masking it. Doing so should foster forms of knowing better able to encompass the relation between language and literature upon which the future of literary criticism will depend.

Abbreviations

The following abbreviations are used for works cited frequently in the text; full citations are provided for each in the "Works Cited."

BL   *Biographia Literaria* in *Samuel Taylor Coleridge: The Major Works*, ed. H. J. de Jackson

CPD   *Critical Pronouncing Dictionary* by John Walker

DENG *Dictionary of English Normative Grammar, 1700–1800* by Bertil Sundby et al.

EG   *English Grammar* by Lindley Murray

JK   *John Keats: A Longman Cultural Edition*, ed. Susan J. Wolfson

LRB   *Lectures on Rhetoric and Belles Lettres* by Hugh Blair

RN   *The Reading Nation in the Romantic Period* by William St. Clair

Notes

Introduction

1. For a brief overview of the presence of oratory and its subsequent demise, see Robert Scholes, *Rise and Fall of English* 3–12.

2. See also Kearney, "First Crisis"; Guillory, "Literary Study and the Modern System of the Disciplines."

3. On the larger context of Victorian philology, see Dowling, *Language and Decadence*, esp. ch. 2, "The Decay of Literature."

4. For example, Fish, "What is Stylistics"; Jameson, "Ideology of the Text"; Attridge, "Closing Statement."

5. For a criticism of poststructuralism's relation to linguistics, see Ingham, *Invisible Writing* 5–6.

6. See, for example, MacCabe, *Tracking the Signifier* 113–30; Pratt "Ideology"; Catano, *Language, History, Style* 191–92; DuPlessis, *Genders, Races, and Religious Cultures*, ch. 1, "Entitled New: A Social Philology of Modern American Poetry."

7. "English has undergone continuous and dramatic change throughout its three major periods; Old English (roughly from 450 to 1100), Middle English (from 1100 to 1500), and Modern English (from 1500 to the present)" (O'Grady et al., *Contemporary Linguistics* 289–90).

8. For a good linguistic treatment of developments in English since the eighteenth century, see Beal, *English in Modern Times*.

9. Note the absence of attention to English in two large-scale books on eighteenth-century Britain: Dror Wahrman's *Making of the Modern Self* and Michael McKeon's *Secret History of Domesticity*. It is also given only a brief mention in Roe, ed., *Romanticism: An Oxford Guide*.

10. Foucault, *Order of Things*, ch. 8, "Labour, Life, Language."

11. On the problems that traditional conceptions of the author pose for stylistics, see Catano, *Language, History, Style* 191–92.

12. McKusick, *Coleridge's Philosophy of Language*; Keach, *Arbitrary Power*; Turley, *Politics of Language*. Such works are all indebted to Aarsleff, *Study of Language*. See also Land, *From Signs to Propositions*; Cohen, *Sensible Words*; Bewell, *Wordsworth and the Enlightenment*, Part One, "The Origin of Language" 51–105; Paxman, "Genius of English"; Keach, "Romanticism and Language"; Hudson, "Theories of Language."

13. Smith, *The Politics of Language, 1791–1819*; Barrell, *English Literature in History, 1730–80*; Crowley, *Standard English and the Politics of Language*; Sorensen, *The Grammar of Empire in Eighteenth-Century British Writing*; Mugglestone, *"Talking Proper"*. See also McKusick, "John Clare and the Tyranny of Grammar"; Nattrass, *William Cobbett*; Tony Crowley, *Language in History: Theories and Works*, esp. ch. 3, "War of Words: The Roles of Language in Eighteenth-Century Britain"; Lauzon, "Savage Eloquence"; Fitzmaurice, "Commerce of Language"; Beach, "Creation of a Classical Language."

14. For discussion, see Stillinger's note in *The Poems of John Keats* 667.

15. See textual notes, ibid., for details of the changes (455, 457, 458).

16. Mugglestone, *Talking Proper*, ch. 1, "The Rise of a Standard." Byron, for example, carefully instructs the reader of *The Prophecy of Dante* that "the reader is requested to adopt the Italian pronunciation of Beatrice, sounding all the syllables" (*Complete Poetical Works* 4:501).

17. Jack Stillinger, *Multiple Authorship* 44.

18. For examples, see Levinson, *Keats's Life of Allegory*; Roe, *John Keats and the Culture of Dissent*. For this criticism of historical readings, see Amanda Anderson, *The Powers of Distance*, ch. 1, "Gender, Modernity, and Detachment"; Anderson concentrates on feminist historicism, but her criticism can be extended to historicism more generally.

19. I am here adapting the contemporary scientific model of language use; see Seidenberg, "Language Acquisition and Use."

20. For an overview of contemporary understandings of philology, see Frank, "Unbearable Lightness"; for a critique of the nationalist biases inherent in traditional philology, see Giancarlo, "Rise and Fall."

Chapter 1

1. For a useful discussion of the critique of prescriptivism, see Cameron, "Problems of 'Prescriptivism.'"

2. For classic older accounts, see Fries, "The Rules of Common School Grammars"; Leonard, *Doctrine of Correctness*.

3. Although I will focus in this book primarily on texts from the second half

of the eighteenth century, the English experts were building on a long tradition from earlier in the seventeenth and eighteenth centuries; see Mitchell, *Grammar Wars* 133–64.

4. On this development, see Brewer, *The Pleasures of the Imagination*, esp. ch. 4, "Readers and the Reading Public."

5. For discussion of typography in dictionaries, see Sheldon, "Pronouncing Systems."

6. See also Hall; Walzer, esp. ch. 7, "Correct Usage."

7. See more generally Anderson, *Imagined Communities* 67–79.

8. For more on the connection between English and national identity, see Crowley, *Language in History* 67–73.

9. Author and poem identified in [John Brightland?], *Grammar* [16].

10. On the importance of good English to the Georgian military, see Colley, *Captives* 278–80.

11. For a thorough overview of the progressive attitude toward language in general and English in particular, see Spadafora, *Idea of Progress*, ch. 5, "Language and Progress."

12. On the changes in the mail system, see Vale, *Mail-Coach Men*, ch. 2, "John Palmer."

13. Blair circulation figure quoted from *RN* 581.

14. On the criticism of women's English during the period, see Crowley, *Language in History* 87–97.

15. On Swift's desire for an academy, ibid., 59–67.

16. On Johnson's resistance to prescriptivism, see McDermott, "Johnson the Prescriptivist?"

17. On this tendency, see Jones, *English Pronunciation* 125–29.

18. On earlier dictionaries, see Lancashire, "Dictionaries and Power."

19. For an exemplary discussion of the latter, see Percy, "In the Margins."

20. For the relation of Combe's poem to Rowlandson's drawings, see Savory, *Thomas Rowlandson's Doctor Syntax Drawings*.

21. On counter-prescriptivism, see Sorensen, "Vulgar Tongues."

22. See the discussion and bibliography in Finegan, "English Grammar and Usage"; for a useful reminder about the limits of the prescriptivists' reach, see Auer and González-Díaz, "Eighteenth-Century Prescriptivism."

23. Murray's book crops up in novels as diverse as Charles Dickens's *Nicholas Nickleby*, Herman Melville's *Moby Dick*, and George Eliot's *Middlemarch*; for its history, see Van Ostade, ed., *Two Hundred Years of Lindley Murray*; on Walker's influence, see Sheldon, "Walker's Influence."

24. A legal case about Longman's right to the book is discussed in [Anon.], "Vice-Chancellor's Court, Nov. 10."

25. For Coleridge, see his *Marginalia* 6:38–40; for Byron, see *Beppo*, st. 52.

26. I have filled in Scott's abbreviations.

27. On Cobbett's grammar, see Smith, *Politics of Language* 239–48; on Hazlitt's, see Tomalin, "'Vulgarisms and Broken English.'"

28. On the growing awareness of prescriptive English in the book trade, see McKitterick, *Print, Manuscript and the Search for Order*, ch. 7, "Re-evaluation: Towards the Modern Book"; Hayden, *Romantic Reviewers* 256.

29. On the role of English in reviewing, see Stanley Jones, "'Bad English.'"

30. Since Addison wrote many of *The Spectator* essays, his combined total is higher than Swift's.

31. On the canon created by the late eighteenth century, see *RN*, ch. 7, "The Old Canon."

32. For the attack on literary language, see Eagleton, *Literary Theory*, "Introduction: What is Literature?"

33. In addition to Miles, *Eras and Modes*, see Bradford, *Linguistic History*; Sylvia Adamson, "Literary Language" in *The Cambridge History of the English Language, Volume 4* and "Literary Language" in *The Cambridge History of the English Language, Volume 3*.

34. For Eliot, see "Byron" and C. S. Lewis's "Shelley, Dryden, and Mr. Eliot" in Abrams, ed., *English Romantic Poets: Modern Essays in Criticism*. Davie notes, "The diction of the Romantic poets is extremely impure" (*Purity of Diction* 25–26).

Chapter 2

1. For the negative associations of Scottish diction, see Sorensen, *Grammar of Empire*; on the historical background of "Resolution and Independence," see Harrison, "Wordsworth's Leech Gatherer."

2. On the tradition of elevated simplicity in English, see Borroff, *Language and the Poet* 32.

3. For a discussion of "Resolution and Independence" that engages some of these issues, see Baron, *Language and Relationship*, ch. 1.

4. Roman Jakobson, "Linguistics and Poetics" 66.

5. From the *Oxford English Dictionary* (online): "Something, n. (a.), and adv., 2.c.": "1711 ADDISON *Spect.* No. 106 p. 6, 'Sir Roger, amidst all his good Qualities, is something of an Humourist.' 1780 *Mirror* No. 70, 'As he was something of a sportsman, my guardians often permitted me to accompany him to the field.' 1802 M. EDGEWORTH *Moral T.* (1816) I. 231, 'I am something of a judge of china myself.'" From *English Verse Drama* (online): John Fletcher, *The Wild-Goose Chase* (1652): "For shame be sorry, though ye cannot Cure her, / Shew something of a Man, of a fair Nature" (4.3.15–16); James Shirley, *The Dvkes Mistris* (1638): "Art thou so ignorant, / Or impudent, or both? let me intreat thee / But to have something of a beast about thee" (5.348–50). From *English Poetry*

Database (online): John Phillips, *Maronides* (1678): "And something of a moldy verse / Hath bred a maggot in my A_____" (6.51–52).

6. On register, see Simpson, *Language Through Literature* 7–19.

7. On this construction, see also van Ostade, *The Auxiliary Do.*

8. For Coleridge's attack on Maturin, see *BL* 466, 470.

9. Coleridge is quoting Pindar; comments in *Etonian* 1 (December 1820): 217–25; quoted in Woof, ed., *William Wordsworth: The Critical Heritage*, 1066–67.

10. For contemporary work on negation, see Horn, *Natural History of Negation*; Ernst, "Phrase Structure"; Baker, "Syntax of English *Not.*"

11. For evidence, see *DENG* 364; van Ostade, "Double Negation."

12. On "nor," see Kjellmer, "On Clause-Introductory *Nor* and *Neither.*"

13. Ibid., 292.

14. For details of this kind of negation, see Hidalgo-Downing, *Negation, Text Worlds, and Discourse* 47.

15. On such rules, see *EG* 210–22.

16. I am influenced here by Horn's "*Duplex Negatio Affirmat*"; see also Hoffmann, *Negatio Contrarii.*

17. A useful contrast to my treatment of Wordsworth is Webb's detailed, more traditionally stylistic treatment of negation in *Prometheus Unbound*; Webb gives considerable attention to the historical context of a word like "unreclaiming" (47), but none at all to the history of negation itself ("The Unascended Heaven").

18. All quotations are from Woof, ed., *William Wordsworth: The Critical Heritage*: Dorothy Wordsworth, letter to Jane Pollard, 16 February 1793, 17; *Analytical Review* (March 1793), 19; the *New Annual Register 1793* (1794), 30; Coleridge, note to "Lines written at Shurton Bars" 31.

19. Ibid.: Losh, Diary for April 1801, 52; Stoddart, reaction noted by Wordsworth in letter to Sarah Hutchinson, late February–early March 1801, 104; Anna Seward, letter to Rev. Robert Fellowes, 31 May 1806, 129; John Taylor Coleridge, review in *British Critic* (February 1821), 799.

20. Ibid.: from R. B. Litchfield, *Tom Wedgwood: The First Photographer* (1903), 120; Letter to Mary Hutchinson, 9–10 March 1801, 98; from *The Diary of Joseph Farington*, 130.

21. See Binnick, *Time and the Verb* (488 n. 44) for a discussion of debate over status of "will" and "shall" as markers of future tense; see also Fleischman, *Future in Thought and Language*; F. R. Palmer, *Mood and Modality* 8–10.

22. I am indebted to Arnovick's discussion (*Diachronic Pragmatics* 41–56); see also Boyd and Boyd, "Shall and Will"; Enns, "Guilliaumian Contribution"; and Traugott and Dasher, *Regularity in Semantic Change* 221–24. Throughout, I will address the will-shall distinction solely in terms of declarative sentences, not interrogatives.

23. For earlier views, see Fries, "Periphrastic Future"; Leonard, *Doctrine of Correctness* 73; for later views, see Taglicht, "Genesis"; Krogvig and Johansson, "*Shall* and *Will*"; Faingold, "Evidence"; Kytö, *Variation and Diachrony*; Facchinetti, "Model Verb *Shall*."

24. See Jespersen, *Modern English Grammar* 4:244–46; see also *OED* (online), "will" v. 13.

25. *OED* (online), "shall" v. 8 b. (b).

26. *OED* (online), "shall" v. 10; Lindley Murray's revision of his 1795 grammar notes that "will" and "shall" "are sometimes interchanged, in the indicative and subjunctive moods, to convey the same meaning of the auxiliary"; since all his examples come from "*if* clauses," he recognizes one of the possible factors influencing "will" and "shall" described in the *Oxford English Dictionary* (*English Grammar* [1824] 90–91). See also Jespersen, *Modern English Grammar* 4:280–83.

27. For more evidence of the connection between will–shall placement and national origin, see *DENG* 190–91.

28. *OED* (online), "will" v.B.I.16. Although the online *OED* is a transcription of the 1989 second edition, it retains the language about "will" and "shall" from the 1933 edition. This edition itself collates the original "fascicles" in which the dictionary was published, along with supplements; the fascicle containing the definition of "will" first appeared in 1926 *OED*, ed. James A. H. Murray et al., 1.xxvi).

29. Another traditional use was the use of "will" in its sense of "insisting on," as in "For the strong hours *will* sway this frail mortality!" (Hemans, *Forest Sanctuary* 2.67) and "Though now and then, a Littleness *will* appear" (Austen, *Sanditon* 332). The category of "transmission" should also include contractions.

30. For an earlier example of what I am calling supersession, see Hannah More's *Slavery: A Poem*: "Will the parch'd negro find, ere he expire, / No pain in hunger, and no heat in fire?" (175–76); "Shall Britain, where the soul of freedom reigns, / Forge chains for others she herself disdains?" (251–52). No semantic distinction is created by using "will" in the first question and "shall" in the second.

31. See Arnovick's careful formulation: "When a speaker wishes to express intention or desires for a future event affecting that speaker or another person, the auxiliary changes along with the personal pronoun to point to the co-referentiality or lack of co-referentiality between agent and goal" (*Diachronic Pragmatics* 49).

32. In listing Wordsworth's "excellencies," Coleridge puts first "an austere purity of language both grammatically and logically" (*BL* 402).

33. For an argument that Shelley's usage is intentional, see Dingley, "Shelley's *Frankenstein*." I see the weakening of the will–shall distinction as characteristic of the Hunt-Shelley circle in a way that David Denison has found the use of the progressive passive to characterize the Lake school (Pratt and Denison, "Language of the Southey-Coleridge Circle").

Chapter 3

1. For discussion of eighteenth-century representation of pronunciation, see McCafferey, *Prior to Meaning* 116–24; Bradford, *Silence and Sound* 103–22.

2. More generally, see Goring, *Rhetoric of Sensibility*, ch. 4, "The Art of Acting: Mid-century Stagecraft and the Broadcast of Feeling."

3. For an overview of the linguistics of literary dialect, see Görlach, *Aspects* 134–43.

4. For such policing, see Bailey, *Nineteenth-Century English*, esp. ch. 2, "Sounds" and 5, "Grammar"; Mugglestone, *"Talking Proper."*

5. On Scottish, see Sorenson, *Grammar of Empire*; John Corbett, *Language and Scottish Literature*; Jones, *Language Suppressed*; on Irish, see Crowley, *Language in History*, ch. 4, "Forging the Nation: Language and Cultural Nationalism in Nineteenth-Century Ireland"; Bartley and Sims, "Pre-Nineteenth Century Stage Irish and Welsh Pronunciation." More generally, see Beal, *English in Modern Times* 199–204.

6. On the status of actual Jews in England during this period, see Katz, *Jews in the History of England*, ch. 7, "Against the Backdrop of Revolution, 1789–1812."

7. Previous work on literary dialects from this period has evaluated them as evidence of actual pronunciation or as transparent derogation: the "contrast between speech in 'formal' English and slaves' 'scant' English . . . emphasizes the 'stupidity' of slaves" (Ferguson, *Subject to Others* 103); "Language marks the foreignness or difference of the Jew, in particular his inability to speak the King's English" (Page, *Imperfect Sympathies* 23).

8. On Jewish speech in eighteenth-century English theater, see Landa, *Jew in Drama*, ch. 9, "Gibberish."

9. For a general treatment of such humor, see Dickie, "Hilarity and Pitilessness."

10. See Michael Ragussis' treatment of the figure of the gentile pretending to be Jewish in Georgian theatre ("Passing for a Jew").

11. Poems collected in Wood, ed., *The Poetry of Slavery*; on the authorship of the poem attributed to More, see Richardson, "'The Sorrows of Yamba.'"

12. For an exemplary and more extended treatment of these novels and their place in the national imagination, see Ragussis, *Figures of Conversion*, esp. ch. 2, "Writing English Comedy: 'Patronizing Shylock'" and 3, "Writing English History: Nationalism and National Guilt"; for more on dialect in the Romantic novel, see Blake, *Non-Standard Language*, ch. 7, "The Romantics."

13. According to this poem's reprinting in Madden, *United Irishmen*, it was written on Nov. 5, 1794 (2:163); Russell was a major figure in the United Irishmen movement and was executed for his participation in the uprising (see Oxford *DNB*).

14. The most complete treatment of the context of Cumberland's play remains van der Veen, *Jewish Characters*.

15. See Siskin, *Historicity*, ch. 5, "The Work of Literature."

16. For insightful treatments of Cowper's complexities, see Goodman, *Georgic Modernity*, ch. 3, "Cowper's Georgics of the News: The 'Loophole' in the Retreat"; Spacks, *Privacy* 201–17.

17. For discussion of Chatterton, see Russett, *Fictions and Fakes*, esp. ch. 2, "Chatterton's Primal Scene of Writing," and Groom, ed., *Thomas Chatterton and Romantic Culture*.

18. On Burns, see Crawford, ed., *Robert Burns and Cultural Authority*; for the larger context of Burns and Scottish poetry, see Stafford, "Scottish Poetry and Regional Literary Expression."

19. For a classic discussion of the background to Burns's poetry, see Butt, "Revival of Vernacular Scottish Poetry."

20. See McLane, "The Figure Minstrelsy Makes."

21. For a stylistic overview of Wordsworth's career, see Rosen, *Power, Plain English, and the Rise of Modern Poetry*, ch. 2, "Wordsworth's Empirical Imagination."

22. In addition to Roe, *John Keats and the Culture of Dissent*, see Cox, *Poetry and Politics in the Cockney School*; Mizukoshi, *Keats, Hunt and the Aesthetics of Pleasure*.

23. As Lynda Mugglestone has noted, in terms of the actual history of pronunciation, Keats's supposed mispronunciations had, by the early nineteenth century, spread throughout the social spectrum. They had not, however, spread to poetry ("The Fallacy of the Cockney Rhyme").

24. See Turley, *Keats's Boyish Imagination* 1–10.

25. For the philological background to Keats's English, see Turley, *Politics of Language* 111–30.

26. Pfau's entire discussion of Keatsian language is valuable in this context (*Romantic Moods* 365–78).

27. For Byron's relation to genius, see Felluga, *Perversity of Poetry*, ch. 3, "Byron's Spectropoetics and Revolution."

28. For a thorough discussion, see Pat Rogers, "Theories of Style."

29. See Michaelson, *Speaking Volumes*, ch. 1, "Women and Language in the Eighteenth Century."

30. See Jane Hodson's illuminating discussion of exclamations, questions, and dashes in eighteenth-century linguistic theory and in Mary Wollstonecraft (*Language and Revolution* 88–96).

31. On the thematization of voice in Hemans, see Saglia, "'A Deeper and Richer Music.'"

Chapter 4

1. See *RN*, ch. 5, "The High Monopoly Period in England."

2. See Gallagher, *Nobody's Story*, ch. 4, "Nobody's Credit: Fiction, Gender, and Authorial Property in the Career of Charlotte Lennox."

3. Such paratextual aids for women writers could also be sites to show their indebtedness to and potential revision of traditionally male forms of writing, like history, and thereby to underscore their authority.

4. See especially, Lynch, *Economy of Character*, ch. 3, "'Round' Characters and Romantic-Period Reading Relations."

5. See Ong, "Romantic Difference and the Poetics of Technology"; Kittler, *Discourse Networks*; Langan, "Understanding Media in 1805"; Goodman, *Georgic Modernity and British Romanticism*.

6. The elocutionists have received scant respect, largely because they have been (mis)understood as part of the history of rhetoric rather than of the history of interpretation. Howell's *Eighteenth-Century British Logic and Rhetoric* notes that they "seem now to have endorsed a futureless idea that was destined against logic and common sense to have a two-hundred year future in England and America" (146). The best available accounts of elocution are Ong's review of Howells; Shortland, "Moving Speeches"; De Bolla, *Discourse of the Sublime*, ch. 6, "Of the Gesture of the Orator"; Bartine, *Early English Reading Theory*; Fliegelman, *Declaring Independence*; Edwards, *Unstoried*; and Goring, *Rhetoric of Sensibility*; also useful is Frederick William Haberman "Elocutionary Movement." Elocution has also been treated by those interested in the history of rhetoric; see Spoel for an extensive secondary bibliography ("Rereading").

7. On Sheridan, in addition to the works cited above, see Mahon, "Rhetorical Value."

8. In my account of the elocutionary movement, I overlook important philosophical and practical differences between its leading figures, largely because these are less central to the history of elocution than the similarities between them. For an excellent discussion of these differences, see Bartine, *Early English Reading Theory*.

9. On the middle-class use of elocution, see Guillory's "Literary Capital: Gray's 'Elegy,' Anna Laetitia Barbauld, and the Vernacular Canon."

10. On speech in the public schools, see Lascelles, "Speech Day"; Elledge, *Lord Byron at Harrow School*.

11. For details, see Beal, "John Walker," in Oxford *DNB*.

12. Herringham q. in "J. O.," "Rev. William Herringham, B. D." 182.

13. The secondary bibliography on the Scottish academics is large; in addition to Howells, *Eighteenth-Century British Logic and Rhetoric*, I would note Miller, *Formation of College English*; Guillory, "Memo and Modernity"; Ulman, *Things, Thoughts, Words, and Actions*; Crawford, ed., *The Invention of English Literature*;

and McKenna, *Adam Smith*. As in the case of the elocutionists, I intentionally overlook important differences among the Scottish academics because I am less interested in the specifics of the texts themselves than in the effects of their reception.

14. On Schleiermacher's distinction, see Rajan, *The Supplement of Reading* 37–45.

15. On this development, see *RN*, ch. 6, "The Explosion of Reading"; see also Ross, "Emergence of 'Literature.'"

16. On the influence of the Scottish academics, see Court, "Early Impact"; Ferreira-Buckley, "Scottish Rhetoric"; on Blair at Oxford, see Wyland, "Archival Study."

17. See Julie Choi's account of the emergence of the voiceless narrator ("Feminine Authority?").

18. For an analogous discussion, see De Bolla's discussion of the tendency of elocution to veer into "a kind of self-indulgence, or indulgence in self that could be seen as far from healthy" (*Discourse of the Sublime* 180).

19. For an analysis that assumes Austen's knowledge of the elocutionists, see Michaelson, *Speaking Volumes*, ch. 5, "Reading Austen, Practicing Speech"; Michaelson focuses on *Pride and Prejudice*.

20. For the process by which the artificiality of elocutionary performance was supposed to result in perceived naturalness, see Fliegelman, *Declaring Independence*, "Natural Theatricality," 79–94.

21. For the drafts of *Michael* written on Coleridge's poem, see *Lyrical Ballads and Other Poems, 1787–1800* 604–88.

22. Ibid., 627.

23. On non-lexical onomatopoeia, see Attridge, *Peculiar Language* 136–47.

24. See Bennett, *Romantic Poets and the Culture of Posterity*, ch. 2, "The Romantic Culture of Posterity."

25. On Thelwall, see Thompson, "'A Voice in the Representation'"; Scrivener, *Seditious Allegories*.

26. See also response by "Telonicus" disagreeing with Ausonius ("A Poetic Test of Pronunciation Not Reducible to Practice").

27. John Honey argues that English-received pronunciation did not really become widespread until after the reform of the educational system in the late nineteenth century ("Acrolect and Hyperlect").

28. In this passage, I have used the LION (Literature Online) database for poems that are not reprinted in the editions noted in the "Works Cited."

29. "Confessor! to thy secret ear" (*Giaour* 1320) vs. "That I have chosen a confessor so old" (*Don Juan* 1.147); "Who can contemplate Fame through clouds unfold" (*Childe Harold's Pilgrimage* 3.11) vs. "Such scene his soul no more could contemplate" (*Lara* 174); "He read the first three lines of the contents"

(*Vision of Judgment* 102) vs. "And quaff the contents as our nectar below" ("To Caroline" 28).

30. "Tomb-Rome" (*Don Juan* 4.101), "dome-Rome" ("Nisus and Euryalus" 405–6); for debate, see entry under "Rome" in *Vocabulary of Such Words in the English Language as are of Dubious or Unsettled Accentuation.*

31. "Shriek-break" (*Lamia* 2.269–70); "break-cake" ("Ode to Fanny" 52–53).

32. "Snake-break-shake" (*Revolt of Islam* 1.13); "break–weak–cheek" (*Adonais* 11).

33. Blake, "Little Girl Found," 5–6; Keats, "Belle Dame Sans Merci," 6, 8.

34. "Nature" ([nejtʃər] vs. [nejtʃuwr]); "empire" ([ɛmpajər] vs. [ɛmpijr]); "satire" ([sætər] vs. [sætajər]); "drama" ([drejmə] vs. [drɑmə]); "knowledge" ([nɑlɨdʒ] vs. [nɑlidʒ]; "privacy" [privəsi] vs. [prajvæsi]; "humble" [hʌmb(ə)l] vs. [ʌmb(ə)l]; "chamber" [(tʃejmbər] vs. [tʃæmbər]); "gold" ([gowld] vs. [guwld]); "legend" ([lɛdʒənd] vs. [lijʒənd]); "hospital" ([hɑspɨtəl] vs. [ɑspɨtəl]); "legislator" (législator vs. legislátor); "sublime" (súblime vs. sublíme); and "horizon" (hórizon vs. horízon). For details, see entries under these words in *Vocabulary.* For a far more extensive list, see MacMahon, "Phonology."

35. See entry under "wind" in *Vocabulary.*

36. Keach, *Arbitrary Power* 53–55.

37. On the pronunciation of "giaour," see Austen, *Persuasion* 121.

38. Walker's *Dictionary* heightens its unsavory overtones by directing that it be pronounced like "bell-damn" (see entry under "beldam").

39. I quote from the *Indicator* version of the poem; in Keats's letter to George and Georgiana Keats, he writes the more distinctively French "merci."

40. For a traditional discussion of Romanticism and voice, see Privateer, *Romantic Voices.*

41. For an important discussion of the thematics of silence, see Wolfson's "Sounding Romantic."

42. On Romanticism and deixis, see Bradford, *Linguistic History,* ch. 4, "Romanticism."

43. See also Langan, "Understanding Media in 1805" 63.

44. See editorial notes to "Nutting" in *Lyrical Ballads and Other Poems, 1787–1800,* ed. Butler and Green, 220.

45. For an overview of such poems that focuses especially on "Casabianca," see Robson, "Standing on the Burning Deck."

Chapter 5

1. For an exemplary work in this vein, see Traugott, *A History of English Syntax.*

2. On this debate, see Williamson, *The Senecan Amble;* Adolph, *The Rise of Modern Prose Style;* Robinson, *The Establishment of Modern English Prose;* Sylvia

Adamson, "Literary Language," *The Cambridge History of the English Language*, *Vol. 3*, esp. section 7.4.3, "Amplifying the Phrase: Periodicity as a Structural Principle."

3. Murray copies this definition verbatim (*EG* 86).

4. See Seguin, *L'invention de la phrase au XVIIIᵉ siècle* 14–18.

5. For an overview, see Levinson and Bock, "Linguistic Relativity."

6. For an example, see the short examination at the end of Collyer, *General Principles* 126–28.

7. On this analysis, see Corbett, "Hugh Blair as an Analyzer of English Prose Style."

8. See *RN* 515; Solomon, *The Rise of Robert Dodsley* 139–44.

9. On the popularity of Blair's sermons, see *RN* 270–73.

10. For a consideration of this moment and its larger textual implications, see Fanning, "Small Particles of Eloquence."

11. For comments, see Rogers, ed., *The Critical Response to Ann Radcliffe*; for Radcliffe's "elegance," see the reviews of *The Mysteries of Udolpho* 19, 22; for the comments about her less labored style in her travel writings, see the reviews of *A Journey . . . through Holland* 41, 46.

12. On this association, see Langford, *Englishness Identified* 85–92.

13. For Grice's maxim, see Grice, *Studies in the Way of Words* 28.

14. On cohesion, see Toolan, *Language in Literature*, ch. 2, "Cohesion: Making Text."

15. See Price, *The Anthology and the Rise of the Novel*, ch. 3, "George Eliot and the Production of Consumers"; and Nicholas Dames, *The Physiology of the Novel*, ch. 4, "Just Noticeable Differences: Meredith and Fragmentation (Discontinuous Form)."

16. The quotation is from George Shelley, *Sentences and Maxims* 50.

17. On this phenomenon, see Lethbridge, "Anthological Reading Habits in the Eighteenth Century."

18. On extraction more generally, see Jackson, *Romantic Readers* 119–20; see also Price, *The Anthology and the Rise of the Novel*, ch. 2, "Cultures of the Commonplace."

19. See *RN* 227, 335, 688.

20. Keach's entire discussion of Shelley's speed is relevant here (*Shelley's Style* 154–83).

21. See Smith, *The Politics of Language*, ch. 1, "The Problem."

22. For discussions of the chaos of Romantic periodical style, see Russett, *De Quincey's Romanticism* 115–19; Nattrass, *William Cobbett: The Politics of Style* 89–118; Butler, "Culture's Medium: The Role of the Review," esp. 143–47.

23. See Beatty, "Macaulay and Carlyle."

24. See also the tributes from working-class readers to Macaulay in Rose, *The Intellectual Life of the British Working Classes* 130–31.

25. On this development, see Ghosh, "Macaulay and the Heritage of the Enlightenment."

26. For a thorough treatment of the essay's place in the politics of the 1820s, see Clive, *Macaulay: The Shaping of the Historian* 74–95.

27. P. L. Carver demonstrates Hazlitt's influence on Macaulay's essay in terms of ideas ("The Sources of Macaulay's Essay on Milton"). Macaulay was strongly influenced by Hazlitt's ideal of a familiar style, which arose from maintaining the abstract ideals of the English experts but realizing them through a much more colloquial style (Tomalin, "'Vulgarisms and Broken English'").

28. See also Madden, "Macaulay's Style."

Chapter 6

1. The majority of the poems in Hughes, ed., *Select Specimens*, are from the nineteenth century; Hughes also includes grammatical questions after many of the poems. Romantic poetry also forms a large part of the selection in Bowman, *Poetry Selected for the Use of Schools*, which is not annotated. Bowen's *Studies in English* includes poetry and prose, largely from the nineteenth century, with very brief biographical notices and occasional historical and verbal glosses; his introduction notes his indebtedness to John Wesley Hales's *Longer English Poems*, which I discuss below.

2. For a good discussion of these early anthologies, see Bauer, "Wordsworth and the Early Anthologies."

3. On Hales, see Palmer, *Rise of English Studies*, 44, 54; see also Hales's own account of his classical education ("Louth Grammar School"), an anonymous obituary ("Obituary"), and the short overview of Hales and his contemporaries in Tillyard (*The Muse Unchained* 24–26). An article by him appeared in the very first issue of *Modern Philology* ("Milton and Ovid").

4. I cite poems by line numbers and Hales's commentary by page numbers in his anthology.

5. On classical pedagogy in the Victorian period, see Stray, *Classics Transformed* 46–58.

6. On Eliot and the Romantics, see Manning, "*Don Juan* and Byron's Imperceptiveness to the English Word"; Chandler, *England in 1819* 490–98.

7. On the need for this middle ground, see Guillory, "Literary Study" 34–35.

8. See Hollingworth, "The Mother Tongue and the Public Schools in the 1860s." Entries in WorldCat for Hales's anthology indicate editions in 1872, 1874, 1875, 1876, 1878, 1880, 1882, 1884, 1885, 1887, 1889, 1890, 1892, 1899, 1903, 1906, 1926, and 1929.

9. For information, see the website of Iqbal Academy Pakistan (http://www.allamaiqbal.com).

10. On Iqbal, see Mustansir, *Iqbal.*

11. Even within medieval studies, the traditional stronghold of philological knowledge, the value of such knowledge underwent prominent attacks, as in J. R. R. Tolkien's classic "*Beowulf:* The Monsters and the Critics."

12. B3151 (as listed on the label): "The Tiger" (Blake), "Westminster Bridge" (Wordsworth), *Samson Agonistes* (Milton), "When to the Sessions of Sweet Silent Thought" (Shakespeare); B3152: "To Sleep" (Keats), "Prospice" (Browning), "Ozymandias of Egypt" (Shelley), "Now Sleeps the Crimson Petal" (Tennyson). I am grateful to the British Library Sound Archive's transcription service for making Clifford Turner's recording available to me on CD.

13. For a thorough discussion, see Perkins, "How the Romantics Recited Poetry."

14. On Victorian reading, see Collins, *Reading Aloud.*

15. On penny readings, see Beaven, *Leisure, Citizenship, and Working-Class Men* 20–24; for a list of works deemed appropriate for such readings, see Yonge, *What Books to Lend and What to Give* 111–15.

16. Alexander Graham Bell, for example, was a professor of "Vocal Physiology and Elocution" at the School of Oratory at Boston University (Gray, *Reluctant Genius* 45–46); although best known as the inventor of the telephone, he also worked on an early version of the phonograph, the "graphophone" (*Reluctant Genius* 228).

17. Examples drawn from Camlot, "Early Talking Books," and from *Great Historical Shakespeare Recordings.*

18. On this development, see Morrisson, *Public Face of Modernism,* ch. 2, "Performing the Pure Voice: *Poetry and Drama,* Elocution, Verse Recitation, and Modernist Poetry in Prewar London."

19. On Clifford Turner and Fogerty, see Cole, *Fogie* 105–6; on the Oxford Recitations, see Sivier, "English Poets, Teachers, and Festivals"; Shields, "Like a Choir of Nightingales."

20. For Masefield's anti-modernism, see his *Poetry;* in his anthology *My Favourite English Poems,* he gives eight pages to Donne, but seventeen to Wordsworth, eighteen to Keats, and nineteen to Shelley.

21. For Masefield's belief in the value of oral recitation, see his *With the Living Voice;* for his history of the Oxford Recitations, see his preface to *The Oxford Recitations* 5–9.

22. For a review of Turner's recording, see "Review of Clifford Turner" in *The Gramophone.*

23. For the dramatic effects of the movement to electronic sound, see Morton, *Sound Recording* 64–67.

24. For some documentation of its decline, see the brief articles collected in Sansom, ed., *Speech of Our Time* 134–51; for poetry on the Third Programme, see Whitehead, *The Third Programme*, ch. 8, "Poetry Programmes."

25. See Alan Bates's recollections in Zucker, *In the Company of Actors* 18; for Peter O'Toole and Albert Finney, see Billington, "Review of Peter O'Toole's *Loitering with Intent*"; for Bikel, *Theo* 40–41.

26. See Turner's *Voice and Speech in the Theatre*; see also Crump, *Speaking Poetry*.

27. See also Clifford Turner's own praise of Keats ("Aesthetic Aspect"; "Verse Speaking").

28. For good accounts of the splitting off of speech and English, see Smith, "Origin and Development of Departments of Speech"; Edwards, *Unstoried*.

29. For an early example, see Eliot, *Three Voices*.

30. For the afterlife of the oral interpretation of literature after it separated from English departments, see Taft-Kaufman, "Oral Interpretation"; on the sex/gender politics of elocution, see Jackson, *Professing Performance*, ch. 2, "Institutions and Performance: Professing Performance in the Early Twentieth Century."

31. For an analysis of this style of speaking, see Tracy, *Colloquium*, esp. ch. 3, "Positioning and Accounting."

32. For examples of such reactions, see the opinions collected in Moulton, ed., *Library of Criticism* 109–115.

33. On this development, see Trachsel, *Institutionalizing Literacy* 65–89.

34. See the record of the debate in Jno. G. R. McElroy's "Matter and Manner."

35. On the continuity of the principles of business English and their relation to the Scottish academics, see Mary T. Carbone, "History and Development of Business Communication Principles."

36. Farrand also describes Carlyle's use as an entrance requirement ([5]).

37. Strunk, ed., *Macaulay's and Carlyle's Essays on Samuel Johnson* xxii.

38. Strunk, *Elements of Style*.

39. On its later revisions, see Minear, "E. B. White Takes His Leave, or Does He?"

40. For an eloquent exposition of the problems of using Macaulay to teach composition, see Rollins, "Macaulay's Essays and the Freshman"; for a late recommendation of Macaulay, see Lynskey, "Imitative Writing and a Student's Style" 398.

41. For a treatment of Stein's sentences that puts her in loftier philosophical company, see Meyer, "'The Physiognomy of the Thing.'"

42. On the importance of background knowledge, see Kellogg, *Psychology of Writing*, ch. 4, "Knowledge."

Works Cited

Aarsleff, Hans. *The Study of Language in England, 1780–1860* (1967). Minneapolis: University of Minnesota Press, 1983.

Abrams, M. H., ed. *English Romantic Poets: Modern Essays in Criticism.* 2nd ed. London: Oxford University Press, 1975.

Adams, James. *The Pronunciation of the English Language* (1799). Facsimile ed. Menston: Scolar Press, 1968.

Adamson, Sylvia. "Literary Language." Ed. Suzanne Romaine. *The Cambridge History of the English Language, Volume 4: 1776–1997.* 589–692.

———. "Literary Language." *The Cambridge History of the English Language, Volume 3: 1476–1776.* Ed. Roger Lass. Cambridge: Cambridge University Press, 1999. 539–653.

Adolph, Robert. *The Rise of Modern Prose Style.* Cambridge, MA: MIT Press, 1968.

Aiton, George B., ed. *"Burns" by Thomas Carlyle.* Chicago: Scott, Foresman and Co., 1898.

Alford, Henry. *A Plea for The Queen's English: Stray Notes on Speaking and Spelling.* London: Alexander Strahan, 1866.

Anderson, Amanda. *The Powers of Distance: Cosmopolitanism and the Cultivation of Detachment.* Princeton: Princeton University Press, 2001.

Anderson, Benedict. *Imagined Communities: Reflections on the Origin and Spread of Nationalism.* London: Verso, 1983.

Arnovick, Leslie K. *Diachronic Pragmatics: Seven Case Studies in English Illocutionary Development.* Amsterdam: John Benjamins, 1999.

Attridge, Derek. *Peculiar Language: Literature as Difference from the Renaissance to James Joyce.* 2nd ed. London: Routledge, 2004.

———. "Closing Statement: Linguistics and Poetics in Retrospect" (1987). Rpt. in *The Stylistics Reader: From Roman Jakobson to the Present.* Ed. Jean Jacques Weber. London: Arnold, 1996. 36–53.

Auer, Anita and Victorina González-Díaz. "Eighteenth-Century Prescriptivism in English: A Re-Evaluation of its Effects on Actual Language Usage." *Multilingua* 24 (2005): 317–41.

"Ausonius." "Poetry or Prose, as the Criterion of Pronunciation?" *Gentleman's Magazine* 68 (April 1798): 290–91.

Austen, Jane. *Northanger Abbey* (1818). Eds. Barbara M. Benedict and Deirdre Le Faye. Cambridge: Cambridge University Press, 2006.

———. *Pride and Prejudice* (1813). Ed. Pat Rogers. Cambridge: Cambridge University Press, 2006.

———. *Sense and Sensibility* (1811). Ed. Edward Copeland. Cambridge: Cambridge University Press, 2006.

———. *Mansfield Park* (1814). Ed. John Wiltshire. Cambridge: Cambridge University Press, 2005.

———. *Persuasion* (1818). Ed. D. W. Harding. Harmondsworth, Middlesex: Penguin, 1986.

"B. P. L. C." "Recording of English." *The Gramophone* (July 1926): 66.

Bailey, Richard W. *Nineteenth-Century English*. Ann Arbor: University of Michigan Press, 1996.

Baker, C. L. "The Syntax of English *Not*: The Limits of Core Grammar." *Linguistic Inquiry* 22 (1991): 387–429.

Baron, Michael. *Language and Relationship in Wordsworth's Writing*. London: Longman, 1995.

Barrell, John. *English Literature in History, 1730–80: An Equal, Wide Survey*. New York: St. Martin's Press, 1983.

Barthes, Roland. "Writers, Intellectuals, Teachers." *Image—Music—Text*. Trans. Stephen Heath. New York: Hill and Wang, 1977. 190–215.

Bartine, David. *Early English Reading Theory: Origins of Current Debates*. Columbia: University of South Carolina Press, 1989.

Bartley, J. O. and D. L. Sims. "Pre-Nineteenth Century Stage Irish and Welsh Pronunciation." *Proceedings of the American Philosophical Society* 93 (1949): 439–47.

Bauer, N. Stephen. "Wordsworth and the Early Anthologies." *Library* 27 (1972): 37–45.

Baugh, Albert C. and Thomas Cable. *A History of the English Language*. 4th ed. Englewood Cliffs, NJ: Prentice Hall, 1993.

Beach, Adam R. "The Creation of a Classical Language in the Eighteenth Century: Standardizing English, Cultural Imperialism, and the Future of the Literary Canon." *TSLL* 43 (2001): 117–41.

Beal, Joan C. *English in Modern Times, 1700–1945*. London: Arnold, 2004.

———. "John Walker (1732–1807)" in *Oxford DNB* (online edition); available at http://www.oxforddnb.com.

Beatty, Richmond C. "Macaulay and Carlyle." *PQ* 18 (1939): 25–34.

Beaven, Brad. *Leisure, Citizenship, and Working-Class Men in Britain, 1850–1945.* Manchester: Manchester University Press, 2005.

Benger, E. O. *Memoirs of the Late Mrs. Elizabeth Hamilton.* 2 vols. London: Longman, 1818.

Benjamin, Walter. "Karl Kraus." *Reflections: Essays, Aphorisms, Autobiographical Writings.* Ed. Peter Demetz. Trans. Edmund Jephcott. New York: Schocken, 1986. 239–73.

Bennett, Andrew. *The Author.* London: Routledge, 2005.

————. *Romantic Poets and the Culture of Posterity.* Cambridge: Cambridge University Press, 1999.

Bewell, Alan. *Wordsworth and the Enlightenment: Nature, Man, and Society in the Experimental Poetry.* New Haven: Yale University Press, 1989.

Bhabha, Homi. "Of Mimicry and Man: The Ambivalence of Colonial Discourse." *The Location of Culture.* London: Routledge, 1994. 85–92.

Billington, Michael. "[Review of Peter O'Toole's *Loitering with Intent*]." *Electronic Mail and Guardian* (June 30, 1997), online at http://www.chico.mweb .co.za/mg/books/may97/26june-otoole.html.

Bikel, Theodore. *Theo: An Autobiography.* Madison: University of Wisconsin Press, 2002.

Binnick, Robert I. *Time and the Verb: A Guide to Tense and Aspect.* New York: Oxford University Press, 1991.

Blackmore, Richard. "An Essay on the Nature and Constitution of Epick Poetry." *Essays upon Several Subjects* (1716). 2 vols. Facsimile ed. Hildesheim: Georg Olms Verlag, 1976.

Blair, Hugh. *Lectures on Rhetoric and Belles Lettres* (1783). Facsimile ed. 2 vols. Ed. Harold F. Hardin. Carbondale: Southern Illinois University Press, 1965.

————. *Sermons.* 3 vols. London: A. Strahan, 1790.

Blake, N. F. *Non-Standard Language in English Literature.* London: Deutsch, 1981.

Blake, William. *The Complete Poetry and Prose of William Blake.* Ed. David V. Erdman. Rev. ed. Garden City, NY: Anchor Books, 1982.

Blank, Paula. *Broken English: Dialects and the Politics of Language in Renaissance Writings.* London: Routledge, 1996.

Borroff, Marie. *Language and the Poet: Verbal Artistry in Frost, Stevens, and Moore.* Chicago: University of Chicago Press, 1979.

Boswell, James. *Life of Johnson* (1791). Ed. R. W. Chapman. Oxford: Oxford University Press, 1980.

Bowen, H. Courthope. *Studies in English, for the Use of Modern Schools.* London: Kegan Paul, 1882.

Bowman, Anne. *Poetry: Selected for the Use of Schools and Families.* London: G. Routledge, 1856.

Boyd, Julian and Zelda Boyd. "Shall and Will." *The State of the Language.* Ed. Leonard Michaels and Christopher B. Ricks. Berkeley: University of California Press, 1980. 43–53.

Bradbury, Jill Marie. "New Science and the 'New Species of Writing': Eighteenth-Century Prose Genres." *ECLife* 27 (2003): 28–51.

Bradford, Richard. *A Linguistic History of English Poetry.* London: Routledge, 1993.

———. *Silence and Sound: Theories of Poetics from the Eighteenth Century.* Rutherford, NJ: Fairleigh Dickinson University Press, 1992.

Brewer, John. *The Pleasures of the Imagination: English Culture in the Eighteenth Century.* Chicago: University of Chicago Press, 1997.

[Brightland, John?]. *A Grammar of the English Tongue.* 2nd ed. London: R. Brugis, 1712.

Brooks, Cleanth. *The Well Wrought Urn: Studies in the Structure of Poetry.* New York: Harcourt, Brace, 1947.

Buchanan, James. *The British Grammar* (1762). Facsimile ed. Menston: Scolar Press, 1968.

Burke, Kenneth. *The Philosophy of Literary Form: Studies in Symbolic Action.* 3rd ed. Berkeley: University of California Press, 1973.

Butler, Marilyn. "Culture's Medium: The Role of the Review." *The Cambridge Companion to British Romanticism.* Ed. Stuart Curran. Cambridge: Cambridge University Press, 1993. 120–47.

Butt, John. "The Revival of Vernacular Scottish Poetry in the Eighteenth Century." Hilles and Bloom, ed. *From Sensibility to Romanticism.* 219–38.

Byron, George Gordon, Lord. *The Complete Poetical Works.* Ed. Jerome J. McGann. 7 vols. Oxford: Clarendon Press, 1980–93. Vol. 6, co-ed. Barry Weller.

———. *Byron's Letters and Journals.* Ed. Leslie A. Marchand. 13 vols. London: John Murray, 1973–82.

Cameron, Deborah. "Problems of 'Prescriptivism'" (1995). *The Routledge Language and Cultural Theory Reader.* Ed. Lucy Burke, Tony Crowley, and Alan Girvin. London: Routledge, 2000. 92–99.

Camlot, Jason. "Early Talking Books: Spoken Recordings and Recitation Anthologies, 1880–1920." *BoH* 6 (2003): 143–73.

Campbell, George. *The Philosophy of Rhetoric.* 2 vols. London: W. Strahan, 1776.

Carbone, Mary T. "The History and Development of Business Communication Principles: 1776–1916." *Journal of Business Communication* 31 (1994): 173–93.

Carlyle, Thomas. "Signs of the Times." *Edinburgh Review* 49 (June 1829): 439–59.

Carver, P. L. "The Sources of Macaulay's Essay on Milton." *RES* 6 (1930): 49–62.

Catano, James V. *Language, History, Style: Leo Spitzer and the Critical Tradition.* Urbana: University of Illinois Press, 1988.

Chakrabarty, Dipesh. *Provincializing Europe: Postcolonial Thought and Historical Difference.* Princeton: Princeton University Press, 2000.

Chandler, James. *England in 1819: The Politics of Literary Culture and the Case of Romantic Historicism.* Chicago: University of Chicago Press, 1998.

Chatterton, Thomas. *The Complete Works of Thomas Chatterton.* Ed. Donald S. Taylor and Benjamin B. Hoover. 2 vols. Oxford: Clarendon Press, 1971.

Chilcott, Tim. *A Publisher and his Circle: The Life and Work of John Taylor, Keats's Publisher.* London: Routledge and Kegan Paul, 1972.

Choi, Julie. "Feminine Authority? Common Sense and the Question of Voice in the Novel." *NLH* 27 (1996): 641–62.

Clare, John. "[Grammar]." *John Clare: Major Works.* Ed. Eric Robinson and David Powell. Oxford: Oxford University Press, 2004. 481.

Clark, Herbert H. *Using Language.* Cambridge: Cambridge University Press, 1996.

Clive, John. *Macaulay: The Shaping of the Historian.* New York: Knopf, 1973.

Cockin, William. *The Art of Delivering Written Language* (1775). Facsimile ed. Menston: Scolar Press, 1969.

Cohen, Murray. *Sensible Words: Linguistic Practice in England, 1640–1785.* Baltimore: Johns Hopkins University Press, 1977.

Cole, Marion. *Fogie: The Life of Elsie Fogerty, C. B. E.* London: P. Davies, 1967.

Coleridge, Samuel Taylor. *Coleridge's Poetry and Prose.* Eds. Nicholas Halmi, Paul Magnuson, and Raimonda Modiano. New York: W. W. Norton, 2003.

———. *Biographia Literaria* (1817) in *Samuel Taylor Coleridge: The Major Works.* Ed. H. J. Jackson. Oxford: Oxford University Press, 1985. 155–482.

———. *Marginalia.* Ed. George Whalley. *The Collected Works of Samuel Taylor Coleridge.* Vol. 12, 6 parts. Princeton: Princeton University Press, 1969.

Colley, Linda. *Captives.* New York: Pantheon, 2002.

———. *Britons: Forging the Nation, 1707–1837.* New Haven: Yale University Press, 1992.

Collins, Philip. *Reading Aloud: A Victorian Métier.* Lincoln: Tennyson Research Centre, 1972.

Collyer, John. *The General Principles of Grammar* (1735). Facsimile ed. Menston: Scolar Press, 1968.

Coote, Charles. *Elements of the Grammar of the English Language.* London: C. Dilly, 1788.

Corbett, Edward P. J. "Hugh Blair as an Analyzer of English Prose Style." *CCCC* 9 (1958): 98–103.

Corbett, John. *Language and Scottish Literature.* Edinburgh: Edinburgh University Press, 1997.

Cornell University Register and Catalogue, 1877–78. Ithaca: Cornell, 1878.

Court, Franklin E. "The Early Impact of Scottish Literary Teaching in North America." *The Scottish Invention of English Literature.* Ed. Robert Crawford. 134–63.

Cowper, William. *Selected Letters*. Eds. James King and Charles Ryskamp. Oxford: Clarendon Press, 1989.

———. *The Poems of William Cowper*. Eds. John D. Baird and Charles Ryskamp. 3 vols. Oxford: Clarendon Press, 1980–95.

Cox, Jeffrey N. *Poetry and Politics in the Cockney School: Keats, Shelley, Hunt, and Their Circle*. Cambridge: Cambridge University Press, 1998.

Crabbe, George. *George Crabbe: The Complete Works*. 3 vols. Eds. Norma Dalrymple-Champneys and Arthur Pollard. Oxford: Clarendon Press, 1988.

Crawford, Robert. *Devolving English Literature*. 2nd ed. Edinburgh: Edinburgh University Press, 2000.

———, ed. *The Scottish Invention of English Literature*. Cambridge: Cambridge University Press, 1998.

———, ed. *Robert Burns and Cultural Authority*. Iowa City: University of Iowa Press, 1997.

Crowley, Tony. *Language in History: Theories and Texts*. London: Routledge, 1996.

———. *Standard English and the Politics of Language*. Urbana: University of Illinois Press, 1989.

Crump, Geoffrey. *Speaking Poetry*. London: Methuen, 1953.

Cumberland, Richard. *The Jew: A Comedy, in Five Acts* (1795). *The London Stage*. 4 vols. London: Sherwood, Jones, and Co., 1825–27. 1:1–16.

Curwen, Henry. *A History of Booksellers: The Old and the New*. London: Chatto and Windus, 1873.

Dames, Nicholas. *The Physiology of the Novel: Reading, Neural Science, and the Form of Victorian Fiction*. Oxford: Oxford University Press, 2007.

Davie, Donald. *Purity of Diction in English Verse*. New York: Oxford University Press, 1953.

De Bolla, Peter. *The Discourse of the Sublime: Readings in History, Aesthetics, and the Subject*. Oxford: Blackwell, 1989.

De Man, Paul. "Time and History in Wordsworth." *Diacritics* 17 (1987): 4–17.

———. "The Return to Philology." *The Resistance to Theory*. Minneapolis: University of Minnesota Press, 1986. 21–26.

———. *Allegories of Reading: Figural Language in Rousseau, Nietzsche, Rilke, and Proust*. New Haven: Yale University Press, 1979.

Deleuze, Gilles. "He Stuttered." *Essays Critical and Clinical*. Trans. Daniel W. Smith and Michael A. Greco. London: Verso, 1998. 107–14.

Denison, David. "Syntax." *The Cambridge History of the English Language, Vol. 4: 1776–1997*. Ed. Suzanne Romaine. 92–329.

De Quincey, Thomas. "Rhetoric" (1828). *Historical and Critical Essays*. 2 vols. Boston: Ticknor, Reed, and Fields, 1853. 2:217–83.

Dibdin, Charles. "Jew Volunteer." *Mirth and Metre*. London: Vernor, Hood, and Sharpe, 1807. 124.

———. "One Negro, wi my Banjer." *A Collection of Songs, Selected from the Works of Mr. Dibdin, Vol. 2*. London: Charles Dibdin, [1792?]. 88.

Dickie, Simon. "Hilarity and Pitilessness in the Mid-Eighteenth Century: English Jestbook Humor." *ECS* 37 (2003): 1–22.

Dingley, Robert. "Shelley's *Frankenstein*." *Expl* 57 (1999): 204–6.

Dodsley, Robert. *The Oeconomy of Human Life* (1750). 7th ed. London: R. Dodsley, 1751.

Dowling, Linda. *Language and Decadence in the Victorian Fin de Siècle*. Princeton: Princeton University Press, 1986.

Downman, Hugh. *Infancy, or the Management of Children*. 6th ed. Exeter: Trewman and Son, 1803.

DuPlessis, Rachel Blau. *Genders, Races, and Religious Cultures in Modern American Poetry, 1908–1934*. Cambridge: Cambridge University Press, 2001.

Dyer, Gary. "Thieves, Boxers, Sodomites, Poets: Being Flash to Byron's *Don Juan*." *PMLA* 116 (2001): 562–78.

Eagleton, Terry. *Literary Theory: An Introduction*. Minneapolis: University of Minnesota Press, 1983.

Easthope, Antony. *Poetry as Discourse*. London: Methuen, 1983.

Edgeworth, Maria. *Harrington* (1817). Ed. Susan Manly. Peterborough, ONT: Broadview, 2004.

———. *Belinda* (1801). London: Pandora, 1986.

Edwards, Paul. *Unstoried: Teaching Literature in the Age of Performance Studies*. *TA* 52 (1999): 1–147.

Elbow, Peter. "The Music of Form: Rethinking Organization in Writing." *CCCC* 57 (2006): 620–66.

Elegant Extracts in Poetry, Selected for the Improvement of Young Persons. London: Rivington et al., 1816.

Eliot, T. S. *The Three Voices of Poetry*. London: Cambridge University Press, 1955.

———. "Byron" (1943). Rpt. in Abrams, ed. *English Romantic Poets*. 261–74.

Elledge, Paul. *Lord Byron at Harrow School: Speaking Out, Talking Back, Acting Up, Bowing Out*. Baltimore: Johns Hopkins University Press, 2000.

Empson, William. *Seven Types of Ambiguity*. 2nd ed. London: Chatto and Windus, 1949.

"English." *Encyclopædia Britannica*. 3 vols. Edinburgh: A. Bell, 1771. 2:497–99.

Enns, Peter J. "A Guillaumian Contribution to a Linguistic Analysis of the Modal *Will* in Contemporary English." Ph.D. Thesis. Univ. Laval, 1999.

Ernst, Thomas. "The Phrase Structure of English Negation." *TLR* 9 (1992): 109–44.

Facchinetti, Roberta. "The Modal Verb *Shall* Between Grammar and Usage in the Nineteenth Century." *The History of English in a Social Context: A*

Contribution to Historical Sociolinguistics. Ed. Dieter Kastovsky and Arthur Mettinger. Berlin: Mouton de Gruyter, 2000. 115–33.

Faingold, Eduardo D. "Evidence of Seventeenth-Century Uses of *Shall* and *Will* Compatible with Markedness-Reversal." *Papiere zur Linguistik* 44–45 (1991): 57–63.

Fanning, Christopher. "Small Particles of Eloquence: Sterne and the Scriblerian Text." *MP* 100 (2003): 360–92.

Farrand, Wilson, ed. *Carlyle's "Essay on Burns."* New York: Longmans, Green, and Co., 1903.

Fell, John. *An Essay Towards an English Grammar* (1784). Facsimile ed. Menston: Scolar Press, 1967.

Felluga, Dino Franco. *The Perversity of Poetry: Romantic Ideology and the Popular Male Poet of Genius.* Albany: State University of New York Press, 2005.

Ferguson, Moira. *Subject to Others: British Women Writers and Colonial Slavery, 1670–1834.* New York: Routledge, 1992.

Ferreira-Buckley, Linda. "Scottish Rhetoric and the Formation of Literary Studies in Nineteenth-Century England." *Scottish Invention of English Literature.* Ed. Robert Crawford. 180–206.

The Festival of Humour; or, Banquet of Wit. London: E. Langley, 1800.

Finegan, Edward. "English Grammar and Usage." *The Cambridge History of the English Language, Vol. 4: 1776–1997.* Ed. Suzanne Romaine. 536–88.

Fish, Stanley. "What is Stylistics and Why are They Saying Such Terrible Things About It? Part II." *Is There a Text in This Class? The Authority of Interpretive Communities.* Cambridge, Massachusetts: Harvard University Press, 1980. 246–67.

Fisher, Ann. *A New Grammar* (1750). Facsimile ed. Menston: Scolar Press, 1968.

Fitzmaurice, Susan M. "The Commerce of Language in the Pursuit of Politeness in Eighteenth-Century England." *ES* (1998): 309–28.

Fleischman, Suzanne. *The Future in Thought and Language: Diachronic Evidence from Romance.* Cambridge: Cambridge University Press, 1982.

Fliegelman, Jay. *Declaring Independence: Jefferson, Natural Language, and the Culture of Performance.* Stanford: Stanford University Press, 1993.

Fogerty, Elsie. *The Speaking of English Verse.* London: J. M. Dent, 1923.

Fogg, Peter Walkden. *Elementa Anglicana* (1792, 1796). 2 vols. Facsimile ed. Menston: Scolar Press, 1970.

Foote, Samuel. *The Lyar.* London: J. Parsons, 1794.

Foucault, Michel. *The Archaeology of Knowledge and The Discourse on Language.* Trans. A. M. Sheridan Smith. New York: Barnes and Noble, 1993.

———. "What is an Author?" *The Foucault Reader.* Ed. Paul Rabinow. New York: Pantheon, 1984. 101–20.

———. *The History of Sexuality, Volume 1: An Introduction.* Trans. Robert Hurley. New York: Random House, 1978.

———. *The Order of Things: An Archaeology of the Human Sciences.* New York: Random House, 1970.

Fowler, H. W. *A Dictionary of Modern English Usage.* Oxford: Clarendon Press, 1927.

Fraistat, Neil. *The Poem and the Book: Interpreting Collections of Romantic Poetry.* Chapel Hill: University of North Carolina Press, 1985.

Frank, Roberta. "The Unbearable Lightness of Being a Philologist." *JEGP* 96 (1997): 486–513.

Fries, Charles C. "The Rules of Common School Grammars." *PMLA* 42 (1927): 221–37.

———. "The Periphrastic Future with *Shall* and *Will* in Modern English." *PMLA* 40 (1925): 963–1024.

Gallagher, Catherine. *Nobody's Story: The Vanishing Acts of Women Writers in the Marketplace, 1670–1820.* Berkeley: University of California Press, 1994.

Ghosh, P. R. "Macaulay and the Heritage of the Enlightenment." *EHR* 112 (1997): 358–95.

Giancarlo, Matthew. "The Rise and Fall of the Great Vowel Shift?: The Changing Ideological Intersections of Philology, Historical Linguistics, and Literary History." *Representations* 76 (2001): 27–60.

Gilman, Sander L. *The Jew's Body.* New York: Routledge, 1991.

———. "Quiet Revolutions and Violent Suppressions: Foreign Language Research and its Rewards in the 1990s." *ADFL Bulletin* 17.3 (1986): 43–45.

Godwin, William. *The Enquirer* (1797). Facsimile ed. New York: Augustus M. Kelley, 1965.

Goodman, Kevis. *Georgic Modernity and British Romanticism: Poetry and the Mediation of History.* Cambridge: Cambridge University Press, 2004.

Goring, Paul. *The Rhetoric of Sensibility in Eighteenth-Century Culture.* Cambridge: Cambridge University Press, 2005.

Görlach, Manfred. *Aspects of the History of English.* Heidelberg: Universitätsverlag C. Winter, 1999.

———. *English in Nineteenth-Century England: An Introduction.* Cambridge: Cambridge University Press, 1999.

———. "A New Text Type: Exercises in Bad English." *Paradigm* 2.7 (December 2003); available online at faculty.ed.uiuc.edu/westbury/Paradigm.

Gosse, Edmund. *A Short History of Modern English Literature.* London: Heinemann, 1907.

Graff, Gerald. *Professing Literature: An Institutional History.* Chicago: University of Chicago Press, 1987.

Graves, Robert. *Good-Bye to All That: An Autobiography* (1929). Ed. Richard Perceval Graves. Providence, RI: Berghahn Books, 1995.

Gray, Charlotte. *Reluctant Genius: The Passionate Life and Inventive Mind of Alexander Graham Bell.* Toronto: HarperCollins, 2006.

Great Historical Shakespeare Recordings. 2 CDs. Franklin, Tennessee: Naxos Audiobooks, 2000.

Grice, Paul. *Studies in the Way of Words.* Cambridge, MA: Harvard University Press, 1989.

Griffiths, Eric. *The Printed Voice of Victorian Poetry.* Oxford: Clarendon Press, 1989.

Groom, Nick, ed. *Thomas Chatterton and Romantic Culture.* Basingstoke, Hampshire: Macmillan, 1999.

Guillory, John. "The Memo and Modernity," *Critical Inquiry* 31 (2004): 108–32.

———. "Literary Study and the Modern System of the Disciplines." *Disciplinarity at the Fin de Siècle.* Eds. Amanda Anderson and Joseph Valente. Princeton: Princeton University Press, 2002. 19–43.

———. "Literary Capital: Gray's 'Elegy,' Anna Laetitia Barbauld, and the Vernacular Canon." *Early Modern Conceptions of Property.* Eds. John Brewer and Susan Staves. London: Routledge, 1995. 389–410.

———. *Cultural Capital: The Problem of Literary Canon Formation.* Chicago: University of Chicago Press, 1993.

Haberman, Frederick William. "The Elocutionary Movement in England, 1750–1850." Diss. Cornell University, 1947.

Hacker, Diana. *A Writer's Reference.* 6th ed. Boston: Bedford/St. Martin's, 2007.

Hales, John Wesley. "The Teaching of English." *Essays on a Liberal Education* (1867). Ed. F. W. Farrar. Facsimile ed. Westmead, Farnborough: Gregg, 1969. 293–312.

———. "Milton and Ovid." *MP* 1 (1903): 143–44.

———. "Louth Grammar School." *The Gentleman's Magazine* 273 (1892): 562–73.

———, ed. *Longer English Poems, With Notes, Philological and Explanatory.* 4th ed. London: Macmillan, 1875.

———. "English Dialects." *Good Words* 8 (1867): 557–60.

Hall, Dennis R. "A Sign of the Human Condition: George Campbell on Grammatical Purity." *ELN* 28.4 (1991): 16–22.

Harrison, Frederic. "On Style in English Prose." *The Nineteenth Century* 43 (1898): 932–42.

Harrison, Gary. "Wordsworth's Leech Gatherer: Liminal Power and the 'Spirit of Independence.'" *ELH* 56 (1989): 327–50.

Hart, J. M. "Rhetoric—Style—Metre." *MLN* 1.4 (1886): 51–52.

Hartman, Geoffrey. *Criticism in the Wilderness: The Study of Literature Today.* New Haven: Yale University Press, 1980.

Hayden, John O., ed. *Scott: The Critical Heritage.* London: Routledge and Kegan Paul, 1970.

———. *The Romantic Reviewers, 1802–1824.* London: Routledge and Kegan Paul, 1969.

Hazlitt, William. "The Late Mr. Horne Tooke." *The Spirit of the Age. The Complete Works of William Hazlitt*. Ed. P. P. Howe. 21 vols. London: J. M. Dent, 1930–34.

———. *A New and Improved Grammar of the English Tongue* (1810). *The Complete Works of William Hazlitt*. 21 vols. Ed. P. P. Howe. London: J. M. Dent, 1930–34. 2:1–110.

Henley, William Ernest. *Lyra Heroica: A Book of Verse for Boys* (1891). New York: Charles Scribner's Sons, 1914.

Hidalgo Downing, Laura. *Negation, Text Worlds, and Discourse: The Pragmatics of Fiction*. Stamford, CT: Ablex, 2000.

Hilles, Frederick W. and Harold Bloom, eds. *From Sensibility to Romanticism: Essays Presented to Frederick A. Pottle*. Oxford: Oxford University Press, 1965.

Hodson, Jane. *Language and Revolution in Burke, Wollstonecraft, Paine, and Godwin*. Aldershot, Hampshire: Ashgate, 2007.

Hoffmann, Maria E. *Negatio Contrarii: A Study of Latin Litotes*. Assen, The Netherlands: Van Gorcum, 1987.

Hollander, John. "Blake and the Metrical Contract." Hilles and Bloom, ed. *From Sensibility to Romanticism*. 293–310.

Hollingworth, Brian. "The Mother Tongue and the Public Schools in the 1860s." *British Journal of Educational Studies* 22 (1974): 312–24.

Honey, John. "Acrolect and Hyperlect: The Redefinition of English RP." *ES* 3 (1985): 241–57.

Horn, Laurence R. "*Duplex Negatio Affirmat...:* The Economy of Double Negation." *CLS 27: Papers from the 27th Regional Meeting of the Chicago Linguistic Society: Part Two: The Parasession on Negation*. Eds. Lise M. Dobrin, Lynn Nichols, and Rosa M. Rodríguez. Chicago: Chicago Linguistic Society, 1991. 80–106.

———. *A Natural History of Negation*. Chicago: University of Chicago Press, 1989.

Howell, Wilbur Samuel. *Eighteenth-Century British Logic and Rhetoric*. Princeton: Princeton University Press, 1971.

Hoye, Leo. *Adverbs and Modality in English*. Longman: London, 1997.

Hudson, Nicholas. "Theories of Language." *The Cambridge History of Literary Criticism, Volume 4: The Eighteenth Century*. Eds. H. B. Nisbet and Claude Rawson. Cambridge: Cambridge University Press, 2005. 335–48.

Hughes, Edward. *Select Specimens of English Poetry with Prose Introductions, Notes, and Questions*. 5th ed. London: Longman Green, 1856.

Hunter, J. Paul. *Before Novels: The Cultural Context of Eighteenth-Century English Fiction*. New York: W. W. Norton, 1990.

Ingham, Patricia. *Invisible Writing and the Victorian Novel: Readings in Language and Ideology*. Manchester: University of Manchester Press, 2000.

Iqbal, Muhammad. *Speeches, Writing, and Statements of Iqbal* (1944). Ed. Latif Ahmed Sherwani. Lahore: Iqbal Academy, 1977.

"J. O." "Rev. William Herringham, B. D." *Gentleman's Magazine* (Aug. 1819): 181–84.

Jackson, H. J. *Romantic Readers: The Evidence of Marginalia.* New Haven: Yale University Press, 2005.

Jackson, Shannon. *Professing Performance: Theatre in the Academy from Philology to Performativity.* Cambridge: Cambridge University Press, 2004.

Jakobson, Roman. "Linguistics and Poetics" (1960). *Language in Literature.* Eds. Krystyna Pomorska and Stephen Rudy. Cambridge, MA: Harvard University Press, 1987. 62–94.

Jameson, Fredric. "The Ideology of the Text." *The Ideologies of Theory: Essays, 1971–1986.* 2 vols. Minneapolis: University of Minnesota Press, 1988. 1:17–71.

Jarvis, Martin. *Acting Strangely: A Funny Kind of Life.* London: Methuen, 1999.

Jay, Timothy B. *The Psychology of Language.* Upper Saddle River, NJ: Prentice Hall, 2003.

Jeffrey, Francis. "[Review of *Characters of Shakespeare's Plays* by William Hazlitt]." *Edinburgh Review* 28 (August 1817): 472–88.

———."[Review of *The Corsair* and *The Bride of Abydos* (1814)]." *Byron: The Critical Heritage.* Ed. Andrew Rutherford. London: Routledge, 1970. 53–64.

Jespersen, Otto. *A Modern English Grammar on Historical Principles.* 7 vols. Heidelberg: Carl Winter Universitätsbuchhandlung, 1931.

Jewsbury, Maria Jane. "[Review of *The Nature and Dignity of Christ* by Joanna Baillie]." *Athenaeum* 187 (May 28, 1831), 337.

Johnson, Samuel. "A Grammar of the English Tongue" (1755). *Samuel Johnson on the English Language.* Eds. Gwin J. Kolb and Robert DeMaria, Jr. New Haven: Yale University Press, 2005. 275–360.

———. "Preface" to *A Dictionary of the English Language* (1755). *Johnson on the English Language.* Eds. Gwin J. Kolb and Robert DeMaria, Jr. New Haven: Yale University Press, 2005. 73–113.

———. "Preface to *The Plays of William Shakespeare*" (1765). *Samuel Johnson: Selected Poetry and Prose.* Eds. Frank Brady and W. K. Wimsatt. Berkeley: University of California Press, 1977. 299–336.

———. *Rasselas* (1759). *Samuel Johnson: Selected Poetry and Prose.* Eds. Frank Brady and W. K. Wimsatt. Berkeley: University of California Press, 1977. 73–153.

Jones, Charles. *English Pronunciation in the Eighteenth and Nineteenth Centuries.* Houndmills, Basingstoke: Palgrave Macmillan, 2006.

———. *Language Suppressed: The Pronunciation of the Scots Language in the Eighteenth Century.* Edinburgh: J. Donald, 1995.

Jones, Stanley. "'Bad English in the Scotch Novels.'" *Library.* Ser. 6. 3 (1981): 202–16.

Kames, Henry Home, Lord. *Elements of Criticism.* 3 vols. Edinburgh: A. Millar, 1762.

Katz, David S. *The Jews in the History of England, 1485–1850.* Oxford: Clarendon Press, 1996.

Keach, William. *Arbitrary Power: Romanticism, Language, Politics.* Princeton: Princeton University Press, 2004.

———. "Romanticism and Language." *The Cambridge Companion to British Romanticism.* Ed. Stuart Curran. Cambridge: Cambridge University Press, 1993. 95–119.

———. *Shelley's Style.* New York: Methuen, 1984.

Kearney, Anthony. "The First Crisis in English Studies, 1880–1900." *British Journal of Educational Studies* 36 (1988): 260–68.

Keats, John. *John Keats: A Longman Cultural Edition.* Ed. Susan J. Wolfson. New York: Pearson Longman, 2007.

———. *The Poems of John Keats.* Ed. Jack Stillinger. Cambridge, MA: Harvard University Press, 1978.

Kellogg, Ronald T. *The Psychology of Writing.* New York: Oxford University Press, 1994.

Kintsch, Walter. *Comprehension: A Paradigm for Cognition.* Cambridge: Cambridge University Press, 1998.

Kittler, Friedrich A. *Discourse Networks 1800/1900.* Trans. Michael Metteer, with Chris Cullens. Stanford: Stanford University Press, 1990.

Kjellmer, G. "On Clause-Introductory *Nor* and *Neither.*" *ES* 60 (1979): 280–95.

Knox, Vicesimus. *Essays, Moral and Literary.* 2 vols. London: Charles Dilly, 1782.

Krogvig, Inger and Stig Johansson. "*Shall* and *Will* in British and American English: A Frequency Study." *SL* 38 (1984): 70–87.

Kytö, Merja. *Variation and Diachrony, with Early American English in Focus: Studies on "Can/May" and "Shall/Will."* Frankfurt: Lang, 1991.

Lancashire, Ian. "Dictionaries and Power from Palsgrave to Johnson." Lynch and McDermott, eds. *Anniversary Essays on Johnson's Dictionary.* 24–41.

Land, Stephen K. *From Signs to Propositions: The Concept of Form in Eighteenth-Century Semantic Theory.* London: Longman, 1974.

———. "The Silent Poet: An Aspect of Wordsworth's Semantic Theory." *UTQ* 42 (1973): 157–69.

Landa, Meyer J. *The Jew in Drama* (1926). New York: Ktav, 1969.

Langan, Celeste. "Understanding Media in 1805: Audiovisual Hallucination in *The Lay of the Last Minstrel.*" *SiR* 40 (2001): 49–70.

Langbaum, Robert. *The Poetry of Experience: The Dramatic Monologue in Modern Literary Tradition.* New York: Random House, 1957.

Langer, Susanne K. *Feeling and Form: A Theory of Art.* New York: Scribner, 1953.

Langford, Paul. *Englishness Identified: Manners and Character, 1650–1850.* Oxford: Oxford University Press, 2000.

Lascelles, B. P. "Speech-Day." *Harrow School.* Ed. Edmund W. Howson and George Townsend Warner. London: Edward Arnold, 1898. 199–204.

Laski, Harold J. *Faith, Reason, and Civilization: An Essay in Historical Analysis.* New York: Viking Press, 1944.

Lauzon, Matthew. "Savage Eloquence in America and the Linguistic Construction of a British Identity in the Eighteenth Century." *HL* 23 (1996): 123–58.

Lennox, Charlotte. *The Female Quixote, or The Adventures of Arabella* (1752). Ed. Margaret Dalziel. Oxford: Oxford University Press, 1998.

Leonard, Sterling Andrus. *The Doctrine of Correctness in English Usage, 1700–1800.* Madison: University of Wisconsin Press, 1929.

Lethbridge, Stefanie. "Anthological Reading Habits in the Eighteenth Century: The Case of Thomson's *Seasons.*" *Anthologies of British Poetry: Critical Perspectives from Literary and Cultural Studies.* Eds. Barbara Korte, Ralf Schneider, and Stefanie Lethbridge. Amsterdam: Rodopi, 2000. 89–103.

Levinson, Marjorie. *Keats's Life of Allegory: The Origins of a Style.* Oxford: Blackwell, 1988.

Levinson, Stephen C. and Philip K. Bock. "Linguistic Relativity." *International Encyclopedia of Linguistics.* 4 vols. Ed. William J. Frawley. 2nd ed. Oxford: Oxford University Press, 2003. 2:459–66.

Lewis, C. S. "Shelley, Dryden, and Mr. Eliot" (1939). Rpt. in Abrams, ed. *English Romantic Poets.* 324–44.

Locke, John. *An Essay Concerning Human Understanding* (1690). 2 vols. 7th ed. London: J. Churchill, 1715–16.

Low, Donald A. *Robert Burns: The Critical Heritage.* London: Routledge and Kegan Paul, 1974.

Lowth, Robert. *A Short Introduction to English Grammar* (1762). Facsimile ed. Delmar, New York: Scholars' Facimiles, 1979.

Luckombe, Philip. *The History and Art of Printing* (1771). Facsimile ed. London: Gregg Press, 1965.

Lynch, Deidre Shauna. *The Economy of Character: Novels, Market Culture, and the Business of Inner Meaning.* Chicago: University of Chicago Press, 1998.

Lynch, Jack and Anne McDermott, eds. *Anniversary Essays on Johnson's Dictionary.* Cambridge: Cambridge University Press, 2005.

Lynskey, Winifred. "Imitative Writing and a Student's Style." *CE* 18 (1957): 396–400.

Macaulay, Thomas Babington. "Preface." *The Miscellaneous Works of Lord Macaulay.* Ed. Lady Trevelyan. 5 vols. New York: Harper and Brothers, 1880. 1:11–12.

———. "[Review of *Joannis Miltoni, Angli, De Doctrina Christiana*]." *Edinburgh Review* 42 (August 1825): 304–46.

MacCabe, Colin. *Tracking the Signifier: Theoretical Essays: Film, Linguistics, Literature.* Manchester: Manchester University Press, 1985.

Mackintosh, Robert James, ed. *Memoirs of the Life of Sir James Mackintosh.* 2nd ed. 2 vols. London: Edward Moxon, 1836.

MacMahon, Michael K. C. "Phonology." Ed. Suzanne Romaine. *The Cambridge History of the English Language, Volume 4, 1776–1997.* 373–535.

Madden, William A. "Macaulay's Style." *The Art of Victorian Prose.* Eds. George Levine and William Madden. New York: Oxford University Press, 1968. 127–53.

Mahon, M. Wade. "The Rhetorical Value of Reading Aloud in Thomas Sheridan's Theory of Elocution." *RSQ* 31 (2001): 67–88.

Manning, Peter J. "'The Birthday of Typography': A Response to Celeste Langan." *SiR* 40 (2001): 71–83.

———. "*Don Juan* and Byron's Imperceptiveness to the English Word." *Reading Romantics: Texts and Context.* New York: Oxford University Press, 1990. 115–44.

Masefield, John. *My Favourite English Poems.* London: Heinemann, 1950.

———. *Poetry.* London: Heinemann, 1931.

———. *The Oxford Recitations.* New York: Macmillan, 1928.

———. *With the Living Voice: An Address.* Cambridge: Cambridge University Press, 1925.

Masud-Ul-Hasan. *Life of Iqbal.* 2 vols. Lahore: Ferozsons, 1978.

Mayo, Robert D. *The English Novel in the Magazines, 1740–1815.* Evanston: Northwestern University Press, 1962.

McCaffery, Steve. *Prior to Meaning: The Protosemantic and Poetics.* Evanston: Northwestern University Press, 2001.

McDermott, Anne. "Johnson the Prescriptivist? The Case for the Defense." Lynch and McDermott, eds. *Anniversary Essays on Johnson's Dictionary.* 113–28.

McElroy, Jno. G. R. "Matter and Manner in Literary Composition." *MLN* 3 (1888): 29–33.

McGann, Jerome. "'Reading Fiction/Teaching Fiction': A Pedagogical Experiment." *Pedagogy* 1 (2001): 143–65.

McKenna, Stephen J. *Adam Smith: The Rhetoric of Propriety.* Albany: State University of New York Press, 2006.

McKeon, Michael. *The Secret History of Domesticity: Public, Private, and the Division of Knowledge.* Baltimore: Johns Hopkins University Press, 2005.

McKitterick, David. *Print, Manuscript and the Search for Order, 1450–1830.* Cambridge: Cambridge University Press, 2003.

McKusick, James C. "John Clare and the Tyranny of Grammar." *SiR* 33 (1994): 255–77.

———. *Coleridge's Philosophy of Language.* New Haven: Yale University Press, 1986.

McLane, Maureen. "The Figure Minstrelsy Makes: Poetry and Historicity." *CI* 29 (2003): 429–52.

"Member of the University of Oxford, A." *Lindley Murray Examined.* Oxford: J. Munday, 1809.

Messer-Davidow, Ellen. *Disciplining Feminism: From Social Activism to Academic Discourse.* Durham: Duke University Press, 2002.

Meyer, Steven. "'The Physiognomy of the Thing': Sentences and Paragraphs in Stein and Wittgenstein." *MoMo* 5 (1998): 99–116.

Michaelson, Patricia Howell. *Speaking Volumes: Women, Reading, and Speech in the Age of Austen.* Stanford: Stanford University Press, 2002.

Miles, Josephine. *Eras and Modes in English Poetry.* Berkeley: University of California Press, 1964.

Mill, John Stuart. "What is Poetry" (1833). *Essays on Poetry by John Stuart Mill.* ed. F. Parvin Sharpless. Columbia: University of South Carolina Press, 1976. 3–22.

Miller, Edwin L. "Literary Study and Character Formation." *School Review* 8 (1900): 295–91.

Miller, Thomas P. *The Formation of College English: Rhetoric and Belles Lettres in the British Cultural Provinces.* Pittsburgh: University of Pittsburgh Press, 1997.

Milman, Henry Hart. "A Memoir of Lord Macaulay." *The History of England by Lord Macaulay, Volume 8.* Ed. Lady Trevelyan. London: Longman, Green, Longman, and Roberts, 1862. 5–28.

Minear, Richard H. "E. B. White Takes His Leave, or Does He? *The Elements of Style,* Six Editions (1918–2000)." *MR* 45 (2004): 51–71.

Minto, William. *A Manual of English Prose Literature.* Boston: Ginn and Company, 1892.

Mitchell, Linda C. *Grammar Wars: Language as Cultural Battlefield in 17th- and 18th-Century England.* Aldershot: Ashgate, 2001.

Mitford, William. *An Inquiry into the Principles of Harmony in Language.* 2nd ed. London: T. Cadell and W. Davies, 1804.

Mizukoshi, Ayumi. *Keats, Hunt and the Aesthetics of Pleasure.* New York: Palgrave/MacMillan, 2001.

Moody, Patricia. "*Shall* and *Will* in English Grammars: A Revised History." *HL* 4 (1977): 281–301.

Morley, John. "Macaulay." *Critical Miscellanies.* 2nd ser. London: Chapman and Hall, 1877. 371–401.

Morrisson, Mark S. *The Public Face of Modernism: Little Magazines, Audiences, and Reception, 1905–1920.* Madison: University of Wisconsin Press, 2001.

Morton, David L., Jr. *Sound Recording: The Life Story of a Technology.* Westport, CT: Greenwood, 2004.

Moulton, Charles Wells, ed. *The Library of Criticism of English and American Authors, Vol. 6, 1855–1874.* Buffalo: Moulton Publishing, 1904.

Mowitt, John. *Text: The Genealogy of an Anti-Disciplinary Object.* Durham: Duke University Press, 1992.

Mugglestone, Lynda. *"Talking Proper": The Rise of Accent as Social Symbol.* Oxford: Clarendon Press, 1995.

———. "The Fallacy of the Cockney Rhyme: From Keats and Earlier to Auden." *RES* 42 (1991): 57–66.

Murray, Lindley. *English Grammar* (1824). Facsimile ed. Delmar, NY: Scholars' Facsimiles, 1981.

———. *English Grammar* (1795). Facsimile ed. Menston: Scolar Press, 1968.

———. *Exercises, Adapted to Murray's English Grammar, Designed for the Benefit of Private Learners, as Well as for the Use of Schools.* 2 vols. in 1. Philadelphia: Asbury Dickins, 1800.

Mustansir, Mir. *Iqbal.* Oxford: Oxford Centre for Islamic Studies, 2006.

Napier, Macvey. *Selections from the Correspondence of the Late Macvey Napier.* Ed. Macvey Napier [Jr.]. London: Macmillan, 1879.

Nares, Robert. *Elements of Orthoepy* (1784). Facsimile ed. Menston: Scolar Press, 1968.

Nattrass, Leonora. *William Cobbett: The Politics of Style.* Cambridge: Cambridge University Press, 1995.

Nevalainen, Terttu and Ingrid Tieken-Boon van Ostade. "Standardisation." *A History of the English Language.* Eds. Richard Hogg and David Denison. Cambridge: Cambridge University Press, 2006. 271–311.

New Joe Miller; or, The Tickler. 2nd ed. London: James Ridgway, [1800?].

O'Grady, William, et al. *Contemporary Linguistics: An Introduction.* 3rd ed. New York: St. Martin's, 1997.

"Obituary: John Wesley Hales." *Journal of Education* 36 (1914): 424.

Ong, Walter J. "[Review of Wilber Samuel Howell's *Eighteenth-Century British Logic and Rhetoric*]." *WMQ* 29 (1972): 637–43.

———. "Romantic Difference and the Poetics of Technology." *Rhetoric, Romance, and Technology: Studies in the Interaction of Expression and Culture.* Ithaca: Cornell University Press, 1971. 255–83.

Opie, Amelia. "The Negro Boy's Tale" (1808). *Poems.* London: Longman, Hurst, Rees, and Orme, 1808. 51–69.

Osborn, James M. *Dr. Johnson and the Contrary Converts.* New Haven: Yale University Press, 1954.

Oxford English Dictionary. Ed. James A. H. Murray et al. 12 vols. Oxford: Clarendon Press, 1933.

Page, Judith W. *Imperfect Sympathies: Jews and Judaism in British Romantic Literature and Culture.* New York: Palgrave Macmillan, 2004.

Palmer, D. J. *The Rise of English Studies: An Account of the Study of English Language and Literature from its Origins to the Making of the Oxford English School.* London: Oxford University Press, 1965.

Palmer, F. R. *Mood and Modality.* 2nd ed. Cambridge: Cambridge University Press, 2001.

Parker, William Riley. "Where Do English Departments Come From?" *CE* 28 (1967): 339–51.

Parrish, Wayland Maxfield. *Reading Aloud: A Technique in the Interpretation of Literature.* New York: Thomas Nelson, 1937.

Pater, Walter. "Wordsworth" (1874). *Walter Pater: Three Major Texts.* Ed. William E. Buckler. New York: New York University Press, 1986. 414–29.

Paulin, Tom. "John Clare in Babylon" (1992). *Romanticism: A Critical Reader.* Ed. Duncan Wu. Oxford: Blackwell, 1995. 401–07.

Paxman, David B. "The Genius of English: Eighteenth-Century Language Study and English Poetry." *PQ* 70 (1991): 27–46.

Pearson, P. H., ed. *Macaulay's Essay on Milton.* Topeka, KS: Crane & Co., 1904.

Pegge, Samuel. *Anecdotes of the English Language, Chiefly Regarding the Local Dialect of London and its Environs.* London: J. Nichols, 1803.

Percy, Carol Elaine. "'Easy Women': Defining and Confining the 'Feminine' Style in Eighteenth-Century Print Culture." *Language Sciences* 22 (2000): 315–37.

———. "In the Margins: Dr. Hawkesworth's Editorial Emendations to the Language of Captain Cook's *Voyages.*" *ES* 77 (1996): 549–78.

Perkins, David. "How the Romantics Recited Poetry." *SEL* 31 (1991): 655–71.

Pfau, Thomas. *Romantic Moods: Paranoia, Trauma, and Melancholy, 1790–1840.* Baltimore: Johns Hopkins University Press, 2005.

"[Pig-Selling Jew, The]." *The Skylark.* London: Vernor and Hood, [1800]. 212–13.

Polwhele, Richard. *Traditions and Recollections: Domestic, Clerical, and Literary.* 2 vols. London: John Nichols and Son, 1826.

Poovey, Mary. *The History of the Modern Fact: Problems of Knowledge in the Sciences of Wealth and Society.* Chicago: University of Chicago Press, 1998.

Pope, Alexander et al. *Peri Bathous: Or, Martinus Scriblerus His Treatise of the Art of Sinking in Poetry. Selected Prose of Alexander Pope.* Ed. Paul Hammond. Cambridge: Cambridge University Press, 1987.

———. *The Poems of Alexander Pope.* Ed. John Butt. New Haven: Yale University Press, 1963.

Pratt, Lynda and David Denison. "The Language of the Southey-Coleridge Circle." *LangS* 22 (2000): 401–22.

Pratt, Mary Louise. "Ideology and Speech-Act Theory" (1986). *The Stylistics Reader: From Roman Jakobson to the Present.* Ed. Jean Jacques Weber. London: Arnold, 1996. 181–93.

"Preface." *Elegant Extracts in Poetry, Selected for the Improvement of Young Persons.* London: Rivington et al., 1816. iii–viii.

Price, Leah. *The Anthology and the Rise of the Novel: From Richardson to George Eliot.* Cambridge: Cambridge University Press, 2000.

Priestley, Joseph. "Observations on Style" in *The Rudiments of English Grammar* (1761). Facsimile ed. Menston: Scolar Press, 1969. 45–63.

Prins, Yopie. "Voice Inverse." *VP* 42 (2004): 43–59.

Privateer, Paul Michael. *Romantic Voices: Identity and Ideology in British Poetry, 1789–1850.* Athens: University of Georgia Press, 1991.

Quigley, Austin E. *Theoretical Inquiry: Language, Linguistics, and Literature.* New Haven: Yale University Press, 2004.

Radcliffe, Ann. *The Italian* (1797). Ed. Frederick Garber. Oxford: Oxford University Press, 1984.

Ragussis, Michael. "Passing for a Jew, On Stage and Off: Stage Jews and Cross-Dressing Gentiles in Georgian England." *The Jews and British Romanticism: Politics, Religion, Culture.* Ed. Sheila Spector. Houndmills, Basingstoke: Palgrave Macmillan, 2005. 41–60.

———. *Figures of Conversion: "The Jewish Question" and English National Identity.* Durham: Duke University Press, 1995.

Rajan, Tilottama. *The Supplement of Reading: Figures of Understanding in Romantic Theory and Practice.* Ithaca: Cornell University Press, 1990.

Rée, Jonathan. *I See a Voice: Deafness, Language and the Senses—A Philosophical History.* New York: Henry Holt, 1999.

Reibel, David. "Introduction." Lindley Murray, *English Grammar Adapted to the Different Classes of Learners.* London: Routledge/Thoemmes, 1996. v–xxiii.

"Review of *Christabel, Kubla Khan, Etc.*" *The Champion* (May 26, 1816): 166–67.

"Review of Clifford Turner." *The Gramophone* (February 1930): 415.

"Review of *Lamia, Isabella, Etc.*" *Literary Chronicle* (July 29, 1820): 484–85.

"Review of *The Monastery.*" *La Belle Assemblée* 21 (1820): 186–88; available online at http://www.british-fiction.cf.ac.uk/reviews/mona20-64.html.

"Review of *Prometheus Unbound.*" *Monthly Review,* 2nd ser. 94 (1821): 168–73.

"Rhetoric." *Encyclopædia Britannica; or, A Dictionary of Arts, Sciences, &c.,* 10 vols. 2nd ed. (Edinburgh: J. Balfour et al., 1778–83), 8:5700.

Rice, John. *An Introduction to the Art of Reading* (1765). Facsimile ed. Menston: Scolar Press, 1969.

Richards, I. A. *Principles of Literary Criticism* (1924). London: Routledge and Kegan Paul, 1967.

Richardson, Alan, "'The Sorrows of Yamba,' by Eaglesfield Smith and Hannah More: Authorship, Ideology, and the Fractures of Antislavery Discourse." *RoN* 28 (2002); available online at www.erudit.org/revue/ron/2002/v/n28/007209ar.html.

Richmond, Legh. *Annals of the Poor* (1814). Boston: Crocker and Brewster, 1829.

Ricks, Christopher. *The Force of Poetry.* Oxford: Clarendon Press, 1984.

Robinson, Ian. *The Establishment of Modern English Prose in the Reformation and the Enlightenment.* Cambridge: Cambridge University Press, 1998.

Robinson, Mary. "A Fragment, Supposed to be Written Near the Temple, at Paris, on the Night Before the Execution of Louis XVI." *Mary Robinson: Selected Poems.* Ed. Judith Pascoe. Peterborough, ONT: Broadview, 2000. 127–30.

Robson, Catherine. "Standing on the Burning Deck: Poetry, Performance, History." *PMLA* 120 (2005): 148–62.

Roe, Nicholas, ed. *Romanticism: An Oxford Guide.* Oxford: Oxford University Press, 2005.

———. *John Keats and the Culture of Dissent.* Oxford: Clarendon Press, 1997.

Rogers, Deborah D. *The Critical Response to Ann Radcliffe.* Westport, CT: Greenwood, 1994.

Rogers, Pat. "Theories of Style." *The Cambridge History of Literary Criticism, Vol. 4: The Eighteenth Century.* Ed. H. B. Nisbet and Claude Rawson. Cambridge: Cambridge University Press, 2005. 365–80.

Rollins, Hyder E. "Macaulay's Essays and the Freshman." *English Journal* 4 (1915): 173–77.

Romaine, Suzanne. *The Cambridge History of the English Language, Vol. 4: 1776–1997.* Cambridge: Cambridge University Press, 1998.

Rose, Jonathan. *The Intellectual Life of the British Working Classes.* New Haven: Yale University Press, 2001.

Rosen, David. *Power, Plain English, and the Rise of Modern Poetry.* New Haven: Yale University Press, 2006.

Rosenberg, Scott. *Dreaming in Code.* New York: Crown, 2007.

Ross, Trevor. "The Emergence of 'Literature': Making and Reading the English Canon in the Eighteenth Century." *ELH* 63 (1996): 397–422.

Russell, Thomas. "The Negro's Complaint" (1794). Richard R. Madden. *The United Irishmen: Their Lives and Times.* 3 vols. Dublin: James Duffy, 1846. 2:162–63.

Russett, Margaret. *Fictions and Fakes: Forging Romantic Authenticity, 1760–1845.* Cambridge: Cambridge University Press, 2006.

———. *De Quincey's Romanticism: Canonical Minority and the Forms of Transmission.* Cambridge: Cambridge University Press, 1997.

Saglia, Diego. "'A Deeper and Richer Music': The Poetics of Sound and Voice in Felicia Hemans's 1820s Poetry." *ELH* 74 (2007): 351–70.

Saintsbury, George. *Specimens of English Prose Style.* London: Kegan Paul, Trench and Company, 1885.

Sansom, Clive, ed. *Speech of Our Time.* London: Hinrichsen Edition Ltd., 1948.

Savory, Jerold J. *Thomas Rowlandson's Doctor Syntax Drawings: An Introduction and Guide for Collectors.* Madison, NJ: Fairleigh Dickinson University Press, 1997.

Scholes, Robert. *The Rise and Fall of English: Reconstructing English as a Discipline*. New Haven: Yale University Press, 1998.

Scott, John. "[Review of *Lamia, Isabella, Etc.* by John Keats]." *London Magazine* 2 (1820): 315–21.

Scott, Walter. *The Monastery* (1820). Ed. Penny Fielding. Edinburgh: Edinburgh University Press, 2000.

———. *Ivanhoe* (1820). Ed. Graham Tulloch. Edinburgh: Edinburgh University Press, 1998.

———. *Waverley, or 'Tis Sixty Years Since* (1814). Ed. Claire Lamont. Oxford: Oxford University Press, 1986.

———. *The Letters of Sir Walter Scott*. Ed. H. J. C. Grierson. 12 vols. London: Constable, 1932–37.

———. *The Poetical Works of Sir Walter Scott*. London: Frederick Warne, [n.d.].

Scrivener, Michael. *Seditious Allegories: John Thelwall and Jacobin Writing*. University Park: Pennsylvania State University Press, 2001.

Sedgefield, W. J. "Records of Recitations." *TLS* (Thursday March 18, 1926): 218.

Sedgwick, Eve Kosofsky. *Touching Feeling: Affect, Pedagogy, Performativity*. Durham: Duke University Press, 2003.

Seguin, Jean-Pierre. *L'invention de la phrase au XVIIIᵉ siècle*. Louvain: Éditions Peeters, 1993.

Seidenberg, Mark S. "Language Acquisition and Use: Learning and Applying Probablistic Constraints." *Science* 275 (14 March 1997): 1599–1603.

"Sentence." *Encyclopædia Britannica*. 3 vols. Edinburgh: A. Bell, 1771. 3:578.

Sheldon, Esther K. "Walker's Influence on the Pronunciation of English." *PMLA* 62 (1947): 130–46.

———. "Pronouncing Systems in Eighteenth-Century Dictionaries." *Language* 22 (1946): 27–41.

Shelley, George. *Sentences and Maxims*. London: Samuel Keble, 1612 [1712].

Shelley, Mary. *Frankenstein, or The Modern Prometheus* (1818). Ed. D.L. Macdonald and Kathleen Scherf. Peterborough, ONT: Broadview, 1999.

Shelley, Percy Bysshe. *Shelley's Poetry and Prose*. Ed. Donald H. Reiman and Neil Fraistat. New York: Norton, 2002.

Sheridan, Thomas. *A Course of Lectures on Elocution* (1762). Facsimile ed. Menston: Scolar Press, 1968.

———. *A General Dictionary of the English Language*. London J. Dodsley, 1780.

Shields, Ronald E. "Like a Choir of Nightingales: The Oxford Recitations, 1923–1930." *Literature in Performance* 3 (1982): 15–26.

Short, Bryan C. "Figurative Language in the Scottish New Rhetoric." *Language Sciences* 22 (2000): 251–64.

Shortland, Michael. "Moving Speeches: Language and Elocution in Eighteenth-Century Britain." *History of European Ideas* 8 (1987): 639–53.

Silliman, Ron. "The New Sentence." *The New Sentence.* New York: Roof Books, 2003. 63–93.

Simpson, Paul. *Language Through Literature: An Introduction.* London: Routledge, 1997.

Siskin, Clifford. "More is Different: Literary Change in the Mid and Late Eighteenth Century." *The Cambridge History of English Literature, 1660–1780.* Ed. John Richetti. Cambridge: Cambridge University Press, 2005. 797–823.

———. *The Historicity of Romantic Discourse.* New York: Oxford University Press, 1988.

Sivier, Evelyn. "English Poets, Teachers, and Festivals in a 'Golden Age of Poetry Speaking,' 1920–1950." *Performance of Literature in Historical Perspectives.* Ed. David W. Thompson. Lanham, MD: University Press of America, 1983. 283–300.

Smeathman, Henry. "Elocution and Polite Literature." *Philosophical Transactions of the Royal Society of London* 71 (1781): 1–6.

Smiles, Samuel. *A Publisher and His Friends: Memoir and Correspondence of the Late John Murray.* 2 vols. London: John Murray, 1891.

Smith, Adam. *The Theory of Moral Sentiments* (1759). Ed. D. D. Raphael and A. L. Macfie. Indianapolis: Liberty Fund, 1984.

———. *Lectures on Rhetoric and Belles Lettres.* Ed. J. C. Bryce. Oxford: Clarendon Press, 1983.

Smith, Charlotte. *The Emigrants* (1793). *The Poems of Charlotte Smith.* Ed. Stuart Curran. Oxford: Oxford University Press, 1993. 131–63.

Smith, Donald K. "Origin and Development of Departments of Speech." *History of Speech Education in America.* Ed. Karl R. Wallace. New York: Appleton-Century-Crofts, 1954. 447–70.

Smith, Herbert Augustine, ed. *Macaulay's Essays on Addison and Milton.* Boston: Ginn & Company, 1902.

Smith, Olivia. *The Politics of Language, 1791–1819.* Oxford: Clarendon Press, 1984.

Solomon, Harry M. *The Rise of Robert Dodsley: Creating the New Age of Print.* Carbondale: Southern Illinois University Press, 1996.

Sorensen, Janet. "Vulgar Tongues: Canting Dictionaries and the Language of the People in Eighteenth-Century Britain." *ECS* 37 (2004): 435–54.

———. *The Grammar of Empire in Eighteenth-Century British Writing.* Cambridge: Cambridge University Press, 2000.

Spacks, Patricia Meyer. *Privacy: Concealing the Eighteenth-Century Self.* Chicago: University of Chicago Press, 2003.

Spadafora, David. *The Idea of Progress in Eighteenth-Century Britain.* New Haven: Yale University Press, 1990.

Spenser, Edmund. *The Faerie Queene* (1590–96). Ed. A. C. Hamilton. London: Longman, 1977.

Spoel, Philippa M. "Rereading the Elocutionists: The Rhetoric of Thomas Sheridan's *A Course of Lectures on Elocution* and John Walker's *Elements of Elocution*." *Rhetorica* 19 (2001): 49–91.

St. Clair, William. *The Reading Nation in the Romantic Period*. Cambridge: Cambridge University Press, 2004.

Stafford, Fiona. "Scottish Poetry and Regional Literary Expression." *The Cambridge History of English Literature, 1660–1780*. Ed. John Richetti. Cambridge: Cambridge University Press, 2005. 340–62.

Stallybrass, Peter and Allon White. *The Politics and Poetics of Transgression*. Ithaca: Cornell University Press, 1986.

Steele, Joshua. *Prosodia Rationalis; Or, An Essay Towards Establishing the Melody and Measure of Speech*. 2nd ed. London: J. Nichols, 1779.

Stein, Gertrude. "Sentences and Paragraphs." *How to Write* (1931). Facsimile ed. New York: Dover, 1975. 23–35.

Stein, Gertrude and Sherwood Anderson. *Sherwood Anderson / Gertrude Stein: Correspondence and Personal Essays*. Ed. Ray Lewis White. Chapel Hill: University of North Carolina Press, 1972.

Sterne, Laurence. *The Life and Opinions of Tristram Shandy, Gentleman* (1759–67). Eds. Melvyn and Joan New. Harmondsworth, Middlesex: Penguin, 2003.

Stillinger, Jack. *Multiple Authorship and the Myth of Solitary Genius*. Oxford: Oxford University Press, 1991.

Stower, Caleb. *The Printer's Grammar* (1808). Facsimile ed. London: Gregg Press, 1965.

Stray, Christopher. *Classics Transformed: Schools, Universities, and Society in England, 1830–1960*. Oxford: Clarendon Press, 1998.

Strunk, William Jr. *The Elements of Style* (1918); available online at http://www.bartelby.com/141.

———, ed. *Macaulay's and Carlyle's Essays on Samuel Johnson*. Rev. 2nd ed. New York: Henry Holt, 1896.

Sundby, Bertil, Anne Kari Bjørge, and Kari E. Haugland. *A Dictionary of English Normative Grammar, 1700–1800*. Amsterdam: John Benjamins, 1991.

Surr, Thomas Skinner. *Richmond, or, Scenes in the life of a Bow Street Officer*. 3 vols. London: H. Colburn, 1827.

Taft-Kaufman, Jill. "Oral Interpretation: Twentieth-Century Theory and Practice." *Speech Communication in the Twentieth Century*. Ed. Thomas W. Benson. Carbondale: Southern Illinois University Press, 1985. 157–83.

Taglicht, J. "The Genesis of the Conventional Rules for the Use of *Shall* and *Will*." *ES* 51.3 (1970): 193–213.

Taunton, William Pyle. *Reports of Cases Argued and Determined in the Court of Common Pleas, Vol. 4*. London: A. Strahan, 1815.

"Telonicus." "A Poetic Test of Pronunciation Not Reducible to Practice." *Gentleman's Magazine* 68 (July 1798): 567–69.

Thompson, Judith. "'A Voice in the Representation': John Thelwall and the Enfranchisement of Literature." *Romanticism, History, and the Possibilities of Genre: Re-Forming Literature, 1789–1837.* Eds. Tilottama Rajan and Julia M. Wright. Cambridge: Cambridge University Press, 1998. 122–48.

Tillyard, E. M. W. *The Muse Unchained: An Intimate Account of the Revolution in English Studies at Cambridge.* London: Bowes and Bowes, 1958.

Tolkien, J. R. R. "*Beowulf*: The Monsters and the Critics" (1936). *An Anthology of Beowulf Criticism.* Ed. Lewis E. Nicholson. Notre Dame: University of Notre Dame Press, 1963. 51–103.

Tomalin, Marcus. "'Vulgarisms and Broken English': The Familiar Perspicuity of William Hazlitt." *Romanticism* 13 (2007): 28–52.

Toolan, Michael. *Language in Literature: An Introduction to Stylistics.* London: Arnold, 1998.

Trachsel, Mary. *Institutionalizing Literacy: The Historical Role of College Entrance Examinations in English.* Carbondale: Southern Illinois University Press, 1992.

Tracy, Karen. *Colloquium: Dilemmas of Academic Discourse.* Norwood, NJ: Ablex, 1997.

Traugott, Elizabeth Closs and Richard B. Dasher. *Regularity in Semantic Change.* Cambridge: Cambridge University Press, 2002.

———. *A History of English Syntax: A Transformational Approach to the History of English Sentence Structure.* New York: Holt, Rinehart and Winston, 1972.

Trevelyan, G. Otto. *The Life and Letters of Lord Macaulay.* 2 vols. New York: Harper and Brothers, 1876.

Turley, Richard Marggraf. *Keats's Boyish Imagination.* London: Routledge, 2004.

———. *The Politics of Language in Romantic Literature.* Houndmills, Basingstoke: Palgrave Macmillan, 2002.

Turner, Clifford. *Voice and Speech in the Theatre.* London: Pitman, 1950.

———. "Verse Speaking." *Journal of Education* 75 (1943): 211–12.

———. "Aesthetic Aspect" in "Speech Training: A Symposium." *British Journal of Educational Psychology* 5 (1935): 21–26.

———. HMV B3152 (1929). Sound recording, 78 rpm. "To Sleep" (Keats), "Prospice" (Browning), "Ozymandias of Egypt" (Shelley), "Now Sleeps the Crimson Petal" (Tennyson).

———. HMV B3151 (1929). Sound recording, 78 rpm. "The Tyger" (Blake), "Composed Upon Westminster Bridge" (Wordsworth), *Samson Agonistes* [excerpt] (Milton), "When to the Sessions of Sweet Silent Thought" (Shakespeare).

Ulman, H. Lewis. *Things, Thoughts, Words, and Actions: The Problem of Language in Late Eighteenth-Century British Rhetorical Theory.* Carbondale: Southern Illinois University Press, 1994.

Vale, Edmund. *The Mail-Coach Men of the Late Eighteenth-Century.* London: Cassell, 1960.

Van der Veen, H. R. S. *Jewish Characters in Eighteenth-Century English Fiction and Drama.* Croningen: J. B. Wolters, 1935.

Van Ostade, Ingrid Tieken-Boon, ed. *Two Hundred Years of Lindley Murray.* Münster: Nodus Publikationen, 1996.

———. *The Auxiliary Do in Eighteenth-Century English.* Dordrecht: Foris, 1987.

———. "'I Will Be Drowned and No Man Shall Save Me': The Conventional Rules for *Shall* and *Will* in Eighteenth-Century English Grammars." *ES* 2 (1985): 123–42.

———. "Double Negation and Eighteenth-Century English Grammars." *Neophilologus* 66 (1982): 278–85.

"Vice-Chancellor's Court, Nov. 10: Longman and Co. v. Dove and Tyson." *The Times* (Nov. 11, 1829), Issue 14068, p. 3, column D.

A Vocabulary of Such Words in the English Language as are of Dubious or Unsettled Accentuation (1797). Facsimile ed. Menston: Scolar Press, 1967.

Wahrman, Dror. *The Making of the Modern Self: Identity and Culture in Eighteenth-Century England.* New Haven: Yale University Press, 2004.

Walker, John. *A Rhetorical Grammar* (1785). Facsimile ed. Menston: Scolar Press, 1971.

———. *Elements of Elocution* (1781). 2 vols. Facsimile ed. Menston: Scolar Press, 1969.

———. *A Critical Pronouncing Dictionary* (1791). Facsimile ed. Menston: Scolar Press, 1968.

———. "Preface to the Index of Perfect and Allowable Rhymes." *A Dictionary of the English Language, Answering at Once the Purposes of Rhyming, Spelling, and Pronouncing.* London: T. Becket, 1775. 672–74.

Walzer, Arthur E. *George Campbell: Rhetoric in the Age of Enlightenment.* Albany: State University of New York Press, 2003.

Warton, Thomas. *The History of English Poetry* (1774–81). 4 vols. Facsimile ed. New York: Johnson Reprint Corp., 1968.

Wasserman, Earl R. *Shelley: A Critical Reading.* Baltimore: Johns Hopkins University Press, 1971.

Webb, Timothy. "The Unascended Heaven: Negatives in *Prometheus Unbound.*" *Shelley Revalued: Essays from the Gregynog Conference.* Ed. Kelvin Everest. Totowa, NJ: Barnes and Noble, 1983. 37–62.

Wellek, René and Austin Warren. *Theory of Literature.* 3rd ed. New York: Harcourt Brace, 1956.

Wesley, John. *Explanatory Notes upon the New Testament.* 2nd ed. London, 1757.

Whipple, Edwin P. "Macaulay." *Essays and Reviews.* 2 vols. 6th ed. Boston: James Osgood, 1873. 1:9–30.

Whitehead, Kate. *The Third Programme: A Literary History.* Oxford: Clarendon Press, 1989.

Wilde, Oscar. *The Complete Letters of Oscar Wilde.* Ed. Merlin Holland and Rupert Hart-Davis. New York: Henry Holt, 2000.

Williamson, George. *The Senecan Amble: A Study in Prose Form from Bacon to Collier* (1951). Chicago: University of Chicago Press, 1966.

Wolcot, John ("Peter Pindar"). "Lord Brudenell and the Eunuch." *The Works of Peter Pindar.* 5 vols. London: J. Walker et al., 1812. 2:153–58.

Wolfson, Susan J. *Formal Charges: The Shaping of Poetry in British Romanticism.* Stanford: Stanford University Press, 1997.

———. *The Questioning Presence: Wordsworth, Keats, and the Interrogative Mode in Romantic Poetry.* Ithaca: Cornell University Press, 1986.

———. "Sounding Romantic: The Sound of Sound." Forthcoming in *Romantic Praxis.*

Wood, Marcus, ed. *The Poetry of Slavery: An Anglo-American Anthology, 1764–1865.* Oxford: Oxford University Press, 2003.

Woof, Robert., ed. *William Wordsworth: The Critical Heritage: Volume 1.* London: Routledge, 2001.

Woolf, Virginia. "The Antiquary" (1924). *The Moment and Other Essays.* New York: Harcourt Brace, 1948. 62–68.

Wordsworth, William. *Lyrical Ballads and Other Poems, 1797–1800.* Ed. James Butler and Karen Green. Ithaca: Cornell University Press, 1992.

———. *The Major Works.* Ed. Stephen Gill. Oxford: Oxford University Press, 1984.

———. *The Excursion* in *Poems, Volume II.* Ed. John O. Hayden. Harmondsworth, Middlesex: Penguin, 1977.

———, and Dorothy Wordsworth. *The Letters of William and Dorothy Wordsworth.* Ed. Ernest de Selincourt et al. 2nd ed. 8 vols. Oxford: Clarendon Press, 1967–1993.

Wyland, Russell M. "An Archival Study of Rhetoric Texts and Teaching at the University of Oxford, 1785–1820." *Rhetorica* 21 (2003): 175–95.

Yonge, Charlotte M. *What Books to Lend and What to Give.* London: National Society's Depository, 1887.

Zucker, Carole. *In the Company of Actors: Reflections on the Craft of Acting.* London: Routledge, 1999.

Index

144–84, 185, 206, 209–11; as social movement, 12–13, 28–29; regarding spelling, 13, 76, 105, 107; regarding syntax, 13, 20–21; regarding vocabulary, 13, 20–21; regarding will-shall distinction, 14–15, 48, 56–63, 68, 70; and women writers, 28, 36, 43, 104–7

St. Clair, William, 170

Steele, Joshua: *Prosodia Rationalis*, 75

Stein, Gertrude: *How to Write*, 210–12; on sentences, 210–12, 237n41

Stephen, Leslie, 167

Sterne, Laurence, 16; *Tristam Shandy*, 156–57, 161, 173

Stillinger, Jack, 9–10, 224nn14,17

Stoddart, John, 55

Stower, Caleb: *The Printer's Grammar*, 37

Strunk, William, Jr.: *The Elements of Style*, 209–10, 212, 237n38

style: and Byron, 101–04; as critical category, 3–4, 6, 9; and education, 186, 190, 206–10; and English experts, 152–55; and Hemans, 104–07; and Keats, 98–101; as response to standardization, 15–16, 40–43, 86, 142; stylization, 61, 66–71, 91; vs. usage, 86–87; and Wordsworth, 54–55

Surr, Thomas Skinner: *Richmond*, 75–76

Swift, Jonathan: on academy for English, 29; "An Argument Against Abolishing Christianity," 154; and English experts, 38, 39, 61, 154

Swinburne, Algernon Charles, 141

syntax: adjective-noun combinations, 8, 12; and sentences, 146–52, 157, 174; standardization regarding, 13, 20–21; subject-verb-object pattern, 47

Tate, Nahum: "Upon this Noble Design of an English Education," 24

Taunton, William Pyle, 27

Taylor, John, 36

teaching of English. *See* English pedagogy

Tennyson, Alfred, Lord: "Charge of the Light Brigade," 141, 196; "Now Sleeps the Crimson Petal," 194, 236n12

Thelwall, John, 131

Thomson, James: *Seasons*, 109

Tighe, Mary: *Psyche*, 110

Times Literary Supplement, 198

"to be" as perfect auxiliary, 46–47

Tolkien, J. R. R.: "Beowulf: The Monster and the Critics," 236n11

Tomalin, Marcus, 235n27

Traugott, Elizabeth Closs: *History of English Syntax*, 4; *Regularity in Semantic Change*, 227n22

Trevelyan, George, 179

Turley, Richard Marggraf, 7, 224n12, 230nn24,25

Turner, J. Clifford, 194, 196–200, 201, 236n12; *Voice and Speech in Theatre*, 199

United States: college entrance requirements in, 207, 209; Cornell University, 191, 207, 209; English in, 27–28, 202, 215, 217; Hales's *Longer English Poems* in, 191; Macaulay and Carlyle in, 207–8; Princeton University, 207; Stanford University, 207; University of Cincinnati, 191; University of Pittsburgh, 201; War of Independence, 22, 119; Yale University, 207–8

Van Ostade, Ingrid Tieken-Boon, 19, 49, 57, 59, 227nn7,11

Vocabulary of Such Words in the English Language as are of Dubious or Unsettle Accentuation, 29

Wahrman, Dror: *Making of the Modern Self*, 223n9

Wales, 7, 21–23, 31, 87–88, 93

Walker, John, 27, 126; *Critical Pronouncing Dictionary*, 8, 23–24, 25–26, 29, 32, 233n38; *Elements of Elocution*, 121; on elocution, 111, 115, 119, 121, 122, 131; on pronunciation,